HURON COUNTY LIBRARY

Date Due

31 'YApr 9 0		
JUN - 5 1990		
MAR 12 1991		
JUN 29		
J _ NOct 92		

BRODART, INC.   Cat. No. 23 233   Printed in U.S.A.

Also by Stephen Hume

Signs Against an Empty Sky, 1980

*And the House Sank like a Ship
    in the Long Prairie Grass*, 1987

GHOST CAMPS

Memory and Myth on Canada's Frontiers

Stephen Hume

NeWest

Canadian Cataloguing in Publication Data

Hume, Stephen, 1947-
  Ghost camps

ISBN 0-920897-67-3 (bound). — ISBN 0-920897-65-7 (pbk.)

1. Canada 2. Canada, Northern. 3. Prairie Provinces.
4. Indians of North America - Canada.
I. Title.

FC60.H85 1989 971 C89-091164-9 F1008.3.H85 1989

Credits

Cover design: Diane Jensen
Maps: Mostly Maps
Editor for the Press: Sylvia Vance
Printing and binding: Hignell Printing Limited, Winnipeg
Financial assistance:
        Alberta Culture
        The Alberta Foundation for the Literary Arts
        The Canada Council

Elements of some essays, in other forms and variations, have appeared in the following periodicals: *Absolute Cannon Review*, *The Martlet*, *Arctic*, *Alberta's Western Living*, *Content*, *Editor and Publisher*, the *Edmonton Journal*, the *Calgary Herald*, the *Ottawa Citizen*, the *Detroit Free Press*, the *Montreal Gazette*, the *Windsor Star* and the *Victoria Times*.

Printed and Bound in Canada

NeWest Publishers Limited
Suite 310, 10359 - 82 Avenue
Edmonton, Alberta
Canada   T6E 1Z9

This book is for Professor Derek Smith,
who taught me how to see.

Kwittri ettounyatcho tit ttrigwitti katundui.
Every heart knows its sorrows.

CONTENTS

ACKNOWLEDGMENTS

This book is not only the product of twenty years of my own experience along the rough edges of something that we call Canada but, also, the shared experiences of others, some living and some dead. In the writing of these essays I am deeply indebted to many people, first among them my wife and fellow writer Susan Mayse. Her free-spirited sharing of unique and otherwise inaccessible material from her own extensive oral and documentary research into the killing of Albert Goodwin makes possible my own cursory remarks upon the matter. I have relied further on her considerable personal knowledge of northern and aboriginal affairs. Other writers to whom I have referred, if not cited in the text, are listed at the end of the book for those interested in reading more widely on the issues discussed. I owe thanks, also, to Genevieve Morrow for the unquestioned sharing of unpublished material relating to her late husband Mr. Justice W.G. Morrow; to Justice William Stevenson for his advice regarding the legacy of Morrow's decisions from the bench; to Stuart M. Hodgson for his frankness in discussing northern affairs; to Arthur W. Mayse, dramatist, novelist and writer of short stories, and to Winifred Mayse, both for their steady encouragement and their sharing of a wealth of undocumented and unofficial history gathered over most of this century; to Professor Gary Geddes of Concordia University for awakening my interest in the national contexts of regional experience; to my father James Hume, reporter, editor, consummate political columnist, who read me the *Odyssey* as a bedtime story, and my mother Joyce Potter Hume, who pushed me to read it for myself. Finally, I am grateful to my four brothers. Timothy, Mark and Andrew spent many years in the Northwest Territories and Yukon as outfitters and artists, writers and photographers, trappers and public servants. Jonathan sailed with the off-shore fishing fleet from the Graveyard of the Pacific to the Aleutian Islands. My own narrative would be incomplete without their stories, criticism and advice.

Waiting for Daybreak

The old woman collected her own blood in her hands and blew it toward the sun. "My soul enters you, too!" she shouted. Since then anyone who kills receives in his body, without wanting or knowing it, the soul of his victim.

From Claude Levi-Strauss, *Mitologica*,
as quoted by Eduardo Galeano, in
Memory of Fire: Genesis.

ABOVE THAT HIDDEN ABYSS

The old woman gazed at me for a long moment. A cold, clear, penetrating stare. Imperious enough to beat my own eyes down to the swirl of sweet, black tea that she had just poured into my battered tin mug. She had caught me watching her when I thought she wouldn't notice, gawking at the *kakiniit* — the livid blue tattoos on her face — making a surreptitious entry in my notebook: twenty-four parallel lines beneath her mouth; eight more swept back across high cheek-bones; the great "V" shape descending from her hairline to the bridge of her nose. Each mark a wound; soot from a lamp, punched into her living flesh with a bone awl. Each pattern a testament, a badge of the beauty that shines through courage.

Everywhere in the High Arctic I had been told stories about the woman who carried a man's name, who hunted the land like a man, who was one of the last living people to have killed a polar bear with a spear and a snow knife, who lived the first half century of her life without encountering white men — *kadlunaat* — or European culture. In my imagination she came increasingly to represent both a connection with the world of our own lost origins and a living metaphor for the contradictions and complexities of cultural evolution in Canada's North. Now, here I was, tongue-tied, red-faced, spying on the legend out of the corner of my eye and snagged like a rabbit in the snare of my own small duplicity.

The spartan quarters bristled with her presence. An old, wrinkled woman with some kind of power in her. She moved closer. When I looked up again from the tea, she stood square before me, seemed to fill the room. In an abrupt, seamless motion, she

stripped off her sweater, displayed herself, naked, proud beyond the embarrassment of stupid convention, amused at my
shock — the stuttering awkwardness of a young man to whom
naked female flesh still embodied some sense of mysterious
taboo. This was her vivid, decisive answer to the unspoken question in my first furtive stare. The blue tattoos did indeed descend to the enigmatic country of her femaleness. Whorls and
spindles coiled to her pale breasts, intricate patterns of lines and
dots marked the soft, still lovely flesh of her throat, shoulders
and upper arms. She gestured at the notebook: permission to
sketch, a concession in service of her importance and my insignificance. And a warning: Your thoughts are transparent to me.

Her grandniece, too little for breasts of her own, watched
beadily from her cross-legged seat in the corner, a kind of impish
familiar. "I will speak for the *kadlunaaq*," she had told me when I
let it be known that I wanted to talk with Atuat, this woman who
survived from the world before white men and European technology. Now, a pretty child's piping tones were the incongruous
bridge between my world of Lear jets and computers and
Atuat's world of spirits, bloodshed and animal powers.

The old woman was not a shaman herself, she had been at
pains to point out, but her own life had been tangled with the
lives of sorcerers from the very beginning. Atuat had been teaching forgotten lullabies to a teen-aged nursing mother when I
made my visit. Suddenly, there were only the three of us in a
silent house — myself, the tattooed woman and the bright-eyed
girl, who seemed adept and yet as unformed as *siksik*, the quick
little ground squirrel. All the others had vanished, as though
into thin air. Later, as I tried to re-create the encounter in the texture of my memory, I could not recall a single other face, just a
vague awareness that there had been others present and, then,
not present.

Atuat seized my hand, placed it upon her body. The raised
pattern of blue bumps in her skin burned under my own. She
began to sing, a guttural, rhythmic chant that I could neither follow nor understand, and then swayed briefly into some small,
ancient dance. Her body slipped from under my hand and my
senses reeled. "*Angekkok*," an Inuit companion told me later. "She
was showing you how the shaman would grow his power." As
quickly as she had begun, she ceased. Pulled her sweater back
on. Laughed, showing long, discoloured teeth. Sat with me to
drink tea. She had opened a window for me. And closed it.

"I had three husbands," she told me. "The *kakiniit* came before
all of them. I was not married yet and I was very much afraid of

the shamans, that one of them would catch me. My mother, Ugulu, gave me the *kakiniit* to make me beautiful so that I could be married. She took soot from the lamps and mixed it with seal oil to make dye. The dye was put on the end of a sharp bone and pushed under my skin."

She turned to the girl, "Young women are lucky today, people think they are beautiful even without *kakiniit*. It was very painful. Ugulu started with my left hand and arm. She made the marks on my arms, then my face, then on the rest of my body. It was not so bad in those days because all Iglulikmiut women had tattoos. The women of Arctic Bay and Pond Inlet were not considered to be as beautiful because they had fewer tattoos."

She turned back to me, "I would like all the *kadlunaat* to have *kakiniit* like these. White men ask too many questions. I would like you to be able to share in feeling how painful it was to be a woman.

"I am named out of blood feud," the old woman said. "My foster mother was Tagurnaag. Atuat was her brother. Iglulikmiut, like me. One day, Atuat hunted walrus. He interrupted a man doing something secret. A Netsilikmiut. He was a shaman, and my uncle had seen him. Atuat was crouched over, stalking the animal, trying to look like a walrus. That Netsilikmiut shaman stood up and shot Atuat in the back — like he was a walrus. He died. Tagurnaag called me Atuat after that.

"That shaman was never caught by anyone. There used to be lots of shamans when I was young. The shamans threw a harpoon and speared people, then they dragged them. Sometimes people would try to stop the shaman, but they were very frightened."

The power of the shaman is difficult for most Europeans to comprehend, distanced as we are from that state of mind by the logical constructions of empirical thought and scientific reason. The contemptuous stereotype of the witch-doctor does little to penetrate the mystery of the spiritual force such individuals were able to command. The *angekkok* cannot be fully understood from outside what one might call the energy field of Inuit cosmology. These individuals were far more than simple magicians, manipulating events with spells and sleight of hand. Both they and their society believed them to be tapped into the original powers of the universe itself, powers which were explained through the metaphors of the spirit world. The shaman was believed to have the power to command these forces, anthropomorphized as spirits, through a complex arrangement of ritual and incantation. Asen Balikci, in his remarkable study of the

Netsilikmiut, points out that the world of the Inuit was a place of constant risk and danger, capable of erupting into violence or accidental catastrophe at any moment. The world of contesting spirits might be seen as a method of internalizing the unpredictable and threatening forces of the physical world. The shaman's importance, then, was not merely his power but also his social role. The shaman served as an instrument by which human culture might rise above its helplessness to deal with the contradictory forces of a hostile world. Nevertheless, the shaman's power enabled him to direct the forces of the supernatural for ill as well as good and made him a person with qualities as sinister as they were admirable. The fear and violence of that world still suffused Atuat's memories in the warmth of her house with its modern appliances.

"My first memory is of men," she said. "Men fighting." That was in another century, in a world the rest of us bury relentlessly in the ethical debris of our own spurious mythologies of progress and civilization. It was one of those brilliant summer days, she told me, the sky was so clear it made her eyes hurt. She was no older than her little niece, playing in the cool shade of the sod and stone hut that her foster-father Padluq had built for the tundra camp. Then came the great noise from outside.

"I am too old. I cannot remember who it was or even if my father or one of my relatives was fighting. All I can remember is the picture in my mind of the two men grappling and swaying as they struggled to kill one another. I cannot say how it turned out. My mother took me back inside."

Atuat suffered my questions. With the voice of the little girl echoing her answers in the foreign tongue, she told me she was eighty-nine. Born near Igloolik around 1884. Government records differ, list her birth as 1892. She shrugged. Neatly turned the tables on my curiosity. What did years matter? How would the government know what she didn't know for certain herself? At her age, the difference was inconsequential and the government couldn't even deliver the community boat that had been promised, smashing in the hull during unloading. Hadn't she herself drawn this to the attention of the Big Boss, the Commissioner of the Northwest Territories? Hadn't he deferred to her? Wasn't this her country, after all?

And what is the nature of her country, set high on the continent's glittering eastern shoulder? First, there are the irresistible imperatives which seem in constant collision with immovable forms. A billion tons of polar ice pack splinters against the sedimentary plates which spill across these far northern latitudes.

They form a necklace of fragments, descending into the Arctic Ocean from a spectacular arc of ancient rock. Earth scientists have their terminologies, but it is equally satisfying to experience the purity of the natural aesthetic: the geological architecture establishes a majestic visual anchor for the world's greatest archipelago. Scattered across an area as great as Europe, the wind-swept islands of Atuat's homeland rise to a sudden wall of peaks almost two kilometres high. These summits, the highest in eastern North America, are clad in ice that is one hundred thousand years old. Most of Canada's freshwater reserves are imprisoned among the rifts and gorges.

Along the whole stunning massif, an array of rocky palisades buckles into Davis Straits, collapsing toward black, storm-torn seas in a cascade of glacial faces, fjords and immense vertical cliffs. Beneath them, powerful currents tear and grind at the heavy shelves of ice that strive to extend themselves over every exposed patch of water. It is one of the earth's great calving grounds for icebergs, a few of them as big as islands themselves, a hundred kilometres square and sixty metres thick. Dense fogs and gales alternately obscure and batter at the coastline. The winds constantly harry the snows, drifting loose powder across the frozen surface in long, ghost-like streamers that pile up by the ton, filling canyons and burying mountains. Wherever moisture from the open water is sucked into the cold, dry air, it forms treacherous ice fogs, spawning bizarre optical illusions and secondary mirages that will surely kill any pilot who loses faith in his instruments.

The ferocity of these conditions challenges even the most sophisticated of our modern technologies. Metal struts go brittle in the cold. Cameras freeze solid and must be worn next to the body, the primitive warmth of the blood keeping the parts moving. Sometimes, it gets so cold that words turn into snow when the mouth opens to speak, the natural moisture in the breath crystallizing in the air. When the wind blows, exposed flesh can freeze solid in thirty seconds.

At Cape Dyer, midway down Baffin Island, stands the eastern outpost of the already obsolete distant early warning line. A long, twisting road snakes back from climate-controlled radar domes on the sea cliffs to the barracks, cafeteria and warehouse huddled along the airstrip. Marking off the distance between are tiny survival huts. One hut for every mile of road. Should a vehicle break down in bad weather, no passenger must walk more than half a mile to shelter, where he can crawl into a down-filled sleeping bag and wait the long wait for rescue.

This is the landscape through which Atuat roamed as a young woman, free as the wind itself, wedded to her environment in a way that seems hardly imaginable in the Canada of a century later. From the north end of the Melville Peninsula she moved southwestward with her new husband to work hunting grounds among the Netsilikmiut, near what is present-day Gjoa Haven. The settlement takes its name from the boat of Roald Amundsen, who wintered there from 1903 to 1906 during the first European voyage through the Northwest Passage. Atuat's two sets of parents, both natural and foster, were to become important informants for Knud Rasmussen's Fifth Thule Expedition, but she was not to meet her first *kadlunaaq* until 1926. She was in her early forties. By then, she had already drifted farther north to the place Inuit call Ikpiarjuq and the federal government calls Arctic Bay. Today the prefab homes of fewer than five hundred people are strung along the shores of Admiralty Inlet, a four-hundred-kilometre slash through the mountains at the top end of Baffin Island.

There is a primal quality to this landscape that leaves the observer with a sense of witnessing the beginning of things. Much of it is polar desert, arid as the biblical wilderness of the empty quarter in the Sinai. In an average year, less than two and a half centimetres of precipitation falls upon the jumbles of rock and ice. The only things moving inland are wind and the rivers of blowing snow that ride it. Vast ice fields, winding glaciers, frozen lakes accumulated over millennia — all sweep around two-thousand-metre towers of rock which look as though they might have been hewn from the earth that same morning. The cliffs drop a sheer kilometre into the sea. At their foot, a crazy, constantly changing jigsaw puzzle of ice and open water stretches away to Greenland. Life seems to have abandoned land for a precarious toehold at the edge of the sea. Even along the coast you can fly for days without seeing any movement other than the scudding form of a polar bear or the tiny flicker of black where a hunter travels through his solitude of pressure ridges, fissures of open water, the whole moving jumble of ice pans.

This is the brutal splendour of *Nunatsiaq* — "the beautiful country." Here, sheltering from the cruel North Atlantic in the lee of Greenland, shining in its mantle of ice five kilometres thick, dwell our people of light and darkness. Some are born here. Some, like Atuat, are here by choice or necessity. Most of the former count themselves among the chosen people of the earth. Of the latter, it is sometimes observed that those not here to find God are often here to hide from Him. It is a place appropriate to that; a landscape of autochthonous forms. For a southerner like myself, the primordial images seem conjured out of pre-Christian mythology. It might be Niflheim, the land of ice, darkness and mist at the edge of the original abyss. In the polar night, one easily imagines the creation of Ymir, the first giant, metaphor for human consciousness, born of snow melting in the black rocks.

This reference to the images of old Norse creation myths is more apt than one might think. Vikings sailed their slender *drakkars* into these waters a thousand years ago and planted colonies in barren Labrador and down the west coast of Greenland. Ari the Learned, writing the *Libellus Islandorum* in Iceland sometime after 1067, records traders' tales claiming the Irish were in the western seas before the Vikings, solitary anchorites of the Celtic church living in the rocks. The Norse settlements themselves became a mystery, enduring on the coast of Greenland for five centuries, then vanishing abruptly from the historical record when generations of wars and pestilence in Europe cut off their contact.

Where did they go when, year after year, the supply ships failed to return? Were they forced to adapt themselves, like the Inuit, to a landscape too austere to support European colonies, dispersing themselves more and more widely? Traces of their weapons, armour and long houses have been found in Newfoundland and even as far west as Atuat's High Arctic Islands. Were they absorbed, eventually, into the aboriginal population, the descendants of Eric the Red enriching the gene pools of isolated Inuit hunting bands? Damiano Goes, a Renaissance Portuguese chronicler, reports "white" Indians in the regions of Newfoundland and Labrador where Basque fishermen had been going since the Middle Ages. John Guy, who traded into Newfoundland in 1612, provides corroboration of a kind, reporting Indians with yellow hair.

Such historical enigma and mystery seem right for this landscape. The whole country offers a concrete expression of the integration of contrasts and opposites: the ultimate balance of sky and earth, light and dark, solid and fluid, permanence and transition, the yin and yang of history and pre-history, reality and myth. At first, it seems barren as the moon, a timeless field of snow that gives way only to glaciated rock and sere tundra, a place so stark and lightless one wonders that any living thing should exist. Yet when night at last sinks below the earth's rim, the snow vanishes in a rush and the dreary tundra explodes into a rich palette of reds and yellows, the immense patterns of copper and green lichen punctuated by drifts of spectacular wild flowers that sweep to the edge of the world. The sky fills with birds, and the seas teem with animals.

In the midst of this, clinging to the southern tip of Ellesmere Island, is the tiny miracle of Grise Fiord, a peculiar statement of national policy which somehow went right for once. Closer to the North Pole than it is to the nearest major community in the south, closer to Greenland than to continental North America, Grise Fiord is farther north than all the land masses of Siberia and Arctic Scandinavia. The only settlements in higher latitudes are the military listening posts at Alert and Thule, the scientific stations drifting on polar ice islands and one isolated settlement in Greenland named Siorapaluk.

Settled in 1953 by the Canadian government, which sought both to assert its claims to sovereignty over the Arctic Islands and to place in an area rich in wild game those Inuit families who wished to pursue traditional ways of life, the community is a lovely anachronism entirely at odds with the twentieth century. In Grise Fiord, the daily calendar is governed not by the timetables of business and bureaucrats but by the machineries of heaven. There is so much waiting to be done. It is the elemental waiting that pre-dates the invention of time, the rational mind's carving of experience into manageable bits. In Grise Fiord, one waits for the ice to go, waits for the snow to end, waits for word from outside to arrive. Waits for the seals and whales to come. Waits for daybreak. Waits for nightfall.

People here live in a satisfying balance with the natural world. What seems a harsh environment is actually the sustaining force of the spirit. At Grise Fiord, children play in a sun which never sets or, conversely, walk to school by the powerful lights of the aurora and wheeling constellations. If housewives may now buy groceries at The Bay, it is only as a supplement to the harvest of caribou and seal, narwhal muktuk and frozen char. If the land is a harsh mistress, she is also a bountiful servant of those who respect her.

Strung along the gently curving beach, Grise Fiord is crowded against the foot of a ragged wall of rock that soars, abrupt and sheer, thousands of metres above the neatly arranged houses. In the other direction, an immense, snow-swept plain of ice rolls off to the thin pen stroke of a horizon that hides the sun during winter months. South of Ellesmere, past the height of Devon Island and beyond the fierce currents of Lancaster Sound, rises the forbidding north shore of Baffin Island. Here are Pond Inlet, Atuat's settlement of Arctic Bay and the self-contained mining camp of Nanisivik. Farther east, facing Greenland, is Clyde River. These tiny communities symbolize the world of human beings perched at the brink of that same abyss one finds at the heart of the Norse sagas.

Christian priests and scientists with their new church of reason notwithstanding, *Nunatsiaq* is where the sun still dies, where the three Frost Giants, cold and storm and night, come into their powerful occupation under skies so dark and yet so full of stars that the Milky Way floods the senses, renders them numb.

Out of this experience emerge those dreams and imaginings which inhabit the furthest reaches of collective human memory. On the north Baffin coast and the southern shores of Ellesmere Island, the descendants of the first Tununirmiut and Akudnirmiut have learned to live with the ice and darkness for a hundred generations. Arguably the toughest and most resourceful people on the planet, they live on the foundations of people who came here a hundred generations before their own ancestors. Atuat's connections to those ancestral people of the Dorset and Thule cultures were tangible and intense. She told me how she killed the bear.

It was midwinter, and her husband had built a snow house near the mouth of Admiralty Inlet. They were asleep inside, wrapped in their skin robes, when they were awakened by the barking of their dogs, staked out in a drift near the igloo. Outside, they found a polar bear stalking the team. There was no question of delay, she told me. The life of a hunter is movement. If the bear killed the dogs, essential for finding the breathing holes of seals, there would be no more food. Worse, deprived of their only source of travel, Atuat and her husband would die also. He took one of the two harpoons in camp, she took the other. The bear charged the dogs and her husband charged the bear. It knocked him down and advanced on Atuat. She taunted it. The bear attacked. She planted the stock of the harpoon and let the bear's momentum impale it on the point.

The story was as plain and unadorned as the bone handle of a skinning knife. She dismissed suggestions of heroism. Any courage, she said, was born of simple necessity: "I had no choice. I had to stand my ground. When you are attacked by a polar bear, it's either him or you. Once you give ground, you are finished."

Her words might be a parable for the world view of a practical and ingenious people, their lives balanced for all of memory on the thin edge that separates wisdom from miscalculation and efficiency from disaster. Long before the Pharaohs were turning the sharpness of their intellects to the vanity of the pyramids, the Inuit were turning theirs to the integration of technology with environment. They chose to occupy the margins of the world, an austere country where winter rules eight months of the year and where the plunging temperatures freeze seven million square kilometres of ocean in a matter of weeks. Yet if these vast and extreme cycles of nature offer a test for the will, they also offer solutions for an irrepressible imagination.

Donald Marsh, the Anglican missionary who went among the Padlimiut of west Hudson Bay in 1921, five years before Atuat saw her first European, exclaims with joy and wonder his discovery of the paradox that is the great Inuit truth — that the snow and ice themselves are the two most valuable resources of people on the land. The densely packed drifts of the polar desert gave birth to the genius of the igloo, exploiting the insulating qualities of the snow; if temperatures plunge to the range of the blast freezer, fish might be shaped into sled runners for far-ranging travel across frozen seas. Inuit clothing, with its ingenious system of air traps and internally contained environments, provides the concept which later yields the space suit. The sea hunter's kayak — light, highly manoeuvrable, with its streamlined profile, waterproof coverings and low silhouette — remains a favoured vessel for commando units and white-water enthusiasts around the world.

Dawn breaks at high noon during the short weeks of that brief flicker which serves for autumn over Grise Fiord. First, a coral flush scallops the curved edge of the world. Faint petals of light unfurl against the sky and then close again thirty minutes later. Day folds back into the tight calyx of night without the sun mustering sufficient strength to roll up over the line that separates sky from ice-clad sea.

In southern Canada, that foreign country which lies "outside" the normal range of High Arctic perception and consciousness, the brief, almost imperceptible lifting of darkness would not be defined as twilight. It is day, nevertheless. Its importance as a link with the explosion of life that is summer north of the seventy-sixth parallel is always measured, minute by minute, petal by petal, as it fades into the tireless tread of winter. Small wonder that for a man raised on European myths, this place should seem an incarnation of Niflheim, cast in its eternal silence and dark.

Despite some curious similarities in origin myths across the polar latitudes of three continents, *Nunatsiaq* is the country neither of Norse saga nor Siberian incantation. It remains the dominion of Sila, the temperamental and unpredictable ruler of weather, and Sedna, the maimed goddess. Sedna rules all sea creatures, which are descended from her severed fingers and remain spiritual extensions of godhead. Traditionally, Inuit hunters offer the slain seal a ritual drink of fresh water as an act of kindness and respect for the animal soul that is part of the deity. Indeed, because the living creature is connected to Sedna, the decision of every hunter to kill a seal may be seen as symbolizing the decision of humanity to maim her again. So the great goddess suffers continually at our hands, is wounded anew as human beings take their sustenance from the animals which embody her spirit. Thus are we linked to the natural world by the damage we impose upon it. The corollary is a powerful obligation to minimize harm, to limit injury to that required by necessity. This is a sophisticated and morally compelling view of man's complex relationship with the environment.

By comparison, the rest of Canadian society appears spiritually stunted, oblivious to any conception of a contract between ourselves and the natural order. In the waters off Vancouver, scientists discover that most of the bottom-dwelling flat-fish are plagued with tumours and lesions caused by carcinogens in the sediments. The gregarious belugas at Tadoussac on the Saint Lawrence River have been turned into festering, disease-ridden travesties of everything that whales stand for in the popular imagination. In the waters off Toronto, sport fishermen kill but cannot eat salmon so contaminated with cancer-causing chemicals that once dead they are considered toxic waste. Pregnant women are warned to avoid eating fish from the North Saskatchewan River system because of the risk of mutations and birth defects. And in the waters of a lake on Little Cornwallis Island, tailings from a mine threaten the extinction of an unique species of cold-water sculpin. Elsewhere, vast tracts of Alberta farmland are made salt waste through careless irrigation in the service of greed. In the Okanagan Valley, living apple orchards which took three generations to grow are uprooted to make way for condominiums and subdivisions to house retirement couples waiting for death. Around our cities, the best agricultural land in the country is killed forever to make way for parking lots, highways and shopping malls. The impact of this conduct, most evil in its banal heedlessness, reaches to the realm of Sedna herself. The marine mammals of *Nunatsiaq*, the sustainers of human life, have begun to show, in their body fat, bones and neurological systems, concentrations of toxic chemicals from Europe, the Soviet Union and our own prairie watersheds. Inuit mothers' milk is contaminated with PCBs at levels higher than those recorded anywhere else in the world, the nourishing breast transformed by distant technology into a lethal spigot for industrial effluents.

The sin is that we harm the natural world not out of necessity, not within limits prescribed by our contract with the environment, but in the service of unrestrained avarice and gratuitous convenience. Wilful ignorance and the worst kind of expedience characterize our actions. Contrast the behaviour of our "advanced" society with the world view embodied in the relationship between Sedna and humanity, and the attitudes of our ostensibly civilized and Christian Canada toward the land seem almost demented.

Dwelling in her stone cells at the bottom of the sea, her hair trailing in the ocean currents as the foul sediment of our collective sin rains down from the human world above, Sedna may be seen in many ways to resemble the land itself — bountiful despite abuse; suffering always at the hands of those who are her beneficiaries. But there is a warning for us in Inuit understanding of this silent goddess. If she is indisposed to intervene in aid of human kind, she can be merciless to those foolish enough to ignore the rules of conduct. If she chooses not to punish wrongdoers through direct retaliation, she is certainly capable of visiting famine and death by simply withholding her gifts.

Both in my travels across the Arctic and in the reading of earlier ethnologists, I was fascinated to discover that Sedna is considered of far less influence among the Inuit of Alaska. In fact, the powerful deities and spirits of the west are largely male. Sedna's power and the power of those shamans capable of communing with her directly — for only the strongest of *angekkok* may look upon her face and survive — intensifies steadily as one moves north and east to the most remote reaches of the Baffin Region. Is this a matter of mythology transforming its substance to reflect the harshness and austerity of the land itself? Or is it, like the shape of the country, a survival of the Mother Goddess from the dawn of the neolithic, preserved by isolation and as old as the ice which shrouds the highlands and which shielded its people from the worst excesses of European contact? Gordon Marsh, whose observations are recorded in the anthropological papers of the University of Alaska, notes a waning from west to east of the male potency that characterizes so many modern religions. And the Inuit of the High Arctic are "unique among all Eskimo-Aleut people in conceiving one dominant power of the universe which is feminine."

Can such a deity have force in a world of Roman Catholic, Anglican and Pentecostal missionaries, all wrangling over the fate of aboriginal souls? Atuat thought so. She described the ancient religion as the vigorous, living sea beneath the brittle crust of ice. You might build whatever you liked above it, you might put the miracle of television in prefabricated houses, but a few feet below this delusion of stability would yawn the hidden abyss and its irresistible currents. Somehow, she said, her people would always know in some part of themselves that the seals they harvest are the gifts of wounded Sedna: "This is the difference between you and us. This is the difference between human beings and *kadlunaat*."

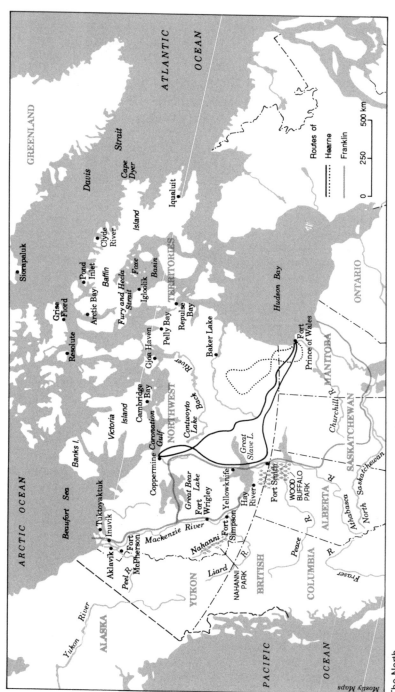

The North

Mosby Maps

TO WALK ON THE WIND

The wind blows and blows. Snow rises from the ground, white shapes emerging out of the earth itself, whirling away in a dance of ice crystals. They seem tireless spirits, singing over the bare rock and off the deep-packed drifts, until the world is suffused with the rasping quality of their sighs and whispers. New ghosts rise over each footfall, one fleeing before me into the night, another rushing behind to fill my tracks, until the trace of passage is that brief instant of each foot lifting for another step forward into a dark that throbs with unseen possibilities.

Overhead, the Milky Way is a luminous river in the black sky. Beneath it, the snowscape glimmers with a strange, pale light and all wild Canada stretches away, empty now as it was two hundred years before, when the man for whom I'd come searching stood somewhere near this place on the ice-fast shores of Hudson Bay, the place once called by the Indian name Keewatin, the home of the north wind. Alone in the polar night, I settle in my tracks, neck prickling under the fine grit of crystals spiked into every crevice of my clothing. Cold seeps into the depths of my down-filled parka, and I stop to squint across the same barren vista that rolled away before him, off to the same distant horizon and twenty-five hundred kilometres beyond it, to the desolate reaches of Coronation Gulf and the beginning of the High Arctic archipelago.

I had come here at the urging of Doug Wilkinson, historian and maker of important National Film Board documentaries about the pre-contact life of people in the High Arctic. I had quickly become infected with his own enthusiasm on the subject. "Don't rely on books," he said. "See what he saw." Wilkinson is right. The power of this vast, stark panorama stuns the senses, terrifies the urban heart. I turn into the wind and struggle back across the little distance I've walked beyond the outskirts of the northern Manitoba town of Churchill.

Today, linked by rail to Winnipeg more than seven hundred kilometres to the south, the place remains strategically significant. Situated near the geographical centre of the country, Churchill is the prairie region's closest tidewater and the only real deep-sea port along Canada's immense Arctic coastline. Although the ice-free days are short, Churchill is the key staging point for resupply of the Northwest Territories region that extends up the west coast of Hudson Bay to the Melville Peninsula and Baffin Island. It remains an important centre for scientific research, particularly for biologists studying polar bear and beluga whale populations, and as a rocket base for research on the high frontier — the ionosphere in which the northern lights are born and which becomes increasingly important as fears deepen regarding depletion of the protective ozone layer and acceleration of the greenhouse effect. Still, Nike-Orion launches by the National Aeronautics and Space Administration aside, the failure of successive Canadian governments to provide icebreakers adequate to winter operations along the world's second longest polar coastline leaves the port of Churchill hostage to the climate, as it was in the days of Napoleon and Nelson. It is there that my imagination walks on this bitter night.

Founded by the Hudson's Bay Company around 1689, the settlement was to become pivotal to fortunes of mercantile empires and the far-flung wars of the European kings who brought it to destruction. Yet, I am less interested in the machinations of distant emperors and czars than in achieving some personal sense of the man who consumes my interest; the man who kept walking out into that darkness where I turned back, who pushed onward into the unknown until he had travelled six thousand kilometres across the heart of an unmapped continent, a journey as exotic and important in its way as Marco Polo's voyage overland to China.

It is in the wreckage of his era that one finds the most substantial evidence of the man's presence. Across the groaning ice of the Churchill River, surrounded by the dwarf trees of a boreal forest giving way to tundra, flanked by immense pressure ridges and the frozen jumbles of sea ice that jam the windward shore of the estuary, stands the stone ruin of a mighty fortress. It is as out of place in this landscape as a modern battle tank at a debutante's coming-out party, but there it stands, oblivious to its oddness. This is the remains of Prince of Wales's Fort, a bizarre colossus that belongs to the age of Marlborough and the wars of the Austrian Succession.

Here was where he scratched his name as a young man full of longing for adventure: "Sl. Hearne, July 1, 1767." He was twenty-two, liberated from a stifling hitch in the Royal Navy into the service of The Governor and Company of Adventurers Trading Into Hudson's Bay and Rupert's Land. Samuel Hearne was to leave a remarkable scientific journal of his adventures, but somehow the words printed for scholarly posterity yield less of the man than the austerity of this inscription etched into a rock. Somehow description carries less force than standing where he stood, knowing the same winter wind, staring out across the same changeless prospect of his epic journey.

Later, I survey the stiff, spidery scrawl of a frost-bitten entry in my own dog-eared notebook, impressions cribbed from memory and the thin air:

> Jealous of its ghosts and its forbidding past, isolated from the mainstream of history by circumstance, geographically aloof from all but the most determined sightseers, Fort Prince of Wales weathers silently back into a remorseless land.
>
> The fortress has been called preposterous — an outlandish symbol of man's arrogance and folly. Certainly it stands as a monument to the vicissitudes of fate. Today it lies echoing beneath the Arctic sky, this immense and futile fortification, with its memories and scars. It belongs as much to the migrating terns and the solitary polar bear as it does to the pageant of Canadian history.

And yet it is to that pageant of history that one must turn to find a frame of reference sufficient to contain Hearne's accomplishments.

The harshness of the land to which Hearne learned to accommodate himself was merciless to those who sought to conquer it with European ways. Reduced to a ragged band of cannibals, shambling down the Arctic coast while amazed Inuit observers watched them fall down and die in their tracks, Sir John Franklin's expedition suffered a fate which testifies to Hearne's intelligence and skill.

Franklin was not the first. Henry Hudson died on the bay he discovered when his mutinous men set him adrift in 1611 after a winter in which they were reduced to eating frogs and moss.

Only eight of the twenty-three-man crew made it home. Sir Thomas Button followed in 1612, the first European to set foot in Manitoba. He wintered in the mouth of the Nelson River after exploring the west coast of Hudson Bay, his crew decimated by sickness and starvation. Seven years later, Jens Munk, in service to the King of Denmark, attempted to winter an exploratory expedition near the present site of Churchill. Fifty-nine of his sailors perished of disease and starvation. Munk and two crewmen somehow survived, digging roots, too weak to bury their dead, and sailed back across the Atlantic to Copenhagen. Their disastrous expedition of 1619 foreshadowed what would befall James Knight, starving with his entire crew on Marble Island in 1719.

For almost half a century, the dangerous western shores of Hudson Bay were shunned by explorers, although a few tentative expeditions charted the northern approaches before turning back. But in Europe, the market for furs was exploding, and the consortium of British merchants that was to become the Hudson's Bay Company was determined to secure its share of the profits. Over the next fifty years, intense and Byzantine commercial struggles developed between the British, the mercantile interests of New France and the hard-nosed Yankee businessmen of New England. For the strategists of the fur brigades, the coast of Hudson Bay was the hinge of success. The British quickly began building fortified trading posts in the region to gather furs from the unexplored watersheds to the south and west.

A hundred years after Munk's grisly misfortune, construction of the Prince of Wales's Fort was begun, and in 1731 it was decided to make the trading post into a military stronghold that might strategically dominate the region. In the middle of the wilderness, up went the huge stone bastions of a classic star-shaped fortress: walls more than ten metres thick and topped with brooding battlements, gun emplacements for forty cannon. Today, two-and-a-half centuries later and under the watchful eye of the federal government, the cannons remain in place not far from the missile range, never having fired a shot in anger.

It was to this tremendous military base that Hearne came in 1767. After the trials of life at sea, it is small wonder that the young man's imagination seemed to open out with the country that lay before him. He was destined to become, before his thirtieth birthday, one of Canada's most remarkable but least celebrated figures. Five years after arrival, almost to the day his company trading sloop dropped anchor in the mouth of the

Churchill for the first time, Hearne was walking back through the main gate of the "preposterous" fortress. It was a typically modest end to what was perhaps the greatest feat of endurance and individual courage recorded in our history.

Using only the crude navigational instruments of his day, Hearne had walked across three hundred and sixty thousand square kilometres of wilderness, much of it not mapped until this century and most of that by aerial survey. Thousands of square kilometres are still virgin territory, some not even walked upon by aboriginal inhabitants. He had survived bloody intertribal warfare, treachery among his native companions, starvation, sickness, plagues of mosquitoes and blackflies and the endless, strength-sapping cold of the barrens.

It is in the nature of materialistic men that they remain blind to the intangible riches of the spirit. In the eyes of his superiors, Hearne was something of a failure. He brought back no gold, no gems or pearls, no word of fabulous mines, no routes to the riches of China or the spice islands. Just a sack of notebooks, and even there his news seemed to his masters to be all of desolation, emptiness, privation and massacre. All he brought back was the most priceless commodity of all, and often the least valued in the world of commerce, the pure knowledge of things witnessed and filtered through a wondering mind.

Hearne was, above all, an adaptable man. Where others struggled against the climate and the terrain, he learned ways to respond to the opportunities they afforded. He watched and listened and immersed himself in the customs of people who knew how to live in the harsh Arctic landscape. His journals are meticulous in noting everything from the patterns of weather to native tricks of survival. He describes the unknown heart of North America in terms of the aboriginal peoples who dwelled upon it, the finely tuned cultures they had evolved to deal with their environment, the richly textured environment itself — geography, climatic conditions, plants and animals. Reading his journals, one is immediately struck by his vision of the landscape. This is not the barren waste confronted by Franklin and looming behind all his scientific reports but a place teeming with life and possibilities. Hearne seems able to step outside the ethnocentric stereotypes that destroyed so many others and to witness the world through the eyes of his Indian guides and mentors.

In his analysis of the death of Franklin's crew, the Arctic explorer Vilhjalmur Stefansson observed in 1938 that game for these British naval expeditions was always procured by hired "hunters." Franklin's journals refer to the wood being provided by the "woodsmen." John Richardson, the Edinburgh surgeon who accompanied the expedition of 1820, notes in his own journals that the British party's supplies and equipment were carried by "porters." While Franklin's group carried their personal belongings, the "porters" dragged canoes weighing 320 pounds and carried individual packs of 180 pounds. Rarely does Franklin bother to record the names of the Indians supporting the expedition. When he does, the names are often quoted from Richardson's journals.

If there is an almost feudal hierarchy revealed by the terminology, it is confirmed in the matter of precisely whom the British leader finds worthy of the simple courtesy of identification by name and who is relegated to the role of anonymous labour. In fairness to Franklin, even his sternest critics acknowledge many of the finer qualities one would expect of a Victorian British gentleman — a sense of natural justice, tolerance, a cheery spirit and a pious nature. The other values are less a reflection upon his character than upon the rigid class structure of his contemporary British society, with each man fixed in the function of his station and inferior to those upper classes to which the young Franklin so fiercely aspired. C. Stuart Houston, the modern editor of Richardson's journals, is of the view that from the first disastrous expedition Franklin "too readily succumbed to the temptation of fame and career advancement." It is this social aspiration and the fear of ruining his reputation which appears to drive Franklin to the feats of endurance and risk for which he is widely celebrated.

Perhaps the harshest critic of Franklin remains Stefansson, the Manitoba-born anthropologist who spent ten happy winters in the Arctic between 1906 and 1918, adapting himself to the ways of the Inuit in the same fashion that Hearne had learned from the Indians:

"Why were the Englishmen, in self-help, a complete dead weight on the [Franklin] party?" Stefansson asks. "Was it beneath their dignity to co-operate in securing food? Was helping the workers, in their minds, detrimental to discipline? Whatever the reason, there is no sign either that they tried to assist in the hunting, or that they studied the methods of the hunt so as to be able to use them later."

Stefansson goes on to observe that when Franklin's starving expedition was lucky enough to find the remains of a caribou carcass that had been stripped to skin and bone by wolves, they had learned nothing from the flourishing native culture surrounding them:

Now skin is as nourishing, weight for weight, as lean meat; but only if you eat it either raw or prepared in one of the ways which we know as ordinary cooking. What the Franklin party did was to scorch the leather until it was at least partly converted to the equivalent of charcoal. They ate the skin after burning some or all of the nourishment out of it. . . . If they had pounded the bones with stone hammers and boiled them, they would have had a rich, nourishing soup. . . . What the Franklin party actually did was to hold the bones in the fire until they were "friable," whereupon they ate them — which means that they let most or all the food value go up in smoke and flame. Then they ate the charcoal.

On Franklin's first expedition of 1819-1821, six Yellowknife hunters were adequate to supply what their chief Akaicho called "the crazy white men" with three thousand pounds of fish, twelve thousand pounds of meat and practical advice about the advent of winter and its risks. The British commander either refused to listen or failed to understand what he was hearing, and his party was reduced to murder and cannibalism before the Yellowknifes provided succour to the survivors. Yet the scientists appear to have learned little from the Indians who thrived around them in identical conditions. How could trained observers fail to notice that scurvy, the dread affliction of so many European explorers, was unknown among both natives and whites who subsisted on the Indian diet? How could they fail to make the connection between the fact that so long as they were eating native food there were no symptoms of scurvy among the Englishmen, despite the fact that their supplies of lime juice had been depleted? Stefansson points out that twenty-five years later, when Franklin's ships were trapped in the ice, his crew huddled aboard the vessels although there were plenty of supplies to provision free-ranging hunting parties which might have brought in sufficient fresh meat to prevent scurvy and ultimate starvation.

University of Alberta anthropologist Owen Beattie, basing his theory on analysis of tissue samples from exhumed remains of crewmen from Franklin's last, fatal expedition, argues that lead poisoning was a critical factor in the disaster. This seems almost certainly true. Lead concentrations that were thirty times the ambient levels in the Inuit population were found in the Franklin party's dead. The expedition had taken advantage of a new technological breakthrough — food preserved in tin cans. The commander's ships carried tons of canned goods, all of which may have been contaminated by the lead solder used to seal the seams. Toxic lead poisoning to the degree measured by Beattie's analysis would almost certainly result in severe physical and neurological impairment.

But if lead was a factor in the catastrophe, it was only that — one factor. In a way, the theory advanced by Beattie helps to confirm Stefansson's thesis. Relying on the so-called superior technology of European civilization, Franklin's two previous expeditions had taught him little. The great success stories in Arctic exploration — Hearne, Rae, Amundsen, Stefansson — are all those of men who learned to read the weather from the natives and to travel light, fast and in small numbers. The numbers on Franklin's expeditions grew bigger not smaller, requiring greater and greater volumes of equipment and supplies. When those supplies failed, large numbers of survivors were thrown into an environment too sparse to support them. Betrayed by his faith in technology, the real killer of Franklin was his inability to see what surrounded him except through the powerful ethnocentric assumptions of his culture regarding the natural inferiority of Indian society.

The contrast of Hearne's attitude is startling: "I have met with few Christians who have more good moral qualities, or fewer bad ones," he wrote of Matonabbee, the man who would guide his great adventure. "To the vivacity of a Frenchman, and the sincerity of an Englishman, he added the gravity and nobleness of a Turk." Filled with an obvious and sincere respect for his Indian companions and their superior knowledge, Hearne understands from his first arrival that he has much to learn. He frequently leaves the relative comfort of the fort to spend bitter nights in the Indian camps, discovering how to survive winter in the open; he continually sharpens his hunting skills; he trains on snow-shoes until he is capable of swift travel in difficult conditions.

Hearne records with gusto a native diet that not only takes advantage of available food sources but provides a steady low-level source of vitamin C to prevent the scurvy which weakened and killed so many who prissily insisted upon their European cuisine. Hearne's journals are filled not with complaints of illness and famine but with sumptuous feasts of raw caribou kidneys, taken hot from the animal's body, with descriptions of how to make an Indian haggis from lungs and liver, with the merits of various animals' stomach linings, with the value of drinking fresh blood from a slaughtered moose, with the succulence of unborn beaver and even with the tasty salad offered by the partially digested moss in a caribou's stomach.

Franklin's journals, while richer in technical information, report native customs with a cultural superiority that leads him to characterize them by the stereotypes that remain with us today: "Vain, fickle, improvident and indolent." He observes these native people with the same perspective that he applies to the animals he records — and with the same detachment. At one point, an old man is dying of starvation in a nearby encampment. Franklin returns several times to watch and seems quite put out when the dying man makes it clear he finds the explorer's morbid curiosity an unwelcome intrusion.

In the end, argues Stefansson, Franklin's crews "perished as victims of the manners, customs, social outlook and medical views of their time." Hearne, on the other hand, his technology and strategies having failed on two previous expeditions, abandoned his European values and submerged himself in the new culture to which he was exposed. He not only endured but prospered.

Who was this tenacious and far-sighted young man who had walked across a continent and back for the sake of entries in a few battered journals?

Samuel Hearne was born into turbulent times. In the year of his birth, 1745, the British colonists of Nova Scotia seized the great French fortress of Louisbourg, while in Britain itself the Duke of Cumberland was marching his army north to put down the insurrection of Bonnie Prince Charlie on the moor at Culloden. An orphan at three in a society without much collective concern for the plight the poor, Hearne grew up in the London of Johnson and Boswell, intellectual ferment and burgeoning empire. In the New World, the French and Indian wars raged as the two empires battled for supremacy, and every year the merchants, traders and explorers pushed back the limits of the world known to Europeans in Africa, Asia, North and South America.

If the expectations of the age were that Hearne should aspire to be a country gentleman, or at least a successful businessman, with some small position in London society, he would have none of it. At the age of eleven he bolted, joining the Royal Navy as a midshipman, sailing in the flagship of Admiral Hood and seeing action against the French before the year was out. A decade later, serving as mate on one of the Hudson's Bay Company trading sloops, he was posted to Prince of Wales's Fort.

In 1769, Hearne was commissioned by Moses Norton, the

Métis factor of the post, to lead an overland expedition in search of fabulous mines to the northwest, where Indian travellers said great lumps of free copper could be picked from the ground. The first expedition was abortive, failing when he and two companions were abandoned in the tundra by Indians who had agreed to travel with the party. The Europeans could not continue by themselves and narrowly avoided starvation. A second attempt was quickly mounted and as quickly abandoned, when Hearne's navigational equipment broke in an accident. Both these failures were significant, for they must have enlightened Hearne to the futility of attempting to apply European methods to an Arctic land expedition. It was at this point that he came into contact with the man who would ensure success on his third and final attempt.

Matonabbee, at thirty-three, was already a trusted Hudson's Bay Company man and was respected as a leader among the Indian nations. He had negotiated an end to generations of conflict among the Chipewyan, Cree and Ojibwa. The two men met for the first time while a glum Hearne was trudging back to Prince of Wales's Fort to report yet another failed mission. Hearne was now convinced that if the trip to the fabled Copper River was to be made successfully it would have to be done using the methods and technology of native people and not the British aristocrat's tradition of a stiff upper lip and an empty stomach.

They set out on December 7, 1770. It was winter, but the marshy tundra was frozen. That would make for fast travel before the advent of the bitterest weather in late January and February. Matonabbee led the party westward, staying close to the shelter of the treeline until the milder weather of spring made feasible a dash north across the open barrens. When winter broke, they were south of Great Slave Lake. They turned north and pushed for the Arctic Ocean.

It was during the final descent of what is now the Coppermine River that Hearne learned first hand that wars and brutality were not the exclusive domain of his European compatriots. The Chipewyans in the expedition surprised a band of Inuit camped peacefully at a summer fishing place on a stretch of white water. While Hearne attempted to dissuade his companions, they put on their ceremonial war paint and ambushed the settlement while the Inuit were sleeping. As the naked and defenceless sleepers tumbled from their shelters, Matonabbee and his war party killed every man, woman and child they could catch.

The place is still identified on the maps by Hearne's name,

Bloody Falls. His journals tell of a pretty teenage girl of perhaps eighteen, stabbed in the side and fallen at his feet, wrapping her arms around his legs in a plea for mercy. As Hearne pleaded for her life, two more spears were plunged through her body, and the impaled girl was left pinned to the ground and "twining around their spears like an eel." Farther on, the war party captured an old woman, so blind she was unable to see her enemies. Her eyes were put out, she was stabbed in the arms and legs and cruelly tortured before she was killed.

The vividness of Hearne's description and the violence of the attack was such that Franklin easily verified the incident and its location fifty years later:

> Several human skulls which bore the marks of violence, and many bones were strewed about the ground near the encampment, and as the spot exactly answers the description given by Mr. Hearne of the place where the Chipewyans who accompanied him perpetrated the dreadful massacre on the Eskimos, we had no doubt of this being the place, notwithstanding the difference in its position as to latitude and longitude given by him, and ascertained by our observation. We have, therefore, preserved the appellation of Bloody Falls, which he bestowed upon it.

When the Chipewyans were finished their slaughter, they sat down for a meal of fish stolen from the victims. Hearne was sanguine. Although he later wrote that he wept whenever he imagined the piteous scenes of the girl and the old woman, he had learned the fundamental pragmatism of the Arctic and joined in the meal. Then, under the blaze of the midnight sun, he travelled the final eight miles to Coronation Gulf and became the first known white man of the historic era to gaze upon the Arctic Ocean from the centre of the continent. The copper mines of legend proved mythical, but, ironically, Hearne had passed within spitting distance of the great mineral treasures of Canada's twentieth century — the huge lead-zinc deposits of Pine Point, the goldfields of Yellowknife, the mines of Uranium City, the silver discoveries of Great Bear Lake.

On his return to Prince of Wales's Fort, Hearne was once again made mate of a Hudson's Bay Company vessel — this time a brigantine, a marginal promotion over the sloop that had brought him. But two years later, he was travelling inland again, this time to what is now Saskatchewan, to establish Cumberland House. In 1776, with the American Revolution occupying Britain's military strength in the colonies and the French waiting

delightedly to take advantage, Hearne was called back to take
command of the big, stone fort. Six years later, when the
colossus fell to the French it had been waiting fifty years to fight,
he was still in command.

Supposed to be impregnable, the great fort fell without a shot
being fired. Designed to withstand a siege army, it required an
army itself to man the battlements and gun emplacements. With
only thirty-nine men to defend the walls, Hearne surrendered
Prince of Wales's Fort to another explorer, Jean François de
Galaup, Comte de La Perouse, who had sailed into Hudson Bay
with three French men-of-war and a force of several hundred
scurvy-ridden men. La Perouse spiked the guns and left them to
rust where they stand today. He breached the walls with explo-
sives and sailed back to Europe with Hearne as his captive.

When La Perouse learned of Hearne's great trek across the
barrens to the far Arctic sea, the French commander was
enthralled. He insisted on setting his prisoner free to tell the
story to the world, after extracting an honourable gentleman's
promise that Hearne would ensure prompt publication of the
documents. Hearne returned briefly to Churchill in the fur trade,
but ill health forced him to return to Britain in 1787, and he spent
his last years revising his journals and lecturing on his adventures. He died in 1792, not yet fifty. The gallant La Perouse vanished at sea in 1788 after sailing from Botany Bay on a scientific
expedition to Australia. His fate remained a mystery of the
South Seas to match Franklin's mystery of the Frozen North,
until the wreckage of his ships was found on an island in the
New Hebrides in 1826. And as for Matonabbee, who had been
away in the interior when Prince of Wales's Fort fell to the
French, the capture of his friend proved unbearable and he committed suicide in 1783.

The enduring question remains, Why do Canadians relegate
Hearne to the marginalia of our history? Historians with particular interest may deny it, and there has indeed been some fine
scholarship, but any quick survey of the literature is revealing. A
two-metre bookshelf of histories, journals, reports, adventures
and popular speculations commemorates Franklin, best sellers
still arise a century-and-a-half after his death and documentaries
find spots on national network television. Hearne, on the other
hand, is not considered worthy of an individual entry in the
Encyclopaedia Britannica. In the *Canadian Encyclopedia,* he merits
entries less than a third the length of those devoted to Franklin.

Perhaps this is not so surprising. In Franklin's disaster we
might recognize ourselves — prideful, arrogant, imperious,

convinced by our technological superiority, trapped in the material values of a society that remains incapable of listening to and learning from the aboriginal cultures we first exploited, then smashed and now either ignore or oppress. Indeed, Matonabbee's suicide might serve as a tragic metaphor for the collective grief of his own descendants, who, in the midst of the richest culture in the history of human kind, experience the highest suicide rates, the highest homicide rates, devastating alcoholism, the greatest poverty and the least opportunity. In that most insolent of sophistries, the rest of us find ways to blame the oppressed for their oppression, the poor for their poverty, the wretched for their wretchedness.

Native people today remain excluded from our national consciousness as surely as they were reduced in Franklin's to the inferior status of nameless bearers, capable of teaching nothing to the advancing values of European science and leadership. This attitude permeates our response to the contemporary aspirations of native people to find some kind of self-determination. We begin with the assumption that the only valid political institutions are a legacy of the European presence, as though the native people of Canada existed for twenty thousand years in some strange vacuum devoid of political awareness and culture.

In fact, there is a rich and substantial texture to aboriginal political philosophy that might offer much to help improve our own. Theirs tends to inclusiveness and consensus, where ours is partisan and exclusive; theirs is imbued by the sharing ethic, where ours is characterized by obsession with power and control and ownership; theirs is egalitarian and fundamentally democratic in its belief that even the smallest voice should be heard, ours is hierarchical and pays heed only to the powerful and the wealthy; their traditional leaders ruled by the moral force of example, ours buy power through the shameless offering of false promises and cling to it by bribing the public with its own money.

Perhaps, ultimately, we love Franklin because he is the historic manifestation of a secret national fetish for failure, the same failure which emerges in its most powerful form from our consistent inability to provide just and equitable status to aboriginal peoples. After a century of assuming ostensible responsibility, political life in Canada is still characterized by our deep national contempt for the distinctive aboriginal cultures which struggle for the right to survival and sovereignty on terms different from ours. It is a contempt we struggle to conceal, deceiving ourselves with the lip service of museum displays and art shows, trotting out the wreckage of a culture we first reduced to artefacts and then looted in the name of preservation. But, for all our self-deception, the truth of our attitudes is revealed in the continued exclusion of native people from full participation in Canadian life. Our contempt is profound, and it prevails in our futile bureaucracies, our cruel political process and, above all, in our blind, Franklinesque acceptance of the inevitability of suffering and grief imposed by our wealthy and powerful society upon our native minorities. Yet, native people, as deserving of respect as those embraced by Hearne, might teach us a great deal about the enduring matter of Canada, if only we could bring ourselves to shed our illusions. What might they teach us, if we could open our hearts and minds?

We might obtain from them some sense of ourselves as integrated beings in a vast and complex arrangement of living things. We might acquire some sense of the precarious nature of this little oasis of life to which we all cling, surrounded by the icy void. We might learn to confront the vanities of our technological prowess: a power which permits us to split the atom and walk upon the moon, but which we use to poison the seas with plutonium, the heavens with fluorocarbons, the lakes with sulphuric acid and, even, the fragile Arctic, where the polar bears and seals and the mother's breast itself are now contaminated with pesticides, toxic chemicals and heavy metals.

We might even learn something of our spiritual connection to the organic world and of our moral obligations to all those living creatures with whom we share our planet and our country and who depend upon us to save them — the animals who cannot hide in bunkers when the ozone layer depletes and who cannot cloak themselves in illusion when their habitats are destroyed. We might choose not to strip the last virgin forest basin of its trees; we might choose not to dam the last wild river in the watershed; we might choose to nurture the delicate flowers of little nations within our own.

Myself, I prefer the ghost of Hearne to that of Franklin. Samuel Hearne was a man with the vision to see beyond his cultural stereotypes, big enough to take the wisdom of his Indian friend Matonabbee for his talisman, gliding across the vast Northland of our national spirit with the grace of those wind-borne shapes of snow, rising and dancing and becoming one with the landscape itself.

A WAR STORY

This is no accounting of Exocet missiles and shipboard infernos hot enough to burn the very metal. Nor is it a romantic tale of battles at the thinning edge of the atmosphere, fought on radar screens by post-adolescent computer jockeys. There is no Top Gun, no planes with names like *Eagle* and *Mirage*, no tanks, no Blitzkriegs, no massed armies weltering in the carnage of machine guns, mud and poison gas. The victims may be counted in hundreds, not millions, although they are certainly just as dead as their counterparts at Phnom Penh and Stalingrad. In their death, they are a lesson to the living, a small compensation for the futility of their extinction.

This is a story about genocide of a kind, if that emotionally charged term has not been so singularized by the Holocaust that it ceases to have meaning for any other. I use it here to describe war policies that result in the vengeful disappearance of an entire nation.

My story is about imperialism and the consequences of it, although the people who practised it likely would not have understood our concept, resonant as it is with echoes of the ancient world and the modern homages paid to Rome by European colonialism and its strange heir, the American idea of manifest destiny and hegemony in the free world. This ongoing American conception, that of a free world compelled occasionally to brutalizing extremes in the defence of liberty — arming terrorists in Nicaragua, for example, or supporting the governments of death squads and torture in Chile and El Salvador — this is itself a disturbing echo of the ancient world. The island of Melos had been a free state for seven hundred years when the great cold war between Sparta and Athens broke out. In 416 B.C., the Athenian democracy sent a naval task force to persuade the Melians to end their strict neutrality and join the free world of the Delian league. The subsequent negotiations and their consequences are recorded by the historian Thucydides. The Melians preferred their neutrality but in the end surrendered unconditionally to the Athenians, who promptly — in the name of national security, no doubt, like the commander in Vietnam who found himself forced to destroy the village in order to save it for democracy — executed every male citizen big enough to carry a weapon and dispersed the remaining women and children into slavery. As any reader of the Peloponnesian War is aware, the Athenians soon followed their victims into ignominious decline and defeat.

Ultimately, although it is as Canadian as the beaver pelt, my story is the same story, one that has played itself out many times in the human experience. It serves as a living proof, if you like, of George Santayana's observation that those who do not remember the past are condemned to repeat it, an idea descended from Ranke, who likely got it from Thucydides, who probably appropriated it from Euripides. It is the story of a society which embraced the warrior's creed — and paid the price that societies have paid for such decisions throughout history and continue to pay in a world incapable of learning the lessons of its collective past. Most important, this is a story about what we forget when we begin to weave the fabric of our pasts into the myths we stitch together to sustain us in the present.

It is a true story. A story about the real face of a social catastrophe from a time which some among us feel compelled to propagandize as a golden age of peace and friendship. A perfect, golden age in which the people lived as one with nature until the natural harmony among native peoples was forever shattered by the arrival of rapacious Europeans. The European invaders of North America were indeed brutal, violent and avaricious. They were imperialists in every sense of the word — culturally, militarily, economically, socially, linguistically. But there are no Europeans in this story, except as keepers of the fragmentary records.

The sources of my story are widely scattered in the ledgers of fur traders, the journals of travellers, the field reports of surveyors and explorers. Perhaps the best source for the general reader seeking basic documentation of these events is an article by Beryl Gillespie. The paper is one of sixty-six on the subarctic collected in volume six of the twenty-volume series planned for the Smithsonian Institution's fine and scholarly work, *The Handbook of North American Indians*. For primary sources, one must scour the reports of Samuel Hearne, George Back, Sir John Franklin and John Richardson and the Hudson's Bay Company archives. For all that, much of the story must be inferred from oblique references, from the folklore of the Chipewyans, Dogribs and Slaveys of the Dene nation.

The story has murky beginnings, and, for the most part, we can rely only on the indirect references and dispersed reports of outsiders, for the people who were subjects of the narrative kept only oral records of their wars and the heroes in them. Since they are all dead — like the Trojans, like the Carthaginians — their past has died with them, except for those bits and pieces kept alive by their exulting enemies and the notes of curious travellers. Who speaks today for Hector and Cassandra? A triumphant Greek in *The Iliad*. And Carthage, the granary of the Mediterranean and a state famed for its libraries, who speaks for it? The Roman conquerors sowed the fields of Carthage with salt and erased the culture. Aside from the fragments uncovered by archaeology, we know little of the people who once ruled the western Mediterranean. We know that a certain Mago once wrote a book about agriculture and that an adventurer named Hanno wrote an account of his voyages to the Pillars of Hercules and beyond to the western coasts of Africa.

This story is not so different. We begin with an obscure notation in Hudson's Bay Company records, dated some time between 1718 and 1721. It marks the visit of a group of Chipewyan Indians to Fort Prince of Wales, the great stone trading fortress that still stands on the icy shores of Hudson Bay near the port of Churchill, Manitoba. They were accompanied by two "Copper Indians." They came from the heartland of a vast, dark continent, still largely unexplored by European fur traders and map makers. These emissaries were the first tangible evidence of a mysterious country to the northwest, known only from tales and traditions among local Indians. It was thought to be inhabited by a powerful people who used metal for their tools and weapons at a time when their neighbours used only flint and bone.

For half a century, the trading company ruminated and speculated over vague reports from Indians trading into Fort Prince of Wales. The visitors told of a rich country far to the west where copper lay about to be picked in pure lumps from the ground. Then, in 1771, a young man named Samuel Hearne was sent to find the fabled land. For two years, he walked The Barrens, and he did indeed find the land of the Copper Indians. It was nothing like what legend had led him to expect, but it was impressive nonetheless. The Copper Indians' territory was huge, almost as large as Europe itself. They ranged over three hundred thousand square kilometres, from the Arctic Coast in the north to Great Slave Lake in the south, from Great Bear Lake in the west to the Thelon River in the east.

Hearne's meticulous journals record contact with the Copper Indians and the location of the copper mines, although they were hardly the riches his masters hoped to find. The names of one of Canada's major rivers and the settlement of Coppermine still bear witness to his voyage. Already, the Yellowknifes, as Hearne's Copper Indians were to become known, were in conflict. They remained isolated from the Hudson's Bay Company, cut off from contact because of hostilities with the Chipewyan nation on their southeastern flank. In the late 1700s, Hearne records reports of distant fighting between the Yellowknifes and the Dogribs, far to the southwest.

By 1800, the new and boisterous North West Company was trading into the country explored a generation earlier by Hearne. At the time of Hearne's trek, the Yellowknifes were without firearms, and Franklin reports them "oppressed" by the better-armed Chipewyans to the south. But the competition between the two fur companies had made trade guns available to the Yellowknifes. The power and militancy of the expansionist Yellowknifes was on the rise. Around 1810, a war party descended the Coppermine River to its mouth and destroyed a large encampment of Inuit, killing about thirty people. In 1812, while Upper and Lower Canada fought a war with the Yankees in the east, there are reports of widespread plundering of Dogrib, Hare and Slavey Indians throughout the Mackenzie Region. The Hudson's Bay Company records Yellowknife war parties slaying Hare Indians on Great Bear Lake in 1815. Five years after that, the Yellowknifes provide guides and provisioners for the first Franklin expedition and the British commander reports a chief named Long Legs trading for ammunition. The explorer reports great fear among any Dogribs or Chipewyans who encounter them. The fearful had good cause.

The next we hear of the Yellowknifes is in Hudson's Bay Company reports which indicate that Dogrib women have been massacred near Fort Providence and the southwest end of Great Slave Lake. The Dogribs of Lac La Martre are reported fleeing westwards toward Fort Simpson, deep in the territory of the Slaveys, to escape the ferocious war parties of the Yellowknifes.

There are further reports of the Yellowknifes pillaging the Hare Indians of Great Bear Lake and even Colville Lake, farther to the northwest. For the rest of the decade, Dogrib and Hare nations are driven from the eastern ranges of their traditional lands because of constant fear of ambush and attack by Yellowknife warriors.

The Dogribs waited to take their revenge. They struck back with a terrible blow of their own. It happened at the very height of Yellowknife ascendancy, but it clearly marked the beginning of the end. With an early northern winter closing in, the Dogribs trapped Long Legs, the powerful Yellowknife leader who had hunted for Franklin, in a camp near Hottah Lake, just south of Great Bear Lake. In October of 1823, they slaughtered the whole encampment. The slain comprised a full 20 per cent of the Yellowknifes' estimated population.

Although sporadic fighting continued for decades more, European accounts thereafter describe the Yellowknifes as demoralized, suffering from starvation, disease, privation and population decline. As early as 1825, Akaicho, the chief who had supplied meat for Franklin's earlier expedition, was refusing to travel "to those parts where the bones of our murdered brethren lie." By 1848, the Yellowknifes had retreated from their vast northern and western territories to a shrunken toe-hold on existence. It ran from the site of the present Northwest Territories capital, which commemorates their name, to the eastern arm of Great Slave Lake. By 1914, records show they had ceased even to call themselves Yellowknifes, preferring to shelter under the name of the powerful Chipewyan neighbours to the east whom they once terrorized. An influenza epidemic swept through the region in 1928. While it had a terrible impact upon the whole northern population, it devastated the Yellowknifes, finishing the slide into extinction that had begun with the violent adventures of Long Legs and his warriors a century before.

We should think about the Yellowknifes whenever we hear calls for the preservation of native culture that are based on romantic illusion and reconstructed myth. There is indeed a rich and important aboriginal culture, and the broader collaboration that is Canadian society is morally compelled to ensure the survival of that culture in all its diversity. But all of us should be certain of what it is we are talking about. Is life on the trap-line traditional native culture? Trapping was the necessity of an ephemeral and largely artificial economy imposed by cosmetic demand in Europe. The morality of killing creatures to sustain community life is clear in the aboriginal culture, but what is the morality of killing rare and beautiful animals like the lynx so that a Parisian woman might be fashionable? And if there is a question about the morality of such commercial pursuits, wrongly identified as the traditional native economy, what is the ethical implication of Canada's appalling failure to provide alternative economic choices to native communities? Life on the reserve? The stationary community was invented by nineteenth century bureaucrats as an instrument of administrative control. It was, to all intents and purposes, a concentration camp for nomadic peoples. The ancestors of the present reserve communities fought to abandon them, to escape from the misery of an alien sedentary life. Now, reserves are fundamental to the political objectives of their descendants. The concentration camps have become the archetypes not of oppression but of cultural sovereignty. These so-called traditional lifestyles may certainly be worth preserving. The reserve system may be essential to the survival of native culture, but let us not be mistaken about their origins or about the ironies and paradoxes inherent in what they have become.

The neglected rights of aboriginal people, their consistent abuse at the hands of the dominant society, make profound demands of the national conscience. They insist that the cultural integrity and political emancipation of our native peoples become our central priority as a nation. But all of us should think hard and long about the commonly held assumptions and attitudes both of the dominant society and of the aboriginal minorities now submerged within it. The confusion of tradition with culture, the blind acceptance of stereotype, the brazen propagandizing with romantic myths which distort the past and cloud the present — these continue to be the major obstacles facing native peoples in their long journey into political awareness and social action.

Many of these confusions flow from the selfish myths forged in the guilty consciousness of European society. I say selfish, because these myths are imposed upon native peoples struggling to articulate their own identity and their own terms of participation in the mainstream of Canadian society. This is an insidious form of cultural imperialism. The aboriginal past is recreated to serve the ends of the dominant society, a revision which justifies and articulates the useless feelings of guilt which one generation bears for the actions of earlier generations. People, many of them in our churches, distil these romantic myths to shield themselves from the tough intellectual work of wringing difficult decisions from the ambiguities of the human condition. It is far easier to invoke the values of a golden age than to grasp the nettle of precisely how one group of human beings with great power may negotiate a sharing of that power with the same minority which the powerful oppresses. Thus we have the spectacle of earnest Christian priests lamenting the dismantling of traditional cultural values in native communities. They lament the loss while remaining unable to acknowledge that they themselves represent an enormous assault upon the framework of spiritual values once at the heart of those communities. Missionaries, no less than traders, served as shock troops in the destabilizing of aboriginal culture. Where traders substituted European economies, missionaries substituted European religion for aboriginal spiritual systems.

Perhaps, this failure to acknowledge responsibility triggers guilt. Perhaps, this is why the new myths often spring from those among us who hold the best and most sincere intentions, the people most desirous of seeing native peoples achieve their political goals. One of the most pernicious of these new myths is the view that native society had existed in exquisite harmony with itself and the land for millennia prior to the brutal intrusion of European colonists, priests and missionaries excepted, for the myth holds that they were employed in the salvation of aboriginal culture and that they were somehow distant and detached from the destructive process of colonization.

European culture, of course, is easier to excoriate when it is presented as an one-dimensional model of savage imperialism. Its necessary obverse is the quasi-utopia of aboriginal societies which inhabited the Eden-like world before contact. This is a convenient picture descended in ignorance from Rousseau's idea of the noble savage, with its implications of childlike innocence in the face of decadent European sophistication. But it is simply not true. Or, at least, it is only a partial truth. European colonists were certainly brutal. They had superior weapons and a social organization better adapted to effective use of those weapons. More importantly, they had developed the sophisticated economic infrastructures required to support their colonial aspirations. One has to look some distance to find a more cynical and cruel conquest than that of the Spanish in Mexico. Yet, when reading Bernal Diaz's eyewitness account of *The Conquest of New Spain,* one is surprised by the rebellions of client states against the oppressive rule of Montezuma's Aztecs. These subject peoples preferred the clear hazards of an alliance with harsh Cortes to a continuation of the status quo under the tyranny of their own Indian emperor.

And native peoples who lived in nature's balance did so not because of an inherent philosophy of conservation as our own society understands it — that is, a European concept which evolved to sustain the recreational pleasures of the noble classes — but because their killing instruments were too crude to permit major ecological disruptions. The European invaders must bear responsibility for the industrial extinction of the buffalo, but to believe this environmental obscenity occurred without the compliance, and even assistance, of the newly armed Indian and Métis hunters is naive. Today, in many areas of Canada's North, the coupling of traditional hunting rights with high-powered rifles and snowmobiles has been followed by precipitous declines in localized game populations. Hunters in many communities must travel farther and farther to find their prey.

The indiscriminate slaughter by native hunters of pregnant cow moose driven by deep snow to the roadside is not a practice which speaks to environmental harmony. I once counted nineteen partially used carcasses in one twelve-kilometre stretch of road and listened to the argument that such wilful mismanagement of the resource was a right guaranteed by the Indian Act. More recently, the extermination of an entire herd of rare bighorn sheep in the Rocky Mountains in 1987 was accompanied by an invocation of traditional hunting rights and insistence by a local chief that his people remained natural conservationists, despite this aberration by hunters from another reserve. Similar invocations accompany the aerial slaughter of caribou and the black market trade in Pacific salmon, harvested by the non-traditional but efficient fishing method of "the CIL spinner," tossing a stick of dynamite into a river pool. While such acts are not commonplace, neither are they so infrequent as to be extraordinary. What is significant about them is their similarity to those acts so often cited as proof of the dominant culture's greed and insensitivity to the natural world.

North American aboriginal cultures practised slavery long before the European invaders arrived. Franklin reports that Akaicho was accompanied by a "personal servant" from among the Dogribs. His surgeon John Richardson is more blunt in describing the man as Akaicho's slave. One can visit the museum of anthropology at the University of British Columbia and look at totem poles with the characteristic markings that indicate a slave was killed and buried underneath for ceremonial purposes. Even today in the Northwest Pacific native community, one may hear the shameful comments intended to identify families and individuals who are descended from slaves, usually offered as an explanation for personal failure or a justification of inferior social status. While such views are far from common, neither are they rare. What is significant about them is the ironic way in which they parallel similar class distinctions and discriminatory stereotypes in the dominant society.

Wars of genocidal intent between tribal groups are reported in the accounts of European explorers, some of them occurring almost within living memory. Hearne, dispatched by a Hudson's Bay Company which employed many of those Scots dispossessed during the Highland Clearances, himself watched in horror as his Indian friends and companions ignored his protests and made sport out of butchering old women and children on the Coppermine River. Change the place names in Hearne's account of the incident at Bloody Falls and it might be a record of Lieutenant William Calley and his men slaughtering the civilians at My Lai in Vietnam.

It is worth remembering that while it is true that Europeans encouraged the taking of scalps as a form of terrorism during their own wars of colonial expansion, it is equally true that the warrior tribes of the Great Plains took up the practice with uninhibited enthusiasm. Ghastly tortures to equal anything devised by the Inquisition or the Death Squads in Argentina are widely reported.

Does any of this diminish the moral imperative which drives the emerging political and cultural aims of native people in Canada? Does this human truth somehow absolve the dominant society from its deep obligations to assist in the preservation of distinct aboriginal cultures? Of course not. It is merely a reminder that racially based myths and a romantic indulgence in them are not constructive elements in the process of enlightenment and reconciliation.

Our brutal past establishes only the commonality of human cultures in Canada, a constant reminder of our own capacities for evil and of the enduring consequences of our acts toward others. In that commonality — recognition that while European and aboriginal societies are distinct and unique we are also the same — is rooted our conception of the indivisible right to self-determination which accrues to all who are party to a true democracy. Yet, this knowledge comes with a warning. People who desire to chart the course of their own destiny must navigate by the true landmarks of their history. Too much of the discussion over how native peoples might fully define and achieve their goals is characterized by the erection of false landmarks;

the self-congratulatory myth, the self-serving distortion and the egregious stereotype.

The definitions which will guide native peoples to their future will emerge from their past. Thucydides chronicled with a cold eye the self-destructive follies of his own Athenians because he knew that only through an exact knowledge of what had gone before might the future be interpreted. It is for this reason that all Canadians have a duty to take ownership of those things done in the name of progress. Those who trade the painful truth of their past for the romantic myth that sustains present stereotypes soon find they have no past at all — and that is the sure path to cultural oblivion.

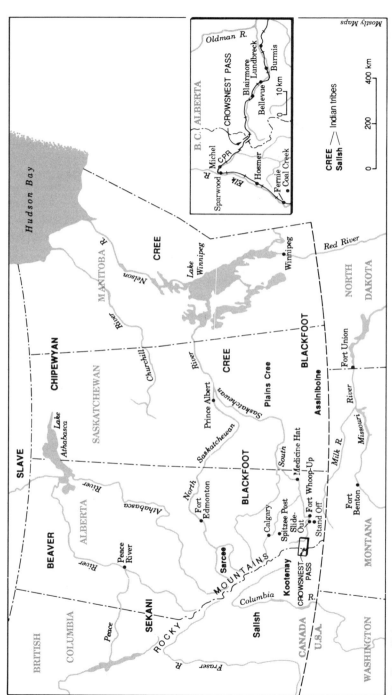

The Great Plains

Mostly Maps

Oldman R.

CROWSNEST PASS

Blairmore
Lundbreck
Bellevue
Burmis

B.C. | ALBERTA

Michel
Sparwood
CPR
Elk R.

Hosmer

Fernie
Coal Creek

0   10 km

CREE
Sallish Indian tribes

0   200   400 km

Hudson Bay

CREE

MANITOBA

Nelson River

Lake Winnipeg

Winnipeg

Red River

NORTH DAKOTA

CHIPEWYAN

SASKATCHEWAN

Churchill River

CREE

Plains Cree

BLACKFOOT

Fort Union

Assiniboine

SLAVE

Lake Athabasca

Prince Albert

Saskatchewan River

South

Medicine Hat

Missouri River

Milk R.

Athabasca River

BLACKFOOT

North

Fort Edmonton

Fort Whoop-Up

Fort Benton

BEAVER

ALBERTA

Peace River

Calgary

Spitzee Post
Slide-Out

Stand Off

Sarcee

MONTANA

Peace River

SEKANI

ROCKY MOUNTAINS

Kootenay

CROWSNEST PASS

Columbia R.

BRITISH COLUMBIA

Peace R.

Fraser R.

Salish

CANADA
U.S.A.

WASHINGTON

THE HILLS COME UP LIKE THUNDER

The air in the cab of my four-by-four is sharp with the bitter scent of alkaline dust. It coats the tongue, crusts around the nostrils, leaves a bone-white patina on the slick vinyl surfaces. The dirty windshield has just been awarded its third star by a knuckle-sized rock chewed out of the ruts by the front-wheel drive and flipped up over the hood.

A kind of grimy bronze comet enclosed in its nimbus of flying gravel, my Jeep is lunging and shuddering down a rough side road on the bald prairie. Bald is the appropriate image. This is antelope country, the powder dry heart of Palliser's Triangle, where the last unfenced landscape that was North America's virgin short-grass prairie still clings to life. It rolls off the edge of the world at all points of the compass, the ground swelling to complete the aching emptiness of sky, a physical manifestation of harmonies, the perfect balancing of opposites. Your feet take root in the treeless sweep of grass, you sense that you stand at the foundations of heaven. There are no intruders into this landscape, quite the opposite. Instead, it embraces you, enfolds you, makes you and the point where you stand the thrumming centre of everything, navel of the earth. On a clear day, you can see the earth's curve along the distant skyline. It is less than fifteen kilometres by line of sight to the razored edge of the horizon, yet your vision seems limitless.

I am lost in this, and I am pressing things because the weather is closing in. What light there is bleeds out of the countryside, taking the hue and texture with it and leaving the tawny swell of prairie with a bleached, faded look. Normally, it should be easy to find the coulee I'm hunting. The government has made it a national historic site, improved the road to take heavier traffic and provided road signs. But if one shys from the government track, the world changes. And this is strange weather. The clouds have dropped in like a Halifax fog. They drape this highest corner of Saskatchewan with curlicues of grey mist, and the sky has settled around us like an opaque bowl. Soon there is only a narrow, tubular world between ditches. It extends maybe a hundred feet ahead, even in the gloomy trench carved by the powerful beams of halogen headlights.

I had wanted to come in from the southwest, get a sense of the country as the characters of my imagination saw it, but the gas jockey on the highway warned me not to try the high ridgeways and cattle tracks from the Alberta side, even with my Jeep and a come-along. "What in hell are you gonna hitch it to out there," he said, leaning his greasy Wheat Pool hat in at my window. "She's bare as a baby's ass out where you're goin. Less you plan to catch a cow to pull you out." He sniggered at the prospect. Blushed. Sniggered again.

With a little moisture, even the fog's slight condensation, clay and hardpan turns greasy as a teflon griddle. It can transform into a sickening gumbo that churns over the axle hubs faster than a driver can think about it. So I circled east and came in from the Saskatchewan side. I haven't seen a soul since I came banging south from the highway in search of the place Canada was born.

That's just my unscholarly opinion, of course. Many historians would disagree. They see the creation of the country in more precise terms, taking place six years earlier than my birthing of Canada, amid the oak-panelled rooms of Ottawa and Quebec City — a bloodless phenomenon of diplomacy, statesmanship, politics and power. It serves the national stereotype that springs from central Canada's self-perception to see the nation's construction as a product of intelligent consideration, the inevitable conclusion of a rational process, the cutting of a deal. The idea of our origins being rooted in chaotic slaughter, the stupidity of greed and excess, cuts against the grain of conventional wisdom. The possibility that a major current of national identity finds its source in the wretched fountainheads of political expedience is simply repellent. The thought that Trotsky's observation that every state is rooted in the exercise of force might equally apply to our own country assaults our comfortable illusions about the essential decency of Canada's genteel ascent to peace, order and good government.

Call it a weakness, but to me true history is written in the heart, is written in the language of blood and passion. There is evil in it, and loss, and the endless suffering that places obligation upon triumph. My instincts tell me that the Canada we know today really came to pass here in the heart of the prairie, born in the shocked aftermath of a hail of bullets, sexual assault and mutilation that seems like a grim foretaste of more recent atrocities. If My Lai serves as a metaphor for the corrupted values so central to the American experience in Vietnam, the other, in its day, came to symbolize the illusory nature of Canada's claim to western sovereignty and the brute reality of American rapaciousness in smashing the Plains tribes. In raising that consciousness alone, what came to be known as the Cypress Hills massacre served to chart new directions for Canada's treatment of Indian nations. And if that treatment has proved far from ideal, it at least sought to shield aboriginal people from the obliterating forces wielded south of the border.

The massacre triggered its own international incident and spurred the mobilization and deployment of the North-West Mounted Police, although organization of the force had already been called for in a federal bill. Most important, the Cypress Hills incident wove an appreciation of the Far West and its strategic consequence into the fabric of an only partially framed national awareness. The prior intelligence of nationhood had been almost exclusively centred on the primary wedding of Upper and Lower Canada. It heeded the huge, wild hinterlands of the North-West largely as a source of exotic interest. Captain W.F. Butler, dispatched by the federal authorities in 1870 to make a formal reconnaissance of the region, had filed a shrewdly prescient report on the strategic importance of the High Plains and had called for an immediate, if nominal, military occupation to offset the lawless and increasingly brutal American presence. But by 1873, the idea of an occupying force which sprang from Butler's report seemed stillborn in the fledgling cabinet. There was talk and there was enabling legislation, but there was no action. Royal Canadian Mounted Police historian S.W. Horrall has pointed out that in May of 1873 the new lieutenant-governor of the North-West Territories expressed concerns about the gravity of the situation around Fort Whoop-Up. Ottawa disagreed. The situation at Fort Whoop-Up was not "sufficiently grave to call for the sending of the force there," the lieutenant-governor was instruced in a dispatch from the minister of the interior.

The distant region, at least in the popular imagination, remained the trackless, unmapped country of explorers, fur traders and powerful, warlike Indians. It was a source of traveller's tales and adventures for young men anxious to show their mettle before marrying and settling down to the family business in Brantford and Guelph. And yet, the incident in question changed all that. Indirectly, it caused Canada's military occupation of the High Plains, justified Sir John A. Macdonald's visions of the great transcontinental railways, set in motion the settling of the West and accomplished with the tools of civilization what had been started with the repeating rifle — the final destruction of the Indian nations' hegemony over the prairie region.

On the basis of muddled documentary evidence and the conflicting, self-serving reports from eyewitnesses that remain tainted by a host of vested interests, historians now generally agree that the event in question occurred on the Sunday morning of June 1, 1873. It took place in a fragrant fold of the unusual highlands with which the massacre shares its name. Hidden deep in the arid southern grassland, these rolling hills straddle the Alberta-Saskatchewan border high above the plateau that rises toward the Rockies. Even without the attractions of history, this is one of the most significant places in Canada.

Sudden as prairie thunderheads, the Cypress Hills burst up into the vast skies of the open plains. The long drive into this dusty corner of southwest Saskatchewan is worthwhile just for the abrupt, surging power of that first sighting. Beautiful, mysterious and strange, these magical uplands mark the true High Plains of the West, rising to greater altitudes, for example, than those found at the Banff townsite in the Rocky Mountains. A geological peculiarity, they are one piece of Canada that was not ground to rubble under the glaciers of the last ice age. A scant twenty-five thousand years ago, during the glaciation known as the Wisconsonian advance, the Laurentide ice sheets, four kilometres thick, pulverized most of what is now Saskatchewan, Manitoba and Alberta. Somehow, this primordial landscape was spared. Species of plants and animals are found here that occur nowhere else upon the ancient sedimentary bottoms that form the Canadian prairies. It was this richness and beauty that drew the Plains Indian tribes to the region long before Europeans arrived. Cree, Assiniboine, Blackfoot, Salteaux, Sarcee, Sioux, all scudded across the sea of grass, setting the painted hides of their tipis like sails before the wind. All sought periodic refuge in the glades and sheltered meadows that still form the green oasis of the Cypress Hills.

This particular day in mid-October, I pick my way along the

knobby spine of a ridge a full kilometre above sea level. The clouds themselves touch the earth, streaming past on either side. It's a raw day, and a feathering of early snow drifts out of the mist in light flurries, mingling with dust, then changing to mud on the windshield in a transubstantiation of the elements. Later it will streak the ground in bizarre patterns, leaving memories of wind rippled into the dead grass like sand after a high tide. The spectral faces of free-range cattle loom at the roadside, their big, liquid eyes suspended over white muzzles and bodies that seem to dissolve into fog. Startled, these lumbering apparitions scatter before the Jeep and clatter away from the rough shoulders. The coulee I want lies at the end of a long gravel road that comes snaking its way down out of the clouds. It is hidden in a fold of the hills like a small Garden of Eden.

In this parched country, the meanders and oxbows of Battle Creek nourish a variety of trees that could not survive in the open plains. Thickets of suckering poplar and cloned drifts of aspen crowd the stream banks, flanked on higher ground by sombre stands of white spruce and lodgepole pine. The bottom-land is lush with sweet grass and willow. In late spring, the ground here explodes into a Persian carpet of wild flowers and the air becomes hypnotic with the perfume of blue lupine, shooting star, prairie buttercup. Shady hollows are graced by fourteen varieties of orchid. The shrubs rustle and twitter with the calls of warblers, yellowthroats and mountain bluebirds, and the glades and meadows provide a rich habitat for elk, mule deer and more than thirty other warm-blooded species.

Even beneath the heavy overcast which accompanies my visit, the grassy hillsides deflect enough indirect sun that the valley seems to have a luminous quality of its own. It is the loveliest of places, pale branches in the groves and withered grasses in the meadows, all silvered with condensation. One can imagine the feelings of long-dead riders, arriving here after the summer's trek across the baking prairies, saying to themselves, "This is it. This is the place."

The original Fort Walsh is long gone. Indeed, it was abandoned as a patrol post less than a decade after Troop B of the North-West Mounted Police erected the palisades and barracks. But the Mounties maintained it as a horse ranch for half a century afterwards, and the walls and buildings of the fort have been rebuilt. Today, it's a national historic site, white-washed stables and bunkhouses identified and explained by the federal government's neat sequence of plaques and signs.

Just as I had planned, the coulee was deserted on the

afternoon I arrived, the museum closed for the season, abandoned by tourists and staff alike. For me, this is the kind of place that should be experienced in its natural sounds: the skeletal rattle of poplars in an icy wind, the clank of rigging against a bare flagstaff, the cry of Canada geese echoing down the draw, making an eerie counterpoint to the whickering of curious ponies that browse untethered along the creek bottoms. From the shadow of the peeled log palisades, the sound of those horses is an evocation of everything that western Canada once was.

Horses were the currency of events here, events that were to shape the whole future of the country. Alexander Henry, the early fur trader who was among the first Europeans to venture among the relatively unknown tribes of the western plains, records for us the price of a common horse: one gallon keg of rum; twelve feet of new twist tobacco; twenty musket balls and the powder to fire them; one awl; one scalper; one flaying knife; one ice auger; one P.C. glass; one steel; one flint. This might be the bulk of a wandering hunter's possessions and reflects the value placed on a single animal.

The values endure. At the Blood settlement of Stand Off, the houses have none of the manicured suburban lawns that grace the smallest Alberta towns. But every yard sports a hitching post. A tour of the Peigan reserve's settlement with two teenage girls yields a social calendar. The Who's Who of these northern Blackfoot is based on who has horses and how many. And a Cree girl, graduating from college, is faced with a major choice: whether to take a boring job in a windowless basement as a government clerk or to go home to material poverty and "ride my dad's horses and feel the wind."

It was on horseback that the Indians of the High Plains came to greatness as nations, and it was from horseback that they were eventually pulled down. As the culture of the gun advanced with the fur traders of the northeast, the culture of the horse advanced from the Spanish Territories to the south. These two technologies collided in the country of the Assiniboines. Once a tribe known primarily for its skill in the use of stationary buffalo pounds, after the Assiniboines had acquired the horse and firearms they rapidly rose to ascendancy over virtually all of what are now the prairie provinces. In their regalia of fringed moose hide, clad in sleeveless battle jackets quilted and folded six layers thick, their decorative breastplates of bone and porcupine quill, their war shields of painted buffalo hide, each one decorated with the bearer's personal vision of a blessing from the spirit world, these proud Assiniboine warriors must have been as imposing and formidable as any European queen's hussar. They made allies of the Cree and waged relentless war on the Sioux, Mandan, Kootenay, Salish and Blackfoot until, in the words of Canada's great and coolly dispassionate anthropologist Diamond Jenness, "The whole area from the Rockies to the Great Lakes became a perpetual battlefield drenched with the blood of animals and men. War and confusion reigned everywhere." This war fever of raids and counter-raids, each success measured in scalp knots and stolen horses, continued for generations. It was largely unknown to the settled regions of Upper and Lower Canada and remained to the Canadian consciousness as remote and exotic as the excesses of Zulu chiefs and the adventures of Afghan war-lords claiming descent from Alexander the Great.

Pestilence makes a habit of riding at the shoulder of war, so, perhaps, it is not surprising that at the height of conflict smallpox ravaged the Plains. There had been an earlier epidemic in 1781, but the disease which struck in 1837 was of even greater intensity and virulence. Many died without developing the skin eruptions that are the characteristic symptom of smallpox. Witnesses reported massive haemorrhages from the mouth and ears, then fever accompanied by acute delirium. At Fort Union, where the disease was introduced to the Assiniboines through infected clothing and blankets, the dead were collected by the cart-load and dumped into the wide Missouri.

"The prairie all around is a vast field of death, covered with unburied corpses and, spreading for miles, pestilence and infection," wrote one horrified German aristocrat who passed through the region. "The Assiniboines, 9,000 in number, roaming over a hunting territory to the north of the Missouri, as far as the trading posts of the Hudson's Bay Company, are, in the literal sense of the expression, nearly exterminated."

Edwin Denig, who traded in the upper reaches of the Missouri River between 1833 and 1856, corroborates with his own eyewitness accounts of stinking death camps and trails littered with the corpses of those who tried to flee. The horror and despair of what must have seemed like the end of the world can be seen in the reaction of a proud warrior named Little Dog. After the first of his children died in agony, he consulted with his wife and, with her permission, shot all his dogs and horses, then her, then cut his children's throats, then shot himself.

It was with the pathetic, diseased tatters of the once-great Assiniboines and it was over stolen horses that the momentous circumstances of 1873 arose. As is often the way with history's

important events, it began with an incident which by later comparison paled into insignificance, and, like so much of human
history, what transpired was rooted in the human elements of
pride, arrogance, rage, lust and larcenous greed.

The story begins on May 17 with a party of Americans —
traders, say some sources; ill-used trappers and mountain men,
say others; desperadoes, hell-raisers and horse thieves, say still
others; sadistic butchers and rapists, said the victims. In any
event, all were southbound on the Whoop-Up Trail which connected the remote whisky trading forts with those slightly less
disreputable American towns protected by the U.S. army. The
men in question were returning from that region of the rolling
Canadian prairies occupied by the powerful Blackfoot Confederacy. They were going to Fort Benton, where it nestles below
the bluffs of the great Missouri River in Montana. The party was
returning from a winter of wolf-baiting, larding animal carcasses
with strychnine and skinning the poisoned predators that came
in to feed on the carrion. This was an occupation of indiscriminate and wasteful slaughter, viewed with enormous anger and
contempt by the Indians and with only slightly lesser degrees of
disgust by the trappers and hunters who had come to the mountains in earlier days.

About twelve kilometres from Fort Benton, but by no means
out of the dangerous territory controlled by the warlike Blood,
Blackfoot and Peigan bands, the wolfers settled down to camp
for the night. Were they drinking in anticipation of arrival back
at civilization? It seems a plausible speculation. This was the
centre of an enormous and illicit whisky trade. Prohibited in
American territory and policed by troops of U.S. Cavalry, there
was nothing to prevent unscrupulous traders from crossing into
the uncontrolled Canadian zone to sell as much of the vile and
stupefying brew they called whisky as they were able to concoct.
Watered down, the whisky was laced with blackstrap molasses,
tobacco, tabasco sauce, even gunpowder. The whisky trade was
lucrative, but it also set up a profitable sideline. Indians befud-
dled with liquor were more easily cheated in the exchange of
ordinary trade goods, a situation which contributed in no small
way to the hostility and bitterness of the native victims. So there
is little reason to doubt that the wolfers bound for Fort Benton
had access to liquor themselves. There was certainly much
drinking later, with monstrous consequences, and on this night
they failed to take the most fundamental precaution of Blackfoot
country — mounting a watch over their horses.

This failure alone is surprising for men who later claimed to be Plains-wise. The country around Fort Benton was marginally more secure than the heartland of the Blackfoot, but the situation was scarcely stable. The whole Montana territory resonated like a drum, taut and quivering under violent blows and counter-blows, the tensions escalating on a current of greed, whisky and revenge.

Only eight years before, the Peigans had attacked and burned the Indian Agency at Sun River Crossing, chasing the agent to Fort Benton. Another Peigan war party captured two men on their way from Fort Benton to Milk River, stripped them naked and whipped them through the snow until they could go no farther, when they were summarily executed. The following winter, Charles Carson, nephew of the famous scout Kit Carson, was ambushed and slain by a Blood raiding party near Dearborn Crossing. In 1868, the Peigans raided and harassed the Diamond R freighting outfit. In 1869, a wagon train was attacked only sixteen kilometres outside Fort Benton itself. This was classic seasonal guerrilla war as the Indians had always fought it. But where the Indians excelled in the art of feint and run, raid and ambush, their enemies preferred to counter with strategies perfected in the Civil War, indiscriminate campaigns designed to terrorize and crush the national will. The consequence was what one might expect — atrocities that offended even their own sense of propriety.

Newspapers of the day report native suspects hanged from the nearest trees without trial or opportunity to plead their case. Witnesses were dragged from prison cells after giving evidence under the court's protection and lynched. When the brother of a Blackfoot chief and a fourteen-year-old boy were dispatched to Fort Benton carrying special orders from Major Alexander Culbertson of the American Fur Company, they were shot down in the street at first sight. Even Montana's *Hill County Democrat* was shocked: "These two innocent Indians were shot down like coyotes by people who called themselves civilized." The Blackfoot responded with raids that captured more than eight hundred horses and killed many white settlers, including noted frontiersman Malcolm Clarke, himself married to a Blackfoot woman.

In retaliation, in the early winter of 1870, four troops of the U.S. Second Cavalry were deployed from Fort Shaw to attack the Blackfoot. Near the Marias River, with Colonel Eugene M. Baker in command, the cavalry troops came upon the camp, not of the offending Blackfoot but of the friendly chief, Heavy Runner. His band was stricken with smallpox, the lodges filled with sick and dying women and children. Colonel Baker,

condemned by newspaper accounts as being "addled with whisky," ordered his troops to open fire. One of the first men cut
down was Heavy Runner, who had approached the soldiers
holding up the peace treaty he had signed.

"Colonel Baker was too drunk to know what he was doing,"
wrote Dan Conway in an account for the *Hill County Democrat*
years later. Another retrospective newspaper account from the
Montana Newspaper Association simply records that, along
with defenceless women and children, the U.S. Army shot down
the sick and the already dying in cold blood, leaving only twenty
wounded survivors amid the hundreds of corpses. Overlooked
in most of the official army dispatches regarding the "battle" of
the Marias River was one significant fact. Only a single shot had
been fired by the "warlike" inhabitants of Heavy Runner's camp.

In the midst of this and scarcely three years after the mistaken
butchery on the Marias River, it seems incredible that supposedly experienced frontiersmen would bed down with their
livestock unguarded. Apparently, that is what happened. Parallel to the wolfers' track, an Indian raiding party was also afield.
Tradition says it was Cree, and there seems little reason to question this assumption, save for the fact that the raiders were far
south of normal Cree raiding zones. They were obviously hoping for booty from their traditional enemies among the Blackfoot
but were quite happy to settle for American horses. The raiders
ran off eighty of the wolfers' mounts and slipped away, sliding
north across the Medicine Line into Canada with their prizes,
fleeting and insubstantial as the shadows of the racing clouds
that come with the prairie spring.

There is no record of bloodshed in this exchange of horseflesh,
just a tale of red-faced wolfers left to the humiliation of limping
to Fort Benton on foot beneath the undignified burden of their
possessions. It seems likely that some face-saving was in order,
Fort Benton being one of those rough and ready towns filled
with experienced fur traders and trappers who would pride
themselves on not losing their horses to Indian raiding parties
and would certainly heap ridicule on greenhorns who did.

The party of wolfers was led by John Evans, a big, blonde
twenty-six-year-old native of Fort Dodge, Iowa, and Thomas
Hardwick, twenty-nine, a Confederate veteran of the American
Civil War, who was referred to by his contemporaries as The
Green River Renegade. The two men let it be known that they
intended to recover their horses. Hardwick had a reputation for
being a tough and callous man, and Evans had been active with
a gang of vigilantes that had attempted to establish armed

control over the rolling grasslands at the heart of Blackfoot country southwest of Calgary. They set out in mid May, accompanied by, as historians can best determine, Trevanion Hale, John Duval, S.A. Harper, Jeff Devereaux, Sam Vincent, Charles Smith, Charles Ladd, Edward Legrace, James Hughes, Joseph Lange and Xavier Faillon.

The exact make-up of the party will likely never be known. Grant MacEwan, in his biography of Sitting Bull, says the party numbered fifteen. But the record is confused and fragmentary. Harper, for example, is referred to as S.A. Harper by one historian, as Charlie Harper by another, as J.A. Harper in a Montana newspaper, as John Harper by a contemporary report and as C. Harper in the formal deposition of John Duval. Are these references to the same man? To brothers? Alberta historian Hugh Dempsey cites the claim of another man, Fort Edmonton buffalo hunter Donald Graham, that he, too, was with the party, although meticulous federal government historian Philip Goldring remains sceptical in the absence of corroborating evidence. Of one thing Goldring is entirely certain: "Even if we knew nothing of the composition of the party, its actions betrayed its character. Hardwick and his men were impetuous, unscrupulous and more than ready to settle disputes with the Winchester and Henry repeating rifles which all of them carried."

Evans had already shown his willingness to take the law into his own hands. The year before, Dempsey points out in an obscure footnote, Evans had been involved in organizing the Spitzee Cavalry, a kind of vigilante force which attempted to prevent traders along the Belly River from selling repeating rifles to the Blackfoot. Hardwick, on the other hand, had been present with a Crow party during a battle with the Sioux on the Musselshell River in August of 1870. Later that fall, he was reported fighting the Sioux and Assiniboines, and, in February of 1871, Dempsey says, he had killed one of his erstwhile Crow allies in a fight at his trading cabin, wounding another and suffering a grievous injury himself.

The following year, Hardwick was trading whisky and setting out poisoned wolf baits in the Sweet Grass Hills, just south of the Canadian border. Another fight occurred, this time precipitated when Hardwick opened fire on a band of friendly Assiniboines. This occurred "without any warning whatever, or without any hostile demonstrations on the part of the Indians," according to the *Helena Weekly Herald* of the day. These men, denounced in contemporary Montana newspapers as "lawless desperadoes" by A.J. Simpson, the Indian agent for the Milk

River territory along the Canadian boundary, were the leaders of the party that set out to recover the eighty head of missing horses. It is not difficult to imagine the punitive nature of the expedition.

The trail of the missing horses took Evans, Hardwick and their party northeast. They forded the Teton River, swam their horses across the Marias River and pushed across the open plains to the Milk River watershed where it straddles the U.S.-Canada boundary. Once north of the border, the expedition from Fort Benton was beyond the jurisdiction of either American Indian agents or U.S. cavalry units. Whether or not they believed themselves beyond the reach of American justice is a matter for speculation. In practical reality, if these essentially lawless men could muster enough Winchester saddle guns, they became the sovereign power on the Canadian Plains, and, certainly in their own eyes, the law itself. This much we can glean from the attitudes toward Indians that permeate the formal depositions, statements to newspapers and accounts given in evidence at later hearings.

By the time Hardwick's band had arrived at the Cypress Hills, well north of the Canadian line, they had lost the trail of the raiding party which they believed had possession of their stolen horses. There were two trading posts in the vicinity, one operated by Abel Farwell, who was married to a Crow Indian woman and served American trading interests in Fort Benton, the other belonging to Moses Soloman, a whisky trader of sordid and disreputable character. The posts were just over a quarter of a mile apart according to research by parks historian Goldring, situated on a rough east-west axis and separated by Battle Creek. Farther to the south, forming the point of a scalene triangle skewed to the east, was the camp of Chief Little Soldier's Assiniboines. It was separated from Fort Soloman by a dry coulee which was to prove of great strategic importance.

The Assiniboine camp numbered forty tipis, or about two hundred people allowing the standard estimate of five to a tipi, but it was hardly a formidable war party — only three or four men had guns according to some reports. The buffalo were already beginning to disappear from the prairie by 1873, and the industrial slaughter for skins and the predations of men like Hardwick would soon wipe out the great herds. Little Soldier's starving band had struggled in from a disastrous winter camp on the Battle River, almost three hundred kilometres to the north. With him were the ragtag remnants of other bands under Chief Minashenayen and Chief Inihan Kinyen. As Goldring puts it: "They were a sorry lot. The survivors of the winter trek had retained little but their lives. Minashenayen's band had lost all its horses; the Indians were scantily armed with bows and arrows and obsolete firearms."

Hardwick, Evans and their twelve companions, on the other hand, were a formidable force indeed. They were equipped with new repeating rifles and revolvers and rode fresh mounts. Their intentions must have been obvious. The Fort Benton party arrived by dark on Saturday night, but by next morning Chief Inihan Kinyen was warning the Assiniboine camp to expect an attack and urging his band to break camp. Where were they to go? Back into the desolate prairie, on foot and armed with bows and arrows? Instead, they turned to the whisky jugs.

On the other side of Battle Creek, the Fort Benton gang also continued to drink. The belligerence of Hardwick and his party was so patent, according to official depositions taken from survivors by Inspector A.G. Irvine, that two men from a nearby Métis hunting camp went to Little Soldier's band and warned them of impending attack. Women and children began to bolt for cover, drunken warriors grabbed their pitiful weapons and prepared to make a defence. It was at this point that one of Farwell's assistants, a French Canadian named George Hammond, decided that his horse had been stolen yet again by the Assiniboines. He marched into Little Soldier's camp, seized a pair and began to march out again. He was stopped and forced to surrender the horses. Hammond retreated to Hardwick and Evans's position in the coulee, which, probably not coincidentally given the Civil War background, formed a perfect military entrenchment.

Who fired the first shot is not clear. Both sides, naturally, blame each other. Métis observers who testified years later described what seems to have been a ritual challenge by four of Little Soldier's intoxicated young men, charging the hunters' battle position and discharging weapons in the air. Did Little Soldier's warriors fire warning shots and frighten Hardwick's men into retaliating? Did the calculating Hammond, as Farwell later testified, fire unprovoked into the Indian camp? The answer to those questions is not important. From the shelter of the coulee, the Fort Benton gang directed a withering fire through the demoralized Assiniboine camp. Hardwick, the Confederate Army veteran, later clambered up to a flanking position on higher ground so that he could continue to shoot into the camp with greater accuracy and effect. When a group of Assiniboines in turn flanked Hardwick, Ed Legrace came to his assistance and was shot dead by a concealed warrior. He became the only white casualty in the attack.

Assiniboine resistance waned, and the Fort Benton gang entered the camp, killing the wounded and any survivors they found. One of them was Chief Little Soldier himself. Incapable of defending himself, he was shot down like a crippled dog by Vincent. A deposition by Miskotakikotena, one of the survivors, describes how the Americans smashed in the skull of an old man with a hatchet, leaving it embedded in his head, then took a pole and impaled him "from his backside to his head." The decapitated head of an old man named Wankantu was jammed onto a lodge pole and raised over the camp as a grisly trophy. Little Soldier's wife, Wakiuskemo, swore in her affidavit that she was raped repeatedly throughout the night by one of the Fort Benton party — it seems logical to assume either Evans or Hardwick, since whoever it was commanded exclusive access. She said three other old women and a girl captured with her suffered the same way but at the hands of the rest of the men.

Legrace was buried under the floor of Fort Soloman, and the bastion was burned down over him, presumably to hide the grave, as the frightened traders fled south to Fort Benton. Two of Hardwick's men went with a group bound for Montana Territory. The remaining thirteen headed west to Fort Whoop-up, still in search of their horses. They found their Cree suspects, but their belligerence evaporated at the prospect of a serious enemy. The Cree camp was large, heavily armed, ready to fight and extremely dangerous. The Benton gang carefully skirted it. Farther on they encountered a powerful encampment of more than a thousand Bloods and cautiously backed away from a threatened confrontation with the menacing band.

By now, the story was beginning to seep out. An Indian agent sent a wire reporting Hardwick's party had slaughtered almost defenceless men, women and children and "mutilated their bodies in a most outrageous and disgusting manner." The *Ottawa Citizen* broke the story in Eastern Canada and called it murder. It was not a view shared in Montana, where the editor of the *Fort Benton Record* suggested it was self-defence and served as a fine lesson to bellicose Indians. His was a view widely expressed in the popular American press.

But the incident had acquired a momentum of its own. The diplomatic pouches of Britain, Canada and the United States flew back and forth. It was decided to extradite the Hardwick gang to stand trial in Canada for the murder of forty Assiniboines. Popular sentiment supporting the Hardwick gang ran so high in Montana that U.S. federal marshals had to be called in to make the arrests. The hearing was held two years later in Helena, the issue being considered too inflammatory for Fort Benton. As might be expected, the Americans refused to extradite the seven men in custody. Later, a Canadian jury in Winnipeg found reasonable doubt in fragmentary evidence and unreliable testimony and acquitted three others arrested and charged in Canada.

For a politically embattled Sir John A. Macdonald, the Cypress Hills incident could not have occurred at a more propitious time. His administration was mired in the Pacific Scandal and the plans for a national railway were sinking amid charges of corruption and political avarice. The slaughter of defenceless Indians by whisky-sodden Americans was not an unusual incident by the frontier standards south of the border, but the invasion of Canadian sovereignty provided a useful diversion from the government's troubles of the day. More importantly, it provided a stark proof in public perception of just how fragile Canada's claims to jurisdiction over the western hinterlands might be.

The Americans, still fighting an Indian war that would not end until the massacre at Wounded Knee in 1897, had powerful military forces at their disposal. The Canadians had none. Typically, Ottawa had a plan, first presented by Macdonald in 1869, but, equally typically, four years later it seemed no closer to reality than at the idea's inception. A bill was to be introduced establishing the North-West Mounted Police, but in 1871 the prime minister was clearly still thinking in terms of a force of fifty men to assert Canadian sovereignty in the prairie region! The number alone reveals the dream-like public perception of the West in prosperous, settled Ontario. Somehow, fifty men were supposed to control and pacify thirty thousand of the most fierce, personally courageous and warlike Indians on the continent, and they were to do it across a territory of three hundred and seventy-five thousand square kilometres.

Philip Goldring, writing in a federal government paper on the early origins of the North-West Mounted Police, argues that before news of the Cypress Hills incident was published in the *Ottawa Citizen*, Macdonald had already presented his cabinet with a recommendation that the force be organized. He had, but as Horrall points out, the plans had, in effect, been shelved as early as 1870. The massacre had little impact on public policy, Goldring suggests. But this is to consider the incident in isolation when it must be viewed as part of a continuum. Alexander Morris, the lieutenant-governor of the North-West Territories at

the time, held the view that as a consequence of the escalating violence, the Far West was teetering on the brink of an Indian war
similar to that being waged in the United States. Morris warned
the federal cabinet in August of 1873 that without swift steps toward military occupation a national tragedy would occur.

The massacre at Sweet Grass Hills had occurred the year
before, and the accidental slaughter at Heavy Runner's camp
only months before that. With further such incidents, the Blood,
Blackfoot, Peigan and Cree were bound to retaliate against the
nearest enemies south of the border, where the wounds suffered
in a decade of fierce fighting with the Cheyenne, Comanche,
Kiowa and Sioux were still fresh in the army's memory. Such a
state of affairs was an open invitation to American military
adventures in areas where Canada claimed to be sovereign, and
Canadian authorities were powerless to respond with anything
other than the rhetoric of diplomatic pouches sent to Washington. Indeed, the Cypress Hills massacre itself revealed Canadian
weakness most candidly when a judicial response was organized. The arresting officer was a U.S. Marshall, the court and all
its authorities drew their power from Washington, not Ottawa.
Adding to the humiliating sense of powerlessness was a final
insult. Following the extradition hearings in Montana, the Canadian policeman assigned to the case was himself arrested and
imprisoned briefly by the American authorities.

It is in this broader context that the significance of the Cypress
Hills incident emerges, and common sense argues that the image
of American brutality and Canadian impotence could only serve
to spur the formation of the North-West Mounted Police. The
speed with which a mounted force was organized and
dispatched to the turbulent southwestern prairies; the way in
which it was supported and nurtured by the hostile Liberal
government which succeeded Macdonald's Conservatives in the
fall of 1873; both lend weight to the view that a growing public
consensus regarding the importance of national sovereignty in
the Far West empowered politicians to act.

Thus it was, that exactly one year after the extermination of
Little Soldier's band of Assiniboines, the scarlet columns of the
North-West Mounted Police began their great trek westward
across the Plains to assume their central place in the emerging
myth of the Canadian West. That mythology of the Mountie, as
much as anything else, gave form and substance to a national
presence that finally extended from sea to sea in reality as well
as rhetoric. If the new railways bound the nation together with
sinews of steel, the Mounted Police provided the muscle of

moral vision and ethical purpose.

It was in the lovely valley where the bones of Little Soldier and his people were scattered for the foxes and coyotes that B Troop's original garrison of thirty men and thirty horses established Fort Walsh. For five years, the Mounties patrolled the western plains and kept the peace in a country that trembled at the brink of war and bloodshed. In that initial period, not one of them was killed and they did not shoot a single Indian.

Whatever else Fort Walsh may be, it is first of all a place where the Indian nations of the West make true their claim on Canada, and we on them. They have shaped us out of their suffering, as we have transformed them. Canada has been far from perfect in its dealing with the descendants of these nations, but we commit a far greater sin if we deny them an exalted place in the substance of our history.

It was not far from the site of Little Soldier's tragedy that Sitting Bull rode into Canada in 1876 at the head of the Sioux nation. He brought a retinue of three thousand warriors armed with the carbines stripped from the U.S. Seventh Cavalry. They were still exulting in the annihilation of General George Armstrong Custer's five troops at the battle of the Little Big Horn. Sitting Bull was pursued by a whole American army. NWMP Major James Walsh rode into his camp with twelve men. A year later, Walsh was offering sanctuary to White Bird and the Nez Percée, fresh from Chief Joseph's brilliant fighting retreat in a campaign that equals Xenophon's escape from Asia and Mao Tse Tung's Long March.

If Major Walsh deserves a special place in our history for his courage and determination, surely his Indian contemporaries are equally deserving in their restraint and statesmanship, bravery and endurance. Assiniboines, Gros Ventres, Bloods, Peigans, Salteaux, Ogalallas, Minneconjous, Sans Arcs, Hunkpapas, Two Kettles, Sarcee and Blackfoot — our High Plains are rich with the power and resonance of Indian names. Their history is written on the Cypress Hills themselves. It is written in blood, but that is just a paragraph. The full story is written in the throaty language of the wind as it shouts down the coulees and hisses across the endless catspaws of the grass. A clean, clear wind that scours the bone of its sorrows under purifying sky. The names listed among dust devils are not merely those of nations, but of great men: White Eagle, Starblanket, Black Moon, Spotted Eagle, Little Knife, Red Crow, Long Dog, Heavy Runner, Big Child, Crow's Dance, Stone Dog, Crowfoot, Poundmaker, Big Bear, Little Soldier.

MAKE THE STROKE WITHOUT LOOKING

Cloaked in the cold grey mists of Canada's Pacific rim, buried deep in the salal and Spanish moss of rain forests, the sacred messages of dispossessed generations decay into dripping undergrowth. Under their acid red corona of berries, vivid green shrubs of huckleberry set root in the cracks and crevices of punky wood. It is nature herself prying apart the rain-silvered riddles of totem pole and housepost. Anthropologists interpret these disintegrating images with the help of informants who ransack the dimmest reaches of memory, seeking to recover meanings that were already faded even for grandfathers and grandmothers. Yet, however skilfully the academics analyze totem and myth with the methodology of empiricism, struggling to recreate parables and visions in the language of equation and formula, their antiseptic search for meaning assimilates only the barest outlines of the mystery. The hidden power of art and ritual in the full harness of its sovereign expression continues to elude even the most intelligent analysis.

After all, anthropologists are scientists first, and science seeks to deny the presence of mystery, eschews the value of ambiguity, begins with the premise that everything is ultimately quantifiable and knowable, that every poem may be parsed down to the phonemes and glottal stops, evaluated and cross-referenced for symbolic content. This is the foundation of our arrogant belief that the process of analysis equals experience and that cold reason may lay bare the mystical. In this way, the abstract rites of science attempt to depose the old order.

Regardless of science, these great, brooding testaments of dynastic rank, of clan allegiance, of the prideful claims on attributes descended from mythic progenitors, all weather back into the rich, red forest earth from which they sprang in the first place. Perhaps, this is as it should be, as it was intended to be by the makers.

Whatever the creators' intention, it was certainly contrary to that of the conquering authorities, with their obsessive need to transform living art into preserved artefact. One need only visit the village of Kispiox, where totem poles are still raised in the context of their creation, or the abandoned villages of Vancouver Island's west coast, where the houseposts slowly return to the holy earth in the context of their own ancestral presences, to appreciate the deep differences between the culture which gave birth to this art and the culture which subsumed it.

Nowhere is this fundamental difference more evident than at the two great museums created by British Columbians to house the specimens of demolished societies. The two institutions were raised, irony of ironies, from the wealth created by the wholesale rape of the environment that once sustained the people whose ruined history they now preserve. Whole watersheds are logged bare and left to erode in the rain. Streams that once teemed with fish now foam with the tea-brown seeps of logging slash and flow devoid of trout. Whole salmon runs are wiped out to facilitate the manufacture of toilet paper, which is later dumped, along with its accompanying sewage and a host of other poisonous effluents, back into the once-sustaining waters. From Campbell River to the capital city of Victoria, plumes of pollution blossom down the west coast, followed by the march of signs warning of the public health hazard. The rich clam and oyster beds once meant that no band, however poor, went hungry in time of need. Now, raw sewage and industrial chemicals pollute the shellfish and the villages are abandoned. All of this in the expedient service of the material greed and relentless profiteering that provided funds to build museums to display the social debris left behind their activities.

The first of these institutions, the museum of anthropology at the University of British Columbia in Vancouver, is ostensibly in the service of science. The other, the provincial museum in Victoria, panders earnestly in the service of tourism. Both presume to preserve, catalogue, explain. Both are brilliant examples of what they do. Neither offers more than token recognition of the artistic integrity of the work on display.

Although these institutions claim to celebrate what they house, as architecture they appear to have more in common with the triumphal arches of the imperial Caesars. Displaying the booty, whether the severed heads of Gauls or the dancing masks of Kwakiutl shamans — the symbolic statement is impossible to ignore — is an affirmation of conquest that legitimizes the status quo, which is to say the subordination of the culture from which the charged ceremonial objects have been claimed. In transforming the sacramental objects into trophies for display, we deny the magical qualities they claim for themselves. In denying their magic, we debase and deny the values of the culture from which they emerged. Ultimately, the museum structures themselves, typically linear, typically angular, typically reflecting the claustrophobic Western European obsession with enclosures and exclusions, say more about the culture which erected them than about their contents.

In Victoria, the Vancouver Island seat of government that proclaims itself the city of gardens and takes personal credit for the beauty of God's environment, one finds Thunderbird Park. The totem poles are surrounded by blue diesel fumes from the bus depot, hucksters touting souvenir gewgaws and tours in transplanted double-decker buses. Across the street rises that perfect monument to offensive Edwardian toadying, the ivy-clad Empress Hotel. This lickspittle remnant of Empire, complete, at my last visit, with with the skins of endangered tigers on the wall and its waiters obsequiously dressed as lackeys from colonial India, forms the perfect backdrop for the park where the visitor is confronted with carefully painted, government-inspected totems. Here, corralled by a fastidious replica of a long house, the tourists could witness aboriginal art in full bloom as a state-sanctioned spectator sport performed by carvers on contract. Even in these salvings of public conscience, commercial exploitation remains the bottom line.

At the provincial museum next door, the totems are mummified under glass, the explanations carefully precise, the humidity perfectly controlled — science conquering natural process in the same fashion that economics conquered aboriginal societies. Upstairs, there is the cunning reconstruction of the interior of a great clan's long house. Despite the taped sounds and theatrical lighting, something seems oddly absent. The image offers texture without hue, a curious failure of perspective. Then, it dawns. It is the frame of reference. It is the way the structure is enclosed within its industrial warehouse space. The entire building has become one more collectible, removed from any context it may have had and transformed into an effect. The whole thing is a fiction erected to appeal to children and to mask from ourselves the ugly truth of history.

At UBC, the museum is a fine example of architecture from the school that might be called twentieth century brutal — concrete and glass, planes and angles, platforms and ramps, utilitarian, functional, accessible to the wheelchair visitor and completely devoid of soul. Here the icons of science rule. All is numbered, indexed, rationalized. Anthropology does indeed have an important place in the saving of many elements of Northwest Pacific Indian culture that might otherwise have been destroyed, and this role should never be diminished. But it is also important to examine anthropology itself as an extension of the power of an imperial culture, its practitioners as looters of the spirit, finishing the work begun by looters of the material wealth which now fills museums around the world. Museums, of course, are themselves artefacts, betraying the hidden assumptions of the societies which build them. The displays at the UBC museum resemble nothing so much as big trophy cases. Only the most insensitive could evade the impact of a wall on which masks with magical powers are displayed, row on row, like so many scalps. Next come acres of glass cases filled with ceremonial objects that appear to have been accumulated in some bizarre collecting frenzy — which, indeed, was the state of mind of the day.

The Japanese and American tourists flash teeth and Leicas, capturing for their own posterities the already captured posterity of the defeated. The displays are meant to demonstrate the prized place of "First Canadians" in the multicultural mosaic, although these "First Canadians" had not yet managed to achieve a formal place in the constitution 120 years after the founding of Canada. Indeed, they were not offered equal rights with other Canadians until the courts whipped us to it with the Drybones decision. Even at that, our native people were not fully empowered with the vote until 1969. So we see this display of aboriginal art for what it is — propaganda. The plasticized, embalmed art of the conquered serves the purpose of its new masters, persuading everyone of their benign intent.

Few native artists still labour under the slow burden of myth and tradition that was the baseline of the indigenous Northwest Pacific cultures. Of these, how many are merely skilful imitators, trapped in the endless repetition of classical styles prized by non-native collectors with big cheque books? And how many remain fully integrated with the mythic elements that seek expression in their work, breathing new life into old forms and liberating them from the embalming table of European expectations? One of the latter, certainly, was the late George Clutesi, painter, author, singer, actor. When he died at the age of eighty-three in the spring of 1988, he was perhaps best known as a performer, having appeared in more than thirty film and television productions. Yet, his enduring contributions were as a painter and writer, offering articulate expressions of his culture's values.

Janitor at a Port Alberni residential school, he painted with the brushes bequeathed to him by Emily Carr, herself one of Canada's authentic, original and undeniable geniuses of the visual arts. He also wrote the collection of Tse-shaht fables and morality tales entitled *Son of Raven, Son of Deer*. It was subsequently introduced to the British Columbia elementary schools curriculum by an enlightened education minister named Leslie Peterson. George Clutesi was sixty-two when the book was published and became an instant best seller. Two years later he published *Potlatch*, an account of the last such ceremonial among his own people. The rite occurred in 1924, when he was a youth of nineteen and it was a subversive ritual that had been banned by an act of the federal parliament.

In the modern cult of celebrity, fame earned George Clutesi a promotion — from janitor to night watchman — but it also drew attention both to his painting, which he acknowledged had long been "relegated to the basements of sympathetic people," and to his lifelong struggle to persuade his own people that their future was rooted not in the dominant society's interpretation of their cultural traditions but in taking ownership of their own values and asserting them as living embodiments of their sovereign and ancestral rights. For half a century, he worked to preserve the songs and intricate ritual dances, teaching them to children, oblivious to the early scorn and cynicism of his peers.

I first came to know George Clutesi as a boy, my father pointing to him in the rainy streets of Port Alberni and telling me to remember his face, that he would one day be acknowledged as a great man, although his own people didn't know it yet. And, then, after the fashion of nine-year-old boys, I promptly forgot about him until ten years later. It was as an undergraduate anthropology student at the University of Victoria that I heard him speak on the role and place of the Indian artist in a culture which, he told me, seemed numb to signs, visions and the invocation of higher powers. In private conversation afterwards, he told me how he had been marked forever when the whalers of his father's generation went out in their big dugouts in the 1930s just to prove that they could still harpoon a whale. They had a lot to prove. After a century of the white man's governance, the population of those loosely connected groups of bands popularly known as the Nootka had declined from perhaps thirty thousand people to less than two thousand by the time Clutesi was born. The descendants of Maquinna, the great chief who impressed the brightest of the European explorers as their clear intellectual equal, were working as janitors in residential schools where children were forbidden to speak their mother tongue, in many cases physically punished for failing to speak the language of their conquerors.

George Clutesi had come to address us at the height of student power on the campuses of the 1960s. Events at the pretentious University of Victoria were among the most turbulent in British Columbia, perhaps, in natural reaction to the stultifying conventions of its surrounding city. The students, occupying administration buildings and faculty clubs, were to dethrone three presidents in less than a decade. There was Student Power, Black Power and, looming on the horizon, we thought, another ally in rebellion against authoritarian oppression, Red Power. I talked to the artist and writer about the suffering of his people and expected the fiery rhetoric of the revolutionary. Instead, I got urgings to gentleness and a mild optimism about the future that was beginning to unfold.

He did not share the political vision of the advocates of Red Power and the American Indian Movement which was to lead to tragedy at Wounded Knee, but he admired their personal courage. He was not happy with the insensitive incompetence that had marked the federal Indian Affairs department in the past, but he believed the department was sincerely trying to change for the better. He was dismayed that there was little of the traditional respect for elders in contemporary native communities, but he believed that progress would depend upon the wisdom, knowledge, eloquence and patience of the elders themselves in serving a youth which groped for identity in a changed world.

He talked about his writing, which he said he had undertaken not for personal gratification but to correct the half-truths, inaccuracies and failures of understanding that marred so much of the writing by non-Indians about native culture and social customs. Ever courteous, he apologized to me for his latest book; he said he didn't think it would please the anthropologists. He was right. It failed to meet the portentous expectations of those who prefer the complex and opaque analysis afforded by the school of Claude Lèvi-Strauss. It was dismissed by many academics as a kind of peculiar West Coast Aesop's fable, although, as the provincial education minister of the day astutely recognized, it spoke to children with clarity and power. Children, it often seems, are frequently better instinctive judges of truth than university professors and their students.

On the basis of Clutesi's remarks, I determined to pursue this conversation about the perceptual gaps between our two cultures, the different ways of experiencing the creative process. I thought about it for most of the next term and, then, one February day, persuaded my girlfriend to join me in cutting lectures. She agreed to give me a ride north in her notorious and unreliable Volkswagen bug, which had never been right since floating downstream while attempting to ford an island brook. Susan took me up the twisting Island Highway and over the icy passes to Port Alberni, a pulp and paper town which huddles under the stink of its money at the head of a long, deep fjord surrounded by mountains sequentially stripped, hillside by hillside, of the forests demanded by the mills' insatiable appetites.

Originally an outpost established by the army of imperial Spain, the port of Alberni was strategically placed in the fertile flood plain of the Somass River, which in itself was valued for its heavy runs of massive tyee salmon weighing sixty pounds and more. The Alberni Canal reaches all the way out to the open Pacific, where the great white combers from Japan thunder through the picture-book islands of the Broken Group and boom into the chutes and caverns of the rocky coast. This was where George Clutesi's grandfathers had sailed so easily the same seas that sank more than two hundred of the white man's great ships.

To our ancestors, it was The Graveyard of The Pacific, a cold hell to be endured only in the pursuit of profit. To Clutesi's ancestors, it was a beautiful Eden filled with the bounty of heaven. His people moved across the sea's face in hand-carved canoes imbued with the attributes of magic animals. Their art was an animate art, made to be used and consumed in the act of living a life, an art that served as decoration upon the process of life itself. Today, those canoes are cracked and dessicated specimens in museum cases accompanied by equally dried-out explanations from curators about the significance of this pattern or that.

George Clutesi was surprised at my arrival on his dripping doorstep. In the brash enthusiasm of a youth who has seen the light, I had thoughtlessly neglected to keep to my appointment and was suddenly tongue-tied and blushing over my lateness. But it was not in his nature to suffer another's mortification. He read my chagrin with a sharp eye and graciously insisted on granting an interview anyway. By formalizing the conversation, he had absolved me of responsibility for the personal faux pas. Thus do the old ways survive into a present that fails to recognize them.

He wanted to be interviewed because I was a good person, he told me. How did he know that? Well, if I was a bad person, his old dog would most certainly have bitten me, he said. The dog, with grizzled fur and arthritic joints, had cracked one red eye on my arrival and returned to sleep. As toothless as he was old, he looked incapable of biting anyone. Next to the kitchen range, the air was redolent with the rich scent of a stew made of salmon heads, that part of the fish I've watched countless white fishermen leave to rot under the docks.

If, in hindsight, my questions seem the simplistic and romantic expressions of a twenty-year-old student, his answers were not. They were solemn, careful and filled with wisdom and respect for my own desire to learn. I have preserved my edited transcript of that interview and his voice rings true from beyond the grave.

HUME: What do you feel the place of the Indian artist is in contemporary society?

CLUTESI: It is going to be very difficult for the Indian artist to be really himself. If he goes to the art schools as a youngster they are going to change him completely — unless they can realize that the Indian is a bit different to the commercial artists. Although all artists today are more or less commercial — they are doing it to sell — the Indian prior to this generation did something to express his feelings and whether it was paid for or not didn't matter. The contemporary Indian is just as commercially minded an artist as the next person, but the art schools will just develop more white artists — of a different colour.

HUME: Do you think then that the Indian artist should be trained by other Indian artists?

CLUTESI: Oh, absolutely. The Indian artist, and when I say artist I include the carvers, paints something like the old masters did in that he paints with feeling — they make the strokes without visual contact. It is a feeling the artist puts on the cedar, and today it is a feeling he puts on canvas. We make the stroke without actually looking at it. I want to apply that stroke according to the feeling that is in my inner sight, if I can use the term, whereas the logical thing to do would be to follow a distinct path. But that breeds the feeling that if you go past that path you are not good enough, and this type of creating tends to stiffen your work.

If you insist on following a path you're going to be stiff and you're not going to achieve what I call the continuation of movement. There will be abutments all through your work. As far as I can see, the contemporary white artist loves abutments and acute angles. He tries to achieve this rather than continuation of movement, and this is very much removed from the Indian way of thinking or feeling.

HUME: Why do you think the white artist likes abutments so much?

CLUTESI: I think it's because of his way of life. The white artist can't help it. His life is a continual Bang! Bang! Bang! Whites are never still. They are hopping up and down in jerks. Even their speaking is full of jerks. In anything the white artist does, he has to be continually moving. He's got to beat that clock. In fact, he's even got to jump ahead of that clock, and, as far as I can see, the white will never be content with his environment, whereas the Indian . . . I want to do a painting. I want to do a big painting. Instead of plotting out my canvas in squares and oblongs, I retire and I think about it for days and days and days. When I finally think that I've got my plan done in my head, then I begin painting!

The white artist begins by placing blobs of paint very neatly on what he calls his palette, then picks out the proper paint and applies it directly to the canvas, square by square, and so on, until he gets his absolutely correct composition. The Indian, if he's an Indian, squeezes the paint out of his tubes and applies it directly to the canvas. Why? Because he already has it finished in his mind and he knows what he's trying to achieve, while the white artist has to follow the pattern that he has worked out.

The white works according to the rules. This is why I say it is going to be hard for the young Indian today to develop into what is really his own self in his own mind and heart. He's going to attempt to please his white friends.

HUME: It has been pointed out that before contact with the white man, Indian life was intensely spiritual. What effect was there on the Indian artist?

CLUTESI: Yes, it was intensely spiritual before the coming of the white man, but this is neither here nor there — most human beings are spiritual. The important thing was that the Indians realized they were not all-powerful gods, or demi-gods, or whatever you want to call it. They realized that there is room for a call for some help, of one kind or another. While the Indian said: "You must believe in a God," he didn't specify. He just said you must believe in a God, and if you don't you're not going to be happy.

Before the white man, the Indian artist expressed himself with the feeling that was in his heart. Rather than just make a bear, for instance, he'd make a bear according to the way he thinks its spirit ought to be. In line drawings, it wasn't actual reproduction of the image of the bear. This went for any other animal or form.

I think the Indian artist today is very much afraid of the set rules of white artists.

HUME: Very often it seems the white artist is influenced largely by intellectual forces rather than what you might call spiritual or environmental forces. How much do you think intellectual abstractions apply to your art as a reflection of Indian art and how much of your art is influenced by your spiritual environment?

CLUTESI: I am neither an Indian artist, as far as the original Indian artists were, nor am I recognized as a product of the white art world. I'm in between. And I'm not really happy. I'd much rather paint in my own ancestor's way of expressing themselves, but I'm afraid, for instance, to use distortion and grotesqueness because I know I will be accused of copying my ancestors.

But I don't want to follow the way of teaching in the contemporary white art world. I'm not one or the other as far as the art world is concerned. Because of this feeling, I'm not happy with my work, really; I know that I can do better.

HUME: What do you plan to do about this state of affairs?

CLUTESI: There is very little I can do. There is going to be a change and nothing can stop it. The only thing I can do is paint and leave behind what I can — I certainly can't instruct the powers that are instructing the Indian artist today. I can't influence one way or the other because white art is, as far as I can see, completely against what I believe myself.

HUME: You think that what makes a piece of art valid is whether feeling has gone into it rather than intellectual process?

CLUTESI: I believe a man should paint according to his own

feelings and not according to his instruction. Give him the pot of paint and let him go ahead with whatever he wants to do — if you don't like it, that doesn't matter. Let him have his head in that way and maybe he'll come up with something original.

HUME: There's an essential difference between stereotyping and working from tradition. We see all kinds of stereotyping with the carvers who make little poles for American tourists. What do you feel is the difference between stereotyping and the judicious use of tradition?

CLUTESI: Stereotyping is the production of something, whether totem poles or paintings, in order to sell. And the more the outlet is assured, the more contemporary Indian carvers think in terms of dollars and cents, and they won't put in the time to produce something they want to.

I think there are very few Indian carvers today who are artists. Indians today are carving because there is no other way of earning money.

HUME: How much influence do dollars and cents have in your art?

CLUTESI: I don't think it has any influence. When I do a painting, I do it according to my own feeling.

HUME: How much influence does spirituality have in your work, and in what ways?

CLUTESI: I try very hard to keep my work beautiful — colourful and harmonized. Think beautifully. Act beautifully. Teach beautifully and preach beautifully. Although I may not consciously practice this today, I believe that it shows in my work. I produce eerie plays on canvas, but even then there is beauty in the canvas [which is] emphasized rather than the stark eerieness.

HUME: You are a Nootka. How much influence do Nootka traditions have on you compared to, say, Tlingit, or Haida, or Kwakiutl?

CLUTESI: I have not gone out of the Nootka tradition. I haven't adopted outside influences or tried to follow other traditions at all. I limit my work to my local area's traditions entirely.

HUME: Is there a general resurgence in West Coast Indian art? For a long time, both socially and economically, the white man has denied the Indian any real form of independence, and it has denied the Indian any real form of independence, and it seems that for the first time Indians are starting to assert their independence — especially the younger ones.

CLUTESI: I think Indian art almost died completely. It would have died but for a very few Indians saying, "I've got my own art and I'm going to show it to you." These persistent men saved the art form. But I do not think the artist today should stick solely to his traditional forms of line-drawings. I think he should interpret the tradition in his own way, using his own feeling. If he wants to rub the paint into his canvas with his fingers, let him do it! If he wants to mix his paint on the canvas, let him do it! Don't say, "That's no good, the white man doesn't do that!"

HUME: Do you think Indian art is starting to develop now as it would have if the white man had never come?

CLUTESI: I think the Indian was interrupted just when he was on the verge of surrealism. I think if the white man hadn't come the Indian would have developed, or retrogressed, depending on how you look at it, right into surrealism. I honestly cannot say whether this interruption was good or not.

HUME: Before contact, Indian art seemed to be a manifestation of very important mythologies. When the white man interrupted, was the Indian on the verge of breaking away from works completely dominated by myth and making work a more subjective personal experience?

CLUTESI: Yes, but I think it would have been surrealistic, and I'm afraid I don't believe in surrealism. I use traditional Indian form, but I make it into a form that becomes everyday. It's a personal interpretation and it's subjective, but it's not surrealism.

HUME: Do you think the white man, with his art, tends to play intellectual games with it rather than producing art for its own sake or for the sake of a mythology as the Indians appear to have done?

CLUTESI: Yes, but I don't think my ancestors produced art for art's sake. It was a method of recording things. They just did it so well that it became considered an art form.

HUME: Would you say, then, that the concept of Indian art, as art, came from the white man rather than the Indian? That the

Indian just lived with it and accepted it, while the white man came along and said, "Aha! That's art!"

CLUTESI: That's a hard question. The West Coast Indians produced great big murals to record happenings or achievements of a particular house, but on ceremonial occasions they were displayed to the best advantage — I think the Indian looked at them with the idea that they were art forms, but I can't say yes or no.

HUME: Do you have any trouble with people or families that own crests or designs saying, "That's mine and you can't use it?"

CLUTESI: Not any more. There was at first a great deal of jealousy. One of the greatest problems of the West Coast Indian is jealousy among the tribes and clans.

HUME: Is there very much dance and totem ownership still prevalent?

CLUTESI: No. Not very much. Very few are aware of the traditional crests and songs and dances. Many would rather see them die rather than preserve them — just out of jealousy.

HUME: Do you find at all that you are acquiring and having to project the image of George Clutesi as a professional Indian, and finding it not quite so happy as just being George Clutesi, human being?

CLUTESI: When you put it that way, yes. I would rather have just been left alone. But, on the other hand, things are changing and we can't stop it. My father could go down the hill and kill anything he wanted for supper. I can't do that any more — I have to buy butter and I have to buy bread and milk for the children. I have to do something to acquire those everyday necessities.

HUME: How much service do you feel your art is doing the Indian people as a whole?

CLUTESI: After two generations of complete subjugation, I think it is important for the Indians to seek work produced by one of their own and not produced according to the white man's rules.

HUME: It has been estimated there are only five top-rate Indian carvers on the West Coast. Do you think that is an accurate estimate?

CLUTESI: Well, I wouldn't say there are any more than five. There are very few really top Indian carvers who work according to the way they feel inside. Who carve without looking at their strokes.

THE SPIRIT WEEPS

In anticipation of the high international profile Canada would achieve during the 1988 Winter Olympics in Calgary, organizing officials planned a dazzling constellation of parallel events intended to showcase the richness and diversity of our national culture. Writers, poets, musicians and painters were to celebrate the Greek ideal of mind and body with demonstrations of their creative prowess to match the physical performances of athletes. As part of this program, Alberta's Glenbow Institute, backed by the major corporate sponsorship of an oil industry giant, Shell Canada Limited, began preparations for what was to be the most complex and complete display of the art of Canadian aboriginal peoples in world history.

For five years before the Olympic Games began, a committee of six distinguished scholars, each bringing specialized knowledge from one of the six cultural regions of aboriginal Canada, began planning the exhibition. The Glenbow is itself a world-class museum and archive, particularly with reference to the culture and ethnology of Plains Indians. But it was clear from the beginning that the scope and magnitude of the exhibition planned could not be mounted with the resources of the Glenbow alone. Starting with a commitment of $600,000 in seed money from the Olympic Organizing Committee and $1,100,000 from Shell, the curatorial scholars began taking inventory of where Canadian aboriginal artifacts might be located outside Canada and subsequently borrowed for exhibition before national and international audiences. By the time they were finished, the committee had scoured more than one hundred and fifty museums and private collections across twenty foreign countries and arranged the display of more than six hundred artifacts.

The show was staged in two segments. The first took place at the Glenbow itself, preceding and coinciding with the Olympic Games; the second, in association with the new National Museum of Civilization, was mounted three months later in Ottawa, using the former premises of Canada's national art gallery for the eastern venue.

The Spirit Sings proved a curator's tour de force. The committee had mounted a show of stunning power and intensity. All the displays resonated with aesthetic genius and a deep sense of spiritual place. Yet this exhibition of the artistic traditions of Canada's first people, so wonderful in the hermetic context of ethnological display, was also an act of national hypocrisy so shocking as to border on the obscene. It triggered deep anger and hurt among the very native peoples it purported to celebrate and raised profound questions regarding the integrity of Canada's social and intellectual conscience.

Art cannot be detached from the social and historical matrix in which it originates, however much museum curators might desire to do so in the interests of neat classification and compartmentalized analysis, and however much the state might seize upon it as an opportunity for shameless propagandizing and outright lying. And that was the great irony of The Spirit Sings. Mounted in celebration of our first peoples, it used their art to tell the world a fundamental lie about our national concern for their rights and well-being. The exhibits displayed in The Spirit Sings and the powerful controversy surrounding them were testimony not only to the richness and diversity of native culture but also to the rapacious and destructive force of European settlement in North America and the continued brutality of Canadian institutions toward native social and political aspirations.

If much of the early destruction of aboriginal culture was caused by people who were not Canadians but the worst of European adventurers — the ancestors of those who now piously seek to deprive remote and impoverished native communities of their economic base in hunting and trapping — Canadians later had the opportunity to chart a different course. The Spirit Sings exhibited damning evidence of our choice not to do so.

While the relics displayed were the beautiful works of sensitive and intelligent artists, they also represented the debris that we robbed from the rubble of cultures whose traditions we first demolished, then sought to extinguish.

Indiscriminate bombardments of Indian villages by naval

flotillas, massacres of women and children by punitive fur traders, tolerance of the ravages of disease and economic impoverishment, denial of universal access in the law, selective official segregation, the corporal punishment of children for speaking their own language in federal schools, the legal banning of ritual, ceremony and religion, denial of the vote — these are phenomena not of some barbarous Dark Age but of recent Canadian history.

It was significant that while the officials and curators were congratulating themselves on the commercial success and aesthetic quality of their show, Georges Erasmus of the Assembly of First Nations was warning Canadians that a new generation of young native "warriors" may be contemplating armed violence instead of talk, having learned that negotiation in good faith with Canada's political institutions appears to be a failure. Indeed, as Alberta officials basked in the Olympic limelight, the Sioux nation was announcing the appointment of its first formal war chief since Sitting Bull crossed the Medicine Line not far from Calgary, carrying the scalps of Custer's Seventh Cavalry. The Sioux had called back the fifty-nine-year-old great grandson of Chief Standing Bear. Now head of a multi-million-dollar engineering firm, he was to be charged with responsibility for recovering the Black Hills, a sacred spiritual centre for the Sioux nation which was never surrendered by treaty.

In Alberta, while The Spirit Sings talked about the importance of art, no less than a dozen outstanding aboriginal claims awaited some kind of formal adjudication in the courts. Some of them, like the question of title to the lands of the dispossessed — and now conveniently dispersed — Papaschase band, are matters of historic and legal curiosity. The Papaschase lands, now occupied by the University of Alberta and most of the south side of Edmonton, may have been surrendered to land speculators under manipulated, defective and highly questionable procedures. But with no survivors of the band, who might legally re-open the issue? Other aboriginal claims are more immediate, from those among the Peigan of southern Alberta who object that the Oldman River dam constructed by the provincial government destroys their ancestral spiritual centres, to the Lubicons of the north who simply want a settlement after half a century of administrative dithering, legalistic equivocating and political indecision by federal and provincial authorities.

The tiny and isolated Lubicon band, 20 per cent of which had just tested positive for tuberculosis — a disease long banished from the general population — went so far as to attempt political action, demonstrating outside the Glenbow in Calgary and seeking public support for a boycott of The Spirit Sings during the Olympics. The 350 Lubicons were joined in protest by the Mohawks, who went to court in an unsuccessful attempt to block the showing of a sacred ceremonial mask, public display of which amounted to a religious desecration. As the simple, rural Lubicons made their small public protest outside the Glenbow, the racist and abusive remarks of Calgarians entering the exhibition shocked even the worldly correspondent from the *Chicago Tribune*, assigned to cover the show and no stranger to racism. The attitude of the public toward the Indians, of course, marred the Olympic spirit in a far more fundamental way than the Lubicons' protest had. It also revealed the true nature of The Spirit Sings exhibition: not so much a celebration of native culture as self-congratulatory propaganda regarding the importance of such peoples to the Canadian state.

In this context, passing through the opening gallery at The Spirit Sings exhibition and gazing upon the thirty or so pathetic little artifacts that represented Canada's extinguished Beothuk nation in Newfoundland, what manner of person could not feel appalled and shamed that the memory of an exterminated nation should be so evoked in the service of our national pride? What perverted manner of pride could be taken from this? It was as though the Berlin Olympics had put on a display of Jewish religious objects to celebrate the diversity, pluralism and tolerance of Nazi culture.

Staring at the tiny pair of baby's moccasins or, near them, the little effigy taken from the grave of a four-year-old child, I could think only of the story of Demasduwit. She had given birth only two days earlier when she was seized by fur trader John Peyton's party in 1819. Peyton was ostensibly charged with establishing contact with the Beothuks on behalf of the government, although the choice of such a man for any mission of diplomacy reveals the cynicism of the authorities. On one occasion, Royal Navy Lieutenant George Pulling complained to his British superiors about the barbarous way in which Peyton had used one of his steel traps to beat out the brains of a wounded, helpless Indian. This was the man with whom Demasduwit's husband pleaded fruitlessly for his wife's return. When he struggled to free her, he was killed before her eyes like a troublesome cur. Demasduwit's baby was abandoned in the snow to die. The mother was taken off to be civilized. A month later, in an act of unusual generosity, her corpse was returned to her dwindling people in a coffin — a gesture intended, no doubt, to emphasize her captor's civilized concern with appearances. Ten years later, the last of her people had died in captivity and the Beothuk nation was extinct.

Demasduwit had not even the dignity of a quiet grave. In 1827, in the interests of preserving for posterity something of the vanished Beothuk culture, William Cormack robbed the grave of the woman, her husband and the little baby, taking two skulls and the collection of burial offerings. To witness the murdered woman's modest possessions — for murder it most certainly was — displayed in honour of a sports event and Canadian self-aggrandizement, is to sense the trivialization of a tragedy of enormous proportions.

Elaborate apologies have been written regarding the fate of the Beothuk in Canadian history, dismissing as mere legend the popular accounts of bounties paid for ears and eighteenth century hunting expeditions by European settlers. The Pulling manuscript notes that settlers referred to Beothuk males as "Cock" Indians, as though they were a kind of game animal, and quotes Richard Richmond regarding an expedition in the winter of 1790 in search of Beothuk and in which "we set out with a determination to kill every one we came across both big and small." When the opportunity arose, Richmond admitted, they could not bring themselves to shoot down the defenceless Indians but, although none were killed, two women and a child were made captive.

Newfoundland historian Frederick Rowe, while acknowledging atrocities against Indians by the white newcomers, calls for even-handedness in examining the Beothuk's extermination. He manages to suggest that the Indians brought about their own destruction by provoking settlers with the raids and pilfering of a desperate and starving population. Furthermore, he implies that assigning responsibility for the extinction to the white settlers amounts to a slur against the descendants of Newfoundland's brave pioneers. The book *Historic Newfoundland and Labrador*, published by the provincial government, disposes of Demasduwit's cruel fate as a captive with the bland observation that she and her relative Shanawdithit "both lived among the settlers in various communities," offering no further details. In many cases, the demise of the Beothuk is blamed upon incursions by warlike Micmac, Naskapi and Montagnais neighbours from the mainland. Denial, prevarication and casting of blame upon the victims are typical of the consistent Canadian refusal to take ownership of the ugly parts of our past, although this approach fails to address the simple fact that the Beothuk were a

coastal people when the European settlers arrived, then suddenly fled to a bitter and inhospitable interior that remains
largely uninhabited even today. It was there, as far from the
settlers as they could get, that they finally perished in poverty,
starvation and disease.

The magnificent artefacts of the Beothuk's neighbours in the
Maritime provinces, also displayed by The Spirit Sings, are
equally poignant in forcing our attention to the brutality of European conquest and occupation. Think of their creators' fate this
way: when the most bloodthirsty Roman despots set out to terrorize dissident elements, they would order a decimation in
which every tenth person was executed. Between 1600 and 1700,
not one out of every ten, but nine out of every ten people of the
Micmac and Maliseet nations died or were killed — a number
which makes Caligula seem moderate by comparison. And this
was not by accident. The Micmac were subject to a bounty
placed on their scalps by the governor of the English settlement
at Halifax. When they proved too elusive for the European
hunters, Mohawk mercenaries were employed to help clear the
land for settlement. After the crafts of the Micmac and Maliseet,
one might admire the lovely decoration of deerskin dresses by
Huron women. The Huron population declined by 65 per cent,
from twenty-five thousand to nine thousand people, in little over
a decade. A similar rate of decline in contemporary Canada
would see the disappearance of every person living outside
Quebec. The Huron's major mistake was in becoming an ally of
the French, who lost to the English. By the time the winners were
finished, the Huron were in diaspora, some fleeing as far as the
present state of Oklahoma. This pattern is characteristic of the
Canadian experience. It is estimated by some scholars that the
total native population of the Canadian landmass might have
been as high as one million people at the time of first European
contact. At the turn of the century, it had declined to about one
hundred thousand. This is a cultural destruction that approaches genocidal proportions.

The Spirit Sings exhibition dealt with these unpleasant reali-
ties in an oblique and less than forthright way. It was, after all,
an ethnological display rather than an expression of historical
context. On reflection, it is clear, the show was actually intended
to tell the world and ourselves what a generous and tolerant
country we live in; how quick we are to recognize and honour
the way in which the culture of native peoples has enriched our
broader society. In fact, the social, ethical, political, spiritual and
philosophical values of native culture have been almost

universally rejected by the dominant society. On the other hand, native culture has certainly enriched museums, even if we consistently exclude it from contributing to the mainstream. And many of the museums that have been enriched are not even Canadian. Douglas Cole, an historian at Simon Fraser University in Vancouver, exhaustively documents the patterns of theft and acquisition in his important book *Captured Heritage*. An estimated three hundred thousand artefacts from the Northwest Pacific coastal cultures are now held by international collections — this is looting on the scale of the Visigoths.

The cataloguing and administration of such collections have made fine careers for curators, who by some extraordinary ethical gymnastics find easy praise for the value of native art while remaining strangely ineffectual regarding the social value of the human beings who produced it. But instead of debating the collective responsibility of the collectors, we might consider instead the social context of a selection of wonderful Assiniboine drawings, kindly loaned by their European owner to The Spirit Sings organizers for display in Canada.

The Assiniboines, numbering about twelve hundred lodges and among the great traders of the Plains tribes, ranged across the central Canadian prairies. In 1833, the winter counts of the Teton Sioux, Kiowa and Blackfoot record unusual numbers of shooting stars, generally considered a harbinger of some natural catastrophe. Major Alexander Culbertson at Fort McKenzie confirms the sightings. The native people did not have long to wait. By 1837, horrified European travellers were reporting the whole prairie region littered with the rotting corpses of men, women and children, abandoned equipment, straying horse herds and the encampments that brought a new term to Plains Indian language — the Ghost Camp, where the lodges are occupied only by the dead.

The pestilence and infection of smallpox reduced the Assiniboines to four hundred lodges. They had gone in one season from being the most powerful nation on the Great Plains to a pitiful, ragged remnant, begging for food. They had been, in the reports of appalled observers, virtually exterminated. While the cycle of plagues which ravaged the Plains cultures in 1837 and again in 1864, 1868 and 1883 could hardly be attributed to federal policy, they did offer a convenient clearing of the landscape for unencumbered settlement by the huge influx of farmers that was deliberate policy in Ottawa.

Shortly thereafter, the strategic elimination of the Plains Indians' primary food source occurred. In 1875, the Baker Company of Fort Benton, Montana, shipped seventy-five thousand buffalo hides to the east. Most of them had been taken from the hunting grounds of Canada's Blackfoot, Blood, Peigan and Sarcee tribal groups, the carcasses left to rot in the summer sun, the bones later collected and shipped for fertilizer production. Four years later, dated precisely by North-West Mounted Police dispatch, the buffalo were gone forever from the southern Alberta grasslands and Canadian society marched its native people into the concentration camp.

Today, we call them Indian reserves, sharing our love of the euphemism with the South Africans, who call them homelands, but let us not deceive ourselves about their original function. The rationalization for reserves, of course, was that they were created to save the few aboriginals who managed to survive the dismantling of their economy and the wrecking of their political structure, social organization, religion and family units. Indian reserves were invented by bureaucrats to control the movements of free-ranging people and to concentrate them in one place and bring them under the power of the dominant society. We may wrap ourselves in the comforting belief that reserves were an act of state generosity, seeking to save native nations from oblivion. The cold eye of political science sees that Indian reserves could not have been better designed for the specific purpose of destroying Plains Indian culture, which was predicated upon movement and freedom, so that the land might be carved up by newcomers who could get more productive use out of it by farming. As the topsoil of Palliser's Triangle, the arid region of southeastern Alberta and southwestern Saskatchewan, blows away on the dry winds of drought, demanding more and more dams and irrigation districts, with the attendant hazards of salinization — not to mention the overall tax burden — the definitions of what constitutes productivity require a new evaluation.

The most intense element of The Spirit Sings was its remarkable and moving celebration of the deep and complex spiritual nature of Indian life. In this, too, the exhibition brings shame upon us. Consider all those missionaries, acting in the name of a compassionate Christ, whose objective was the displacement of all the spiritual beliefs the exhibition purports to celebrate.

To this day the church, in its various manifestations, has difficulty bringing itself to acknowledge its role as an agent of cultural destruction. Yet, with all the best of intentions, missionaries representing the two mainstreams of Christian religion waged an active campaign to displace traditional religious belief and value systems among native peoples. At a time when aboriginal societies faced enormous upheaval and change, their societies threatened by the growing military, economic and commercial pressure from the European invaders, the missionaries set about sucking out the glue which held native communities together. By devaluing the moral force of traditional spiritual leaders and co-opting the belief and value systems of native people, the church served as an active agent in fomenting confusion and increasing vulnerability — always there with compassion, of course, to help pick up the pieces and shape them into a Christian and, essentially, European framework.

Evocative examples of the disruptive influence of Christian missionaries can be found almost everywhere. The Inuit settlement of Igloolik, high in Canada's Central Arctic, provides one good example. It was the site of a shameless war for souls which raged between Anglicans and Roman Catholics, as though the numbers of converted were pieces to be captured in a chess game. Fifty years later, a visitor from outside could still witness the scars of sectarian division in a community that had been homogeneous and secure. The Tsartlip Indian Reserve of Vancouver Island is another example. One of its elders told me that the people who eventually became its residents had the early distinction of having been formally converted by visiting priests to Roman Catholicism, Anglicanism and Methodism — all in the same year.

The state certainly concurred with this approach, seeing the church as a powerful instrument of assimilation. Missionaries like William Duncan, who established a mission to the Tsimshian at Metlakatla, off the coast of what is now the Alaska Panhandle, saw traditional native rites as an obstacle to Christian conversion and lobbied for their prohibition. Duncan was particularly offended by the ancient puberty rites that accompanied potlatch ceremonials. By 1885, with the whole-hearted backing of the various churches, Canada's parliament had passed legislation which prohibited the practice of native religious and spiritual ceremonies.

The Canadian state took suppression of native ceremonies seriously indeed. In 1922, following a traditional potlatch at Alert Bay, a prosperous Kwakiutl community located just off the northeast coast of Vancouver Island, a large number of men and women (the Indians say forty-five, the official records say twenty-nine) were arrested for the offenses of making speeches, singing, dancing, arranging and distributing gifts. The police action followed complaints from federal Indian agent William

Halliday, who, in a gross conflict of interest, conveniently doubled as magistrate for the trial. The arresting officer, an RCMP
sergeant, took the role of prosecutor. In this perversion of justice,
twenty of the men and women arrested were sentenced to
prison terms of two and three months. Fines were levied in the
form of their ancestral ceremonial regalia, which was seized by
the federal government. Halliday reported more than four hundred and fifty items filling three hundred cubic feet of space.
Some, according to Cole, he sold off to a foreign collector for
$291, the rest went to the curators at the National Museum in
Ottawa, the forerunner of the same Museum of Civilization
which hosted The Spirit Sings.

These officials salved their conscience in the matter by assigning arbitrary commercial values to the items and sending
cheques to the Indian agent for distribution. Cole points out in
Captured Heritage that some Indians claim never to have received
a penny's compensation for the priceless material — one item
was believed by the Indians themselves to have a value of 18,250
Hudson's Bay Company blankets. Just at the retail value of quality blankets today, it would be worth more than $4 million. Ulti-
mately, part of the stolen property was returned after sixty-six
years and a legal battle, but much of it has been lost to the owners and, in any event, as Cole points out, "The charges and convictions, the surrenders and imprisonments, were a severe blow
even to so resilient a culture as that of the Kwakiutl. . . . But the
forced cessation of the public potlatch, the feasts, and the dances
was a more severe blow."

This essential contempt by the collectors of artefacts for the
validity of traditional cultural values which the material items
represent continues today. At the Calgary segment of The Spirit
Sings, the curators insisted on displaying sacred objects in bald
defiance of the wishes of those who consider them sacred.
Sacred objects, it seems, are merely property, and in Canadian
society ownership is nine-tenths of the law. Would the Pope and
the Archbishop of Canterbury feel this way about the sacra-
ments and holy relics of their faith, one wonders. At the Ottawa
segment of the exhibition, at least, the authorities reportedly
decided not to include the false face mask of the Mohawk nation,
public display of which the Indians had fruitlessly sought to
block by court action. One wonders, however, whether this decision had more to do with the proximity of angry Iroquois to
Ottawa than with real understanding or compassion for the ethical issue.

At the Glenbow exhibit in Calgary, which is surrounded by

the Blood, Peigan, Sarcee, Blackfoot and Stoney reserves, cards were provided for observers to record their feelings.

"Sometimes our spirit has wept," wrote one viewer. "Sadness for my people who lost so much of their spirit when their ceremonial objects were laid down or taken away" — an interesting irony considered in the context of the consistent robbing of native cultural items in order that museums might provide evidence of the "preservation" of native culture. This juxtaposition of the aboriginal view and the official view says much about Canadian values. It confirms what has long been clear, that we actually prefer our native culture in museums. We certainly do not prefer it running the Department of Indian Affairs or the Department of Fisheries. Nor do we prefer native culture announcing the news on national television or determining its own political destiny.

"Where are the natives whose heritage this is?" asked another observer in Calgary. "Couldn't you find ANY to guide us through THEIR history . . . the spirits must be crying." This, too, draws attention to the wretched lie at the heart of The Spirit Sings. We prefer native culture that we may put on display when it conveniences us, called out for ceremonies that make us appear magnanimous — whether the creators of the artefacts like it or not.

"Why get upset, it's all in the past," one young white observer said to me after hearing my feelings about the show. "We didn't do it, somebody else did. Don't expect me to feel guilty for my great grandfather." This view I did not find surprising. It is the constant bleat of Canadian society with respect to native peoples. It was somebody else's fault. It is somebody else's responsibility. This familiar refrain lies at the very heart of Northern Alberta's Lubicon band dispute, still festering at the time of writing after fifty years of political buck-passing and evasion of moral responsibility by the federal and provincial governments.

"It's all in the past."

Tell that to the people of Peerless Lake, where on March 10, 1986, six young people died after drinking methyl hydrate — children erasing their futures with reproducing fluid.

Tell it to Richard Cardinal, the Cree teenager who hanged himself in despair after being shunted through twenty-eight foster homes and institutions in his brief seventeen years of life.

Tell it to Donald Marshall, imprisoned for eleven years for a crime he did not commit because of a justice system that made more assumptions about his racial origins than the evidence.

Tell it to the relatives of Helen Betty Osborne in The Pas, Manitoba. She was abducted, raped, stabbed fifty times with a screwdriver and left dying in the snow by four white teenagers. For sixteen years, the murderers were sheltered from the law by their community. Testimony at the trial made it clear that the identities of Helen's abductors were no secret in The Pas — but, then, the victim was only an Indian.

Try telling the Lubicons that the injustice is all in the past, they who struggle today to defend their tiny cultural enclave against the encroachments of the very same oil industry that so sanctimoniously sponsored The Spirit Sings exhibition in honour of native culture.

All of this adds up to the old Canadian story. Native culture is nice, but not if it gets in our way. Native culture is important, but not in terms of the people in whom it resides, only in the artefacts — the *things* we can collect and display in museum cases.

In the context of what The Spirit Sings claimed to say about the importance and value of native culture, Canadians need to ask some pointed questions of ourselves and our governing authorities. We need to ask why, in a province as wealthy as Alberta, we permit continuation of the conditions which lead to a death rate among Indian infants that is more than twice what it is for the general population? Why, in a country prepared to spend millions of dollars telling the world how much we value native culture, we tolerate conditions in which native people are four times as likely as the rest of us to die before reaching their life expectancy? Why is it acceptable that aboriginal Canadians are three times as likely to die by violence?

We need to ask how we can accept the conditions under which native people are ten times as likely to be diagnosed as alcoholics? Why it was possible, for nearly a decade, for the suicide rate for native people in northern Saskatchewan to remain fifteen times greater than the national average? What landscape of sorrow and despair do such people inhabit?

Why do 75 per cent of native students in the Northwest Territories abandon school between Grade 7 and Grade 12? Is this a failure to be blamed on the victims, or is the failure in the structure of a system which can neither visualize nor address their needs? How can it be that only 2 per cent of the Canadian population provides 10 per cent of the prison inmates — perhaps because the unemployment rate for native people consistently runs about 800 per cent higher than that deemed acceptable for mainstream society?

Whatever we put on display in the glass cases, the numbers betray the lie. These statistics provide the reality behind the self-serving falsehoods of exhibitions like The Spirit Sings. They reveal far more about the hypocrisy of the dominant culture than they do about the propensities of aboriginal people. They tell us that far from honouring native culture, Canadian society dismisses it in all its living forms.

Made invisible by our denial of the worth of their own cultural values, excluded from real economic participation in the dominant culture, squeezed into ghettos at the least productive margins of society, cheated of their promised patrimony, cheated of an equal opportunity at life itself and fully cognizant of our hypocrisy, aboriginal people are far from the honoured participants in Canadian society that exhibitions like The Spirit Sings would have the world believe. They remain deeply estranged from the social and political process of this nation. How long before, as Georges Erasmus warns, the sorrow and despair becomes rage and vengeance?

The tragedy, unfortunately, is not all in the past. It is all in the present. It is not somebody else's responsibility. It is Canadians' responsibility. If The Spirit Sings served one purpose, it was to remind thinking Canadians that the pathetic remnants of the Beothuk should be on display all right. They should be on display in a national shrine of shame and humility. The very first act of every prime minister should be to kneel before them and pray to the God that we invoke in our national anthem — both for national forgiveness and that Canada itself may never suffer what was suffered by the Beothuk, the Micmac, the Huron, the Assiniboine.

Earth, Air, Fire and Water

"Bedd pwy ydy hwn?
Gowin i mi, mi ae gwn."

"Whose grave is this? Ask me, I know it."

Stanzas of the Graves
Ninth century Welsh, anonymous

AFTERDAMP

Joseph Brown settles himself wearily among the shiny patches
that age has mapped into the plush of his battered sofa and surveys me with a glittering eye. Behind me, the balding furniture
sports antimacassars and lumpy cushions. Sepia photographs
jam the mantle. The wan light of a hazy Vancouver afternoon
seeps in around bleached chintz curtains. This whole room
might be a painter's metaphor for the faded elegance of an age
receding from memory.

It is an Edwardian woman's room, this front parlour cluttered
with bric-a-brac and properly skirted furniture, yet it manages to
ache with the sense of that woman's absence. The polished shine
of bare linoleum where there should be rugs, the mechanical
odds and ends carefully aligned on a corner Parson's table, the
thin layer of undisturbed dust among the pictures — the room is
a kind of reliquary, an old man's shrine to the passing of his life.
And all the small signs, the small austerities of male intrusion,
all these things speak to the woman's absence.

Joe leans suddenly into my space, a tough jaw, glinting with
silver stubble but fighting a tremor, controlling it with a precise
will which knots the muscles down the whole horizon of his
face. His hair has gone past white into that curious range of yellow that resembles aged ivory. He taps me on the knee, lets me
know he can read the thoughts in my face. "You bet I'm old," he
says. "Know how old I am? I'm older than the income tax."

And indeed he is. Joe Brown is so old that his first track boss
was a man born in the 1840s, a man who laid steel for the very
first transcontinental railway, punching through Indian territory
from the factories of the east to the markets of Sacramento and

the California gold fields. In Joe's own childhood, the Kootenay and Siksika were still moving camp from the high country to winter quarters, passing down the ridges above his father's house, their dogs carrying packs, the horses dragging travois, the men with their Winchesters in the saddle boots.

Joe, as he is fond of pointing out, had already been working a full year himself when the government brought down the income tax — an act of treachery that confirms the eternal duplicity of political life. That tax was a temporary measure to finance the mounting losses of 1917 campaigns mired in the bloody quagmire of Flanders. His father had saved him from the fate of millions, pleading with him not to enlist, to go down pit instead, where the jobs were considered strategic and the risks, however great, were at least known.

And the risks were enormous. Almost four hundred men had been killed in the coal mines between the time Alberta became a province and the outbreak of World War One. Three years before, just a few miles up the road, 189 men had perished in Canada's worst mining disaster. Four years before that, right across the valley, thirty men had been killed. Fernand Capon had been twelve years old the day they stacked the dead from Hillcrest Mine in a mass grave. His father had taken him to bear witness to history, leading his son through the long rows of coffins. "Son," he's reported to have said, "take note of this and never go down the mines." But that was in the high summer of 1914, and the armies of Europe had just begun to mobilize. Two months later, the sons of miners across southern Alberta and British Columbia would be embarking on the grand adventure of World War One. In the aftermath of the carnage at Hillcrest and Bellevue, it must have seemed a glorious opportunity to avoid the pit.

All through the boundary country, down the Crowsnest and out across the foothills and plains, young men were clamouring to join regiments with Kiplingesque names like the Kootenay Borderers, the Rocky Mountain Rangers, Lord Strathcona's Horse, the B.C. Dragoons. In British Columbia 10 per cent of the province's total population would enlist and serve overseas. But all too quickly the veil of romance lifted from the face of grisly nightmare. The spirited names of the regiments were replaced by numbers as the war was changed utterly by the statistics of attrition. The 1st Battalion, then the 31st, the 50th, the 222nd. Of the forty-three thousand young men that British Columbia was to give to the Empire, almost twenty thousand were to be killed or wounded. As Joe Brown came of age, the monthly casualty lists for the British Expeditionary Force were averaging thirty-five thousand names a month. His father begged him not to enlist. On October 26, 1917, the 46th Battalion that had mustered as the South Saskatchewan Regiment lost 70 per cent of its men in one afternoon. Ever after, it was to be known as The Suicide Battalion. A few days later, the 49th Battalion from Edmonton lost 75 per cent of its men. These were enormous losses for small communities. In Medicine Hat, for example, one out of every five people wound up as a name on the cenotaph. By the autumn of that year, the severely wounded survivors of Passchendaele began coming home. Sixteen thousand Canadians had become casualties in that battle, a fight for territory that was abandoned just six months later. The trickle of disabled veterans had turned into a torrent of maimed bodies and mutilated minds. Joe heeded his father and went down the pit. There was death in the mines, but for the most part it was fast and clean.

"I'm still here and it's still here," he says of the war tax he started paying for the privilege of working. The point behind his observation is witty and mischievous. Joe expects to be off to meet his Maker at any moment, but the rest of us will be stuck back here paying the tax the politicians promised would end with that almost forgotten war — the war that was supposed to end war. So much for the promises of politicians. Joe says he's never trusted any of them since.

He looks out the window at some invisible point. His stare drifts off into the oyster-coloured sky above his tranquil suburban neighbourhood. It is an industrial design engineer's sky, grey on grey, one that admits a diffuse, indirect light, rendering the world beneath it curiously featureless, washing out the sharp relief of shadow. Joe muses on it, "I might be in another world the next time you come." He'd had a slight stroke two weeks before and thought he was bound for The Other Side right then and there. Somebody, he says, had second thoughts and decided not to call him over.

Joe laughs about his struggle to reach a telephone and call for help. Alone in the house, trapped in the body he'd once known so well, known with the athlete's precise inner sense — that mental contour map, the mysterious awareness of every muscle, every tendon; that fine body betraying him, refusing him. He dragged himself to the stairs and slid down step by step on his backside, "Bump! Bump! Bump! Like a baby! Like a damn baby!" He laughs.

You get nonchalant about these things when death visits your friends so frequently. Live long enough and death visits all of them. You wake up one morning and the familiar community of the living has transformed itself to the austere community of the dead; you find yourself lost in the primal mysteries of transubstantiation, a ghost of physical presence at the fringes of a world of memory, the unheard revenant who may never enter. All the ordinary values of material possession are changed. Things take on importance only as icons through which you may evoke the insubstantial. You wait patiently to become a memory yourself.

"I read the obituaries all the time now," Joe says. "I'm not morbid. When I see those names, they come back to me. They come back clear as when we were young, when I knew them seventy years ago."

He is able to conjure them for strangers, too, sitting in the parlour under the clear-eyed stare of that absent lover, the gaze of friends, formal portraits of children and grandchildren, snapshots of the neighbourhood youngsters he bravely walked to school every day while police hunted desperately for mass child murderer Clifford Olsen. His eyes brim with tears as the mute people from a distant past become vivid on his tongue: The freed slave who came to Canada as a steel-driving navvy on the railways and ended his days as a wealthy — but always silent, always fearful — landlord and hotel owner: "Oh yes, the Ku Klux Klan burned a cross in our valley." Bob Dugdale and Bill Miller, strikers from the Hillcrest football team he dreamed of beating as a boy. Joe's long-dead wife: "Oh, she was a smart, beautiful woman. An intelligent woman. A tough woman. I'm just lingering here."

In this room of ghosts, I realize that it is to a ghost to whom I owe my encounter with Joe. There are parts of my country just like this room, defined by what is not there, made real only by the flickering play of dreams and fictions upon the screen of memory. The ghost of my visitation is the town were Joe grew up, vanished now into willow and underbrush, a footprint in the trackless Canadian bush, traced only in the faint outline of a path beside a cascading stream. Brindled trout hang in the shadows of boulders among clear pools; here and there a rusted twist of cable juts from gravel bars, sometimes the blackened timber of a collapsed bridge. Back in the dappled shade of alders, you find the eerie carapace of decayed industry: black ruts of coal-dust roads, sudden drifts of slag, the dank breath of the underground and the odour of abandonment mingling in the concrete shells of hoist rooms and washer sheds.

I came upon the place almost by accident, led there by my wife Susan, who was doing research for a book. I was along only to provide the four-wheel drive she needed to explore the back roads in the Crowsnest Pass where it breaches the Rockies between Lundbreck, Alberta, and Fernie, B.C. It seems strange to locate the towns of this unusual and beautiful region in different provinces. The whole pass has its own distinct sense of geography. It has its own history, its own economy, its own precise sense of place in the tides of fortune and tragedy. Joe's roots are here in the mining camps and boom towns that roared and ranted into being when the mountains rang with their enterprise, when coal was king.

The main streets of Blairmore and Coleman, Hillcrest, Fernie and Bellevue tell part of the story. Their big boulevards trumpet big dreams, born in the conviction that prosperity would endure as long as men could cut the best coking coal in the world. The richness of the seams and the quality of the coal drew entrepreneurs and developers and flim-flam operators from all over the world. On their heels came the miners from Yorkshire, Wales, Italy and France. Labour radicals and political dissidents in exile flavoured the air with revolutionary fervour and socialist idealism.

If it had less of the romantic glitter of the gold and silver stampedes that preceded it, the Crowsnest coal boom was no less vigorous and wild. Cities sprang up overnight and vanished as quickly. The men and women who peopled them were tough as rawhide, and the society they forged was fraught with hardship and violence and sudden death. The Crowsnest region between Fernie and Blairmore was so rough that it chewed up half-a-dozen British Columbia Provincial Police constables in just over a year. The cables between the town of New Michel and police headquarters in Victoria tell the story best: On January 24, 1911, Constable Bulger is discharged due to ill health. His replacement, Constable MacCuish, resigns when he cannot find a suitable place to dwell. Constable McLeod lasts until April 3. His replacement, Constable Hughes, lasts a matter of days. Constable McMillan takes up his duties on April 3. On April 15, he gives two weeks notice: "I am sick of this district. As you are aware, there are no people that a man can associate with, with the exception of the hotel keepers, and I wasn't long in finding out that if a man becomes familiar with them that they will take advantage of him."

The reluctance of these officers to accept a posting to the new towns of the Crowsnest Pass is not surprising. The turbulent stew they were expected to police was afflicted with the brutality of meagre wages and the extortions of the Black Hand, the cruelty of the brothels and the avarice of the bootleggers, labour strife that frequently erupted into violence and intimidation. And the horrors of the mine accidents. Always, the mine accidents.

The fire that ripped through the Hillcrest Mine in the twinkling of an eye was a present danger in all the pits. At Hillcrest, deep in what they called The Old Level workings, a heavy rock fall struck sparks, igniting the methane gas in the tunnel roofs and flashing through the explosive coal dust. It triggered three blasts so powerful they blew the rope-riders out of the pithead to the height of a six-storey building and pulverized eight-inch concrete walls. Joseph Atkinson later said he never even heard the explosion, just suddenly went deaf. In a matter of seconds, the firestorm had consumed all the oxygen in the mine and replaced it with poisonous carbon dioxide, the invisible, odourless, lethal afterdamp.

On November 9 of the year that Joe Brown went to work at his own mine just up the valley, a series of tremors rumbled through the mountain. Nine men escaped, but John Janiack was "left entombed." Five months later, an explosion flashed through the drifts at Coal Creek Number Three, killing thirty-four. In Europe, the Great War raged, and, through the Crowsnest Pass, Canada's secret police hunted Bolsheviks, enemy aliens and draft evaders. Military intelligence intervened in the form of spy chief Sir Percy Sherwood himself when the district coroner blamed the blast at Coal Creek on a bomb conspiracy by enemy saboteurs, although miners on the rescue teams scoffed that it was just the usual accident. Irish Republican agitators from Sinn Fein whipped up anti-British sentiment among workers on the CPR, and just south of the border, in the state of Washington, there was bloodshed and heavy fighting between the International Workers of the World and a hundred armed Everett businessmen.

But, in truth, Joe Brown was less concerned with these things than the fact that "Kid" Scaler of Spokane and Coal Creek's local hero, a boxer named McCarthy, had battled to a draw and had scheduled a twenty-round rematch to settle things once and for all. The purse was an unbelievable $100, about ten weeks pay for a miner with a good place.

Not far east of Fernie was the town of Michel, reduced by 1988 to a road house and a few blackened buildings. It boasted the longest bar in the whole country and jobs for six extra bartenders every payday. The owner, Tommy Crahan, was a boomer who plotted the townsite for Morrissey Mines. He left his name on a soccer medal, and the teams that played for it left their mark in legend, teams of uncouth coal miners who played like angels — good enough to conquer professional first division clubs from England.

One of these black-faced dust devils, Dave Turner, who starred with Cumberland United out of Vancouver Island's coal fields, went on to become the Wayne Gretzky of his era. Chosen Canada's male athlete of the half century in 1950, Doc Turner's magic with the soccer ball was so brilliant he won his laurels over Olympic sprint champion Percy Williams; over Cyclone Taylor, Lester Patrick, Lionel Conacher and all the other greats of the more prestigious National Hockey and Canadian Football leagues.

It was a sweaty, virile, exciting time to be alive and in the prime of youth. Joe Brown went to work in a valley where the twenty-two seams of the Crowsnest field were 216 feet thick and covered two hundred square kilometres. Surveys estimated close to twenty-five million long tons of coal available per kilometre, and the pit crews operated round the clock. At Corbin Mines, the output for each man underground was more than two thousand tons of coal — cut by hand over a work year of 291 days. The Crow's Nest Pass Coal Company stuffed that yield into more than a thousand beehive ovens producing premium coke to fire the world's blast furnaces. Canadian and American railways fought a ferocious commercial war to control the freight routes, and the city of Spokane in Washington rose to prominence as a supplier to towns across the Canadian border. Joe and everyone else thought it would never end.

But prideful dreams are made to crumble. Prices collapsed as oil displaced coal. The mines closed, the miners left, poplars suckered up through the house foundations, the camps blew away on the wind and the wild places reclaimed their patrimony as they always do.

Today, the husks of those empty dreams rattle in the memories of small communities. Long arches of coking ovens spill their bricks in the shadow of spoil heaps that blaze with dandelion and goldenrod. Rust-stained fences seal off the mine drifts. The opulent house of the owner's family stands roofless behind the field where his legendary daughter put on her white dress and rode her pony down through the strikers' lines, carrying a secret payroll for the scabs. Across the valley, another kind of legend. The ugly scar that slashes through the yellow carpet of daisies and buttercups is the mass grave for the men killed in the Hillcrest Mine disaster, with seven of the town's fine soccer team among them. There, too, you find the grave of Dave Murray, who survived the blast but plunged back into the holocaust alone to perish with the three sons missing underground. And the graves of the Petrie boys, buried side by side. And the Johnsons, the Dugdales, the Fortunatos and the McKinnons; fathers, sons and brothers; the futures of whole families laid forever in the ground.

Up where Joe was raised in the first years of this century, there is not even a cemetery. Nothing remains but a curious, weed-choked meadow under the shoulder of a mountain stripped to the bone, first by settlers clear cutting timber from its slopes, then by the avalanches that deny regeneration, winter after winter. All that is left of Joe's youth is here. The rectangular meadow is the soccer pitch where he played centre-half for the Coal Creek football eleven when the teams of the Crowsnest Pass matched and defeated the powerhouse professional clubs of Europe.

I knew none of this as we slammed our truck through ruts of coal dust and raw earth, churning down to that sun-dappled field. When we reached the bottom, a surprise. We found the remote meadow filled with people. A reunion of old timers gathered to pay respects to a town etched only in their dwindling recollections.

They invited us to join their picnic, heaped our plates with fried chicken and potato salad, stuck cold beers in our hands and pressed me into the tournament that was unfolding with the stately fierceness only a serious game of horseshoes among old men can inspire. During the tournament, I met Roger Postlethwaite, one of the cool, intellectual experts of a new kind of coal mining. Roger and people like him are creating the next generation of automated, scientific, safety-conscious operations that impress the daylights out of old miners like Joe.

We stood in the tall grass with our blue cans of Kokanee, listening to the clamour of children playing in the creek that once supplied Dolly Varden for the table between paydays when men like Joe earned a dollar a week and were thankful for it. Roger, with his engineer's eye, pointed out the tangle of underbrush where the miner's houses had stood, where Joe had been born in a back bedroom so long ago. Behind us, a pair of old men dallied with a soccer ball. It was one of the heavy leather ones from another age. None of your pretty black and white patterns, just thick bars of durable brown stitched together. Slowly, they booted it back and forth in the rank growth of a football field that once hosted fans by the noisy thousands.

As we idled, Roger told me of his teenage daughter's new gods, Kevin Lowe, Jari Kurri and the Edmonton Oilers. Hockey is the game now, he said. These kids have never heard of Dave Turner. When I got home I sent his daughter some odds and ends of Oilers memorabilia — a few pictures, the *Edmonton Journal's* commemorative edition for the first Stanley Cup. Roger wrote back to thank me and added a laconic note: "If you ever get to Vancouver, look up Joe Brown."

I did. And Joe told me how it was cutting coal in the dark, lying in the narrow seams and listening to the growl and shudder of the mine settling around him in that winter of 1917. Working with the ghosts of 1902, when something happened "in the deeps" of Coal Creek No. 2, and the blast killed 125 men. Working always with one ear cocked for the sounds of a blowout. Worrying every second of every minute about apparitions, about the underground gas demons — blackdamp, afterdamp, firedamp — terrors to asphyxiate the unlucky or sear the skin off the careless. Remembering the clean-up duty after a fault slipped and the mine bumped so hard the floor hit the ceiling and squashed flat the steel wheels of the coal cars, not to mention the flesh and blood of the crews.

Mostly, Joe talked of coming out of the mine still black with grime, skipping supper after a twelve-hour day and racing to meet the special trains down from Blairmore and Hillcrest, wanting only to play his game. Remembering the dream of the youth who would live forever, who ran like a deer and crunched into fearless tackles — down the whole Crowsnest Pass, he owned that centre zone. The youth with pale and slender limbs, who wore the coal dust on his face like a badge of honour among men. Suiting up in the simple team colours and moving out into the midfield of his manhood. Hearing only the great roar of the crowd thrown back by the cold face of the mountain that took his whole life to its unforgiving heart.

END OF THE WORLD TIME

On the unusually close, humid Friday afternoon of July 31, 1987, *Edmonton Journal* news photographer Steve Simon was looking forward to an easy holiday weekend. His shift rotation and the civic holiday activities ahead meant that short of a monumental screw-up he had a guarantee of front page play.

The sultry, dripping heat was oppressive enough to be unpleasant and thundershowers were expected, but the Edmonton Eskimos were playing a crucial professional football game and the city's annual Heritage Festival followed. A two-day kaleidoscope of dance, food and vivid ethnic costumes that draws up to three hundred thousand people for the last long weekend of the summer, Heritage Days was a photographer's dream of action and colour. Heck, with a heavy rain there might even be flooding in the "rat-hole," as local drivers referred to a low-lying underpass. There was an outside possibility Simon might even get the grand slam and ace all four major picture positions — front, city section, sports and entertainment. That was at 2:30. An hour later, Simon was staring down the throat of hell itself. It was not an experience for which the young photographer had been entirely prepared.

A bright prospect who impressed editors with his portfolio and confirmed it with his work as a summer intern, Simon was just about to celebrate his first anniversary as the junior staff photographer in a department studded with award-winning veterans. He'd been dispatched by assistant photo editor Cheryl Shoji to check out reports of freakish weather and hail at the farming village of Beaumont, just south of the city, but stopped to fill the gas tank of his company car at the *Journal*'s fleet control centre in an east-side industrial park.

Simon happened to glance at the sky over Beaumont. What he saw froze his blood. He found himself gaping at an immense vortex of cloud, half a mile wide at the base and reaching a thousand feet into the black sky. The tornado was surrounded by a horrifying nimbus of debris kicked up as it consumed everything in its path. Shredding trees, smashing structures like kindling, the twister moved so fast that survivors later said it seemed to be standing still — until it arrived and swept over them with winds estimated as high as four hundred miles an hour. Simon raced his Chevy Citation twenty blocks farther east to get a better camera angle, set himself squarely in the twister's path as it roared toward him out of the southwest and — not exactly calmly — braced himself against the buffeting wind and shot the picture that claimed front pages across the continent.

Back at the *Journal* newsroom, photo editor Steve Makris had just emerged from the statistical boredom of his monthly departmental budget meeting and was joking with managing editor George Oake about whether the sudden downpours pounding across the city might make a stand-up picture for Saturday's paper — "Weatherman Ruins Holiday Weekend" kind of stuff. The weatherman, in fact, along with other meteorological staff at Environment Canada's weather office, was cowering in the basement as the immense twister stormed by a scant one hundred metres from the atmospheric environment service building.

The meteorologists were the only people in the city who were not totally surprised by the appearance of the tornado, although the size, suddenness and ferocity of the storm that had rolled into Edmonton from the south had shocked even their veteran watchers. Weather scientists across North America, relying on satellite photographs and the readings from stations across the continent, had been watching an ominous build-up down the whole eastern side of the Rocky Mountains of the huge thunderstorms called supercells. As far south as Oklahoma City, square in the middle of the continent's tornado alley, severe weather expert Gary England watched with growing apprehension as the roiling cumulo-nimbus clouds piled up on the satellite pictures, their black anvil-shaped heads flattening out in the cold, dry jet streams of the upper atmosphere.

"We wondered if it was EOTW Time up there in Edmonton," England confessed later. "You could see those clouds piling up. It looked awesome. We call it End of The World Time."

He had been to the end of the world many times before. From

the low-lying Texas coast on the Gulf of Mexico to northern Alberta, the Great Plains corridor that runs up the middle of the continent is the most active severe weather zone in the world. More than twenty-eight thousand tornadoes have been tracked since 1916, an average of seven hundred per year, with fatalities averaging ninety-four per year.

In the turbulent bellies of the towering thunder clouds that moved toward Edmonton through the hot, wet air of the weather front, twisters were being born. They were spawned in the vortex formed by warm air rising and meeting winds blowing at different speeds and in different directions. These jet streams were carrying the air away as it cooled instead of allowing it to fall back to earth. Spinning upward at speeds of up to one hundred kilometres per hour, the updraft created a low pressure area which sucked more and more hot, moist air up into the turning column. Around it, spiralling counterclockwise, a downdraft of dry air eventually formed, cooled and condensed by evaporation. Plunging earthward from as high as twenty-five thousand feet, turning faster and faster on a tighter and tighter axis, the funnel clouds began to sink toward the ground. With violent supercells, heavy rain and powerful hail stuttering across the radar scopes, Edmonton's atmospheric environment experts knew that a witch's brew of bad weather was on the way. The best of them could not have guessed the magnitude of the tornado that was forming in the cauldron of cross-winds, lightning and hail that rumbled toward the city. At 1:40 p.m., the scientists put out a severe weather watch for Edmonton and surrounding districts and mounted a minute-by-minute observation of the rapidly changing conditions. At 2:45 p.m. they changed the watch to a severe weather warning, a small matter of words but a large matter of meaning. In a weather watch, the public is warned to remain alert to the possibility of severe weather developing quickly. A weather warning means that severe weather is expected.

Ten minutes later, at 2:55 p.m., a small-town weather observer reported a funnel cloud northeast of Leduc, twenty-five kilometres south of the city. It was moving toward the suburban outskirts of Edmonton. After ten minutes of analyzing data to corroborate the visual sighting, the weather office put out a formal tornado warning. It was 3:04 p.m. Unfortunately, of the city's four television stations and eighteen radio stations, only one TV and two radio stations had the special receiver required to pick up the broadcast warning that tornadoes were imminent. Luckily, a ground observer at Leduc had the foresight to telephone CBC radio after spotting the funnel cloud. The station broke into its routine afternoon broadcasts and went live with a request that listeners who saw anything similar should phone in immediately and report the location over the airwaves. This public response enabled authorities to track the tornado's destructive path with even more precision than the Environment Canada meteorologists, a critical factor in quick response by civil disaster units.

Yet even if the tornado warning had achieved general broadcast, it is unlikely that the public would have responded in the way official hindsight would like to believe. Although the region running north from Red Deer to Edmonton is Alberta's own tornado alley — one study tracks seven hundred twisters and one thousand destructive windstorms in Alberta and the adjacent parts of Saskatchewan between 1910 and 1960 — in the entire half century only five real, if small, tornadoes had been recorded in the vicinity of Edmonton. Twisters were a curious phenomena, worth a picture and short story in the paper when they knocked over spruce trees, scattered haystacks or took the occasional roof off a farmer's grain shed. In the public imagination, they were nothing to be compared with the television pictures of catastrophe from distant places like Kansas and the Texas panhandle. All that changed abruptly at 3:25 p.m.

It was then that the multi-band radio on the *Edmonton Journal* photo desk erupted with Simon's report that he was fleeing a huge tornado. As Oake, Makris and other newsroom staff clustered to listen in disbelief to Simon's frightened voice describe the monster chewing its way through the eastern suburbs and industrial parks, they realized that the unpleasantly heavy weather was about to become a civic catastrophe. In what seemed like an instant, police, fire and ambulance radio bands on the newsroom monitors were incoherent with a cascade of confused and frequently inaccurate reports of deaths, injuries, damage, missing people and the always-present fear in the oil patch — explosion and fire, deadly gas and toxic chemicals leaking from pipelines or storage tanks ruptured near downed high-tension electrical wires in the refinery district.

At that point, a massive power surge took out the *Journal*'s newsroom computer system, the composing room system and the advertising system that served as back up. All the computer circuits had been fried by the savage spikes in voltage. Telephone communications in large areas of the city crashed next, and managing editor Oake found himself in charge of a newsroom command centre rendered blind, deaf and partially paralyzed, while he frantically sought to co-ordinate a grab bag of more than forty hastily assembled reporters, photographers and editors. They ranged from society columnists to political writers, experienced police reporters to staff from the paper's neighbourhood weekly.

For his own part, photo editor Makris had quickly deployed his eight available photographers in what he called "a classic triangular response — go to the point of origin, get way out in front of it, drop the rest into the middle as widely spaced as possible." Buddied up with reporters whenever feasible, the photographers were able to use the sophisticated mobile radios in their *Journal* vehicles both to report the magnitude of the disaster and to create an unofficial city-wide communications net.

Photographer Ken Orr, an aviation enthusiast in his spare time, was dispatched to the city's municipal airport to get aloft for aerial pictures. He stopped briefly to snap the wreckage of small aircraft on the apron, then took off for what proved an exceptionally brief flight. Caught aloft by another fast-moving supercell, Orr and his pilot banked and raced for the airport. Alberta Member of Parliament Jack Shields, flying his small Beechcraft from Lac La Biche in the north toward Edmonton, was at forty-four hundred feet of altitude when the storm systems roared through. His plane was tossed around like a leaf. Drawing on his long experience as a pilot, Shields managed to set down at the Edmonton International Airport, bruised and frightened by the worst turbulence in twenty years of flying. Twenty-five kilometres to the north, Orr's plane scudded before the fast-moving front like a surf board on a breaker. What he saw from the cockpit confirmed the worst. Skipping through the farm fields from the south, the tornado had slashed a kilometre-wide wound along the entire eastern edge of the city of six hundred and fifty thousand, ripping haphazardly through outlying farms, residential suburbs, rush-hour traffic and major industrial zones.

Reporters and photographers, frequently arriving at disaster sites before police, fire or medical teams, found themselves in a disorienting wilderness of tortured wreckage, crushed vehicles, maimed corpses and stunned survivors. Familiar landmarks vanished, streets disappeared into jumbled heaps of machinery and the strewn remains of disintegrated buildings. Dazed victims stumbled in the ruins.

Photographer Brian Gavriloff, a tough, national class athlete with a first aid ticket, found himself interrupting his shooting to treat the injured and assist the police in conducting body counts.

Gavriloff is no stranger to trying conditions. Only eighteen months before, he had slogged through minus-thirty degree temperatures for weeks on end as the *Journal*'s photographer on a ski trek to the North Magnetic Pole. But those conditions were trivial compared to this.

Shearing through the industrial park, the tornado had exploded buildings, crumpled the metal skin of huge warehouses like used aluminum foil and squashed a huge oil storage tank like an empty beer can. Twenty-ton trucks had been lifted into the air and telescoped back into the ground, trains had been flipped off the tracks. Compounding the hazards, the tornado had knocked down sixty high steel towers carrying live two-hundred-and-forty-thousand-volt power lines to the industrial sites. Another one hundred and fifty wood and steel towers carrying one-hundred-and-thirty-eight-thousand-volt lines had been knocked down farther to the southeast. In the midst of this tangle of sparking high tension wires, propane gas was leaking from a farm of twenty-eight tanks, some of which had ruptured, many of which had damaged valves. Scattered through the rubble were oxy-acetylene welding tanks, leaking refrigeration units, toxic PCBs, explosive fertilizers and poisonous pesticides.

Beyond the industrial park, the tornado smashed across the Sherwood Park freeway, jammed with bumper-to-bumper holiday traffic. After churning the highway into a terrifying junkyard of twisted car hulks and flattened trucks, it blasted through the five hundred fragile trailers of Evergreen Mobile Park. Photographer Mike Pinder found a desolate landscape and the scattered wreckage of two hundred homes. They had been obliterated so completely they might have been hit by a tactical nuclear weapon. A chaff of planks, splintered plywood, shattered siding, shingles, remnants of furniture, insulation and beams trailed away to the northeast, marking the twister's route out into the countryside.

The prefabricated mobile homes were death-traps, disintegrating into a whirling blizzard of deadly debris. Of the people killed, fifteen were among the two thousand residents of the park. Lois Theroux, a twenty-four-year-old mother of two, had been sitting down to watch "The Young and The Restless" on television when she noticed the tornado approaching. She hustled her seven-year-old daughter and a one-year-old baby into her new 1987 Mustang and tried to run for it. The winds picked her car from the ground, first the front end, then the rear end, slamming the vehicle up and down in a kind of demonic dance. Her speedometer read 140 kilometres per hour, she recalled later, but the car did not move. Like many of the victims, she reported a strong sense of everything moving in slow motion, the car filling with a strange, terrible smelling white cloud and the wind whirling around inside the cab, lashing her hair about. Then the car dropped onto all four wheels and she screeched out of the trailer park.

Marvin Reimer and Kelly Pancel were not so lucky. Kelly was just eighteen and the mother of Megan, a three-week-old baby. When the twister slammed into the trailer, she and her brother Brian Bowyer crouched to shelter the infant with their own bodies, but the washer and dryer tore loose and hurled across the room, striking them both. Brian and Megan survived, Kelly died instantly. Marvin Reimer was huddled with daughter Diane, thirteen, and his eleven-year-old twins Darcy and Dawn. When his wife Arlene got to the scene, nothing was left of the trailer. No clothes, nothing. Just Marvin's shed, perfectly intact, with all his tools in it. In the freakish skipping of the tornado, flower beds were found untouched, while the trailers they graced had been lifted and crashed to earth hundreds of metres away. On one trailer pad, a closet full of undisturbed clothing stood in the bare floor of a trailer with the roof and walls ripped off. Three-month-old Cody Grandish was lying in his crib when the twister struck. It whisked the crib out from under him, to vanish in the swirling column of junk that surrounded the central funnel, but deposited the baby gently on the carpet, where he was later found sheltered by rubble.

In other places, objects had been fired through plate glass windows at such velocities that it seemed a glass cutter had made neat holes in the panes. A telephone pole was uprooted and fired like a dart, piercing the foundations of the Evergreen Supermarket. It was this flying debris that claimed most of the victims, and medical examiners were issuing blanket death certificates: "multiple blunt injuries." For the dead at Evergreen Trailer Park, a makeshift morgue for the little community had been located, poignantly, in the Happy Pizza and Steak House. A kilometre to the south, Pinder's colleague Karen Sornberger found residential streets in the suburb of Clareview choked with the wreckage of comfortable split-levels and bungalows.

By now, *Journal* staffers stationed at city hospitals were reporting the human dimensions of the carnage as the injured streamed in — a man with a board through his spine, a three-year-old child with a severed arm, a teenager sucked through the windshield of his van, people disfigured by flying glass, a baby with skull fractures, miraculously alive after being plucked from his mother and dashed to earth four city blocks away. One veteran journalist reported scenes reminiscent of an advanced military field hospital in a major battle zone. Helicopters ferried in the wounded and the dying, their pilots braving the violently gusting winds to land in the street perilously close to swaying lamp standards. Attendants sprinted down the emergency ramps, carrying injured children in one arm and pulling trolleys loaded with injured adults with the other. The fourteen doctors and thirty nurses the hospital had been able to muster in a matter of minutes coped with 127 dazed, confused, highly apprehensive survivors who suffered a bewildering range of serious cuts, fractures and puncture wounds from flying glass and metal. Another seventy similar cases descended on the University of Alberta hospital from the freeway and industrial park to the southeast.

One of the first to arrive at the Royal Alexandra was temporary acting sergeant Bill Clark of the Edmonton City Police. He had been the first officer to arrive at the devastation of Evergreen Trailer Park, where a woman he could not identify handed him a tiny baby wrapped in a soaking blanket. She had found the infant in the debris and did not know where the parents were or what the baby's name was. Clark checked to make sure the baby was alive, pulling its toes to make it cry, then packed his squad car with as many injured as he could carry and raced to the hospital.

The miracle baby, as she was soon named by the rescue teams, was Kristen Gregoire, born only ten days before. When the twister hit, Kristen was in the arms of her grandfather while her sixteen-year-old mother, Monique, had been standing in the hallway of her mobile home. The teenage mother later remembered her brother Bruno yelling at her to take cover, but before she could take a single step the structure around her vanished. Six-pound Kristen was torn from her grandfather's arms and carried away on the whirlwind like Dorothy bound for the Land of Oz. Monique came to her senses buried in mud and wreckage. A frantic search of the area turned up no sign of her baby. But the length of a football field away, on the other side of the trailer park, another survivor heard a baby crying in the debris. It was Kristen. The rescuer pulled her out of the wreckage, wrapped her in a blanket and turned her over to Sergeant Clark.

While the city policeman was struggling to get Kristen and the other wounded to the north side's Royal Alexandra Hospital, Evergreen Trailer Park manager Chico Bulner was crawling out of the only basement on the site. In the shadow of the huge tornado, he had dashed outside and rounded up as many play-ing youngsters and bystanders as he could reach and packed them into his cellar. Thirty of them huddled there as the tornado went over with the sound of a hundred jet planes. When Bulner emerged, he was confronted by the blood-soaked horror of Troy Murdock. The three-year-old's arm had been lopped off near the shoulder and dangled by a shred of muscle. Bulner stayed calm and rushed the bleeding youngster south toward the Royal Alexandra Hospital but had to turn back when his way was blocked by flooding. He kept his head and managed instead to get the child to a medical clinic in a shopping mall on the north-ern periphery of the city. First aid administered there kept Troy alive until he could be moved to the hospital, where an eight-hour operation re-attached the severed arm.

In its forty-minute rampage, the tornado had left twenty-seven people dead or dying and injured another three hundred. At least one thousand people were homeless, and damage was being counted at $300 million or more, the greatest civil disaster in Canadian history.

Bodies still littered the ground in the worst hit areas, where desperate rescue teams picked cautiously through debris up to two storeys deep, slowed by the twenty kilometres of live high-voltage power lines that snaked through the rubble. Major trans-port arteries were blocked by flooding and a growing jam of frightened civilian traffic. Fears that exposed rescue teams might themselves be at risk were intensified by the arrival of a second cell of severe thunderstorms that briefly dropped another tor-nado funnel over the city, accompanied by torrential rain and hail. The emotional impact was so devastating that relief officials later said some traumatized newspaper and television reporters were among those applying for counselling from special psycho-logical aid services set up by government agencies.

"I was shocked by it myself," said one veteran reporter who flew in to cover the disaster for the *Vancouver Sun*. "I've seen some pretty bad stuff but this was the worst. It wasn't so much the violence and destruction as the aftermath in human terms. I watched this long line of refugees in the pouring rain, wrapped in green plastic garbage bags, trudging single file through the wreckage of what used to be their homes. It was the saddest thing. . . . "

Meanwhile, an official emergency command centre had been set up at Edmonton's city hall. Members of the government's emergency response team struggled through the floods and wreckage to take their posts with the planning unit in an almost flawless real-life performance of the exercise they had rehearsed so many times. Most of them were on duty for twenty-six continuous hours before relief was available. If the performance was smooth and professional, what they hadn't counted on was the depth and complexity of the services that had to be addressed after the disaster. A senior communications adviser seconded to the unit from the provincial government said that when they assembled a multi-agency committee to discuss what had to be done for survivors and victims they found they had a committee of about forty people.

"Things just mushroomed," he told me later. "You know you have to get money to people, so you call in a rep from the social services department. Then you have to have somebody from finance to make sure the cheques can be drawn without any red tape. Then you have to get somebody from the post office because a lot of the victims no longer have an address where you can deliver their money. And so on, and so on. . . . Well, you know what they say — nothing is impossible until you refer it to a committee, and the bigger the committee, the less possible it is." Instead, the huge emergency committee set an agenda, came up with a plan and got it implemented in a single six-hour session.

Don Getty, the new provincial premier, as decisive as you'd expect for a former quarterback for the Eskimos professional football team, had come to the committee meeting early and given it clear authority to break whatever rules of bureaucratic procedure were necessary to achieve its goals. He said he'd worry about the rules, they should worry about the victims: "I don't want any of these people waiting in line-ups for help."

The committee took him at his word and called for the setting up of a single central service point, commandeering M.E. Lazerte High School on the city's northeast shoulder. All services for disaster victims were to be concentrated in the school, with trauma counsellors, unemployment insurance experts, household insurance adjusters and financial advisers all available in the same place. This meant the relief agencies were able to respond to 250 families in the first day with virtually no waits for anyone.

While the official response was being organized, the unofficial response was already well underway. Six city hotels in outlying regions had thrown their doors open to shocked victims and survivors seeking food, medical attention and word of missing loved ones. Under the supervision of the Canadian Red Cross, the suddenly homeless flooded into the Sands Inn, the

Edmonton Inn, the two Renford Inns, the Ramada Renaissance
Inn and the Londonderry Inn. Hotel managers like Jason Braun
at Londonderry set up registration for the refugees so that families could be reunited the next day and organized supplies of
dry diapers for babies, clean clothing and bedding. The hoteliers
soon ran out of rooms and began using banquet halls. By midnight, every available space had been converted to a makeshift
dormitory.

Braun also provided a bank of telephones for people
desperate to call hospitals or the homes of friends to inquire
about missing spouses, children and other relatives. And for all
those trying to use the city's wrecked phone system within
Edmonton, worried callers were trying to phone in from outside
and to phone long distance to let distant relatives know that
their folks were okay. Alberta Government Telephones, the
agency responsible for telephone services outside metropolitan
Edmonton, called in six hundred extra long-distance operators
for a shift normally handled by twenty-six. It was a wise decision. At one point, as television news flashed pictures of the
disaster across the country, the AGT long-distance operators
handled twenty-eight thousand calls in a single hour.

If Canadians elsewhere were worried about the extent of the
disaster in Edmonton, the emergency response team was trying
to evaluate the damage in the midst of chaotic local communications. *Edmonton Journal* managing editor Oake, charged with getting information out to the national and international wire services, decided to rely on his own staff in the field for an accurate
measure of the dimensions of what had happened. It was an
astute call. The officials who swiftly assembled and co-ordinated
rescue and relief efforts later acknowledged that the press
played a critical role in providing and disseminating accurate
information while normal communications channels were falling
apart.

Back in the *Journal* newsroom, photo editor Makris and assistant Neil Smalian were now faced with their own emergencies
— both the flood of film pouring in for the picture labs and the
clamour for material by other news agencies around the world.
Over the next few hours, the *Journal*'s darkroom technicians
would process and Makris would edit more than fifteen hundred frames of colour film from staff photographers and
freelancers. He would select and proof seventy of the best for his
own senior editors. At the same time, he would complete twelve
separate projects for Canadian Press, the national wire service.

While Oake struggled to organize his coverage into coherent

form amid dead computers, editor-in-chief Linda Hughes was wrestling with an even greater problem — whether or not the paper could publish. One collateral victim of the twister had been the *Journal*'s modern printing plant, located several miles east of the city core in one of the most heavily damaged industrial zones. It was here that Simon first spotted the funnel cloud. While the tornado skidded past the $35-million plant and its twenty-seven press units, missing it by a narrow 300 metres, it had torn out all the building's power supplies. Plant manager Fred Dicker was already on the phone warning that he couldn't provide the two thousand kilowatts needed to run the presses and their fifteen colour decks, and it was clear that there were no alternative sources. The big Goss Metro offsets were to sit idle for the next twenty-two hours.

When the tornado hit, preparations had been well underway for the next morning's seventy-six-page Saturday edition, heavy with advertising and special feature sections. Now, it appeared there would be no paper at all. News and composing room computer systems had been down for four hours and there was no hope of starting the presses. Hughes, thirty-six, and appointed editor only months earlier, scrambled to find alternatives while her newsroom raced to prepare for an edition that might never see print.

First, the publishers of weekly newspapers in outlying communities were contacted. They volunteered press facilities without hesitation, but their tiny, slow presses couldn't handle the runs required of a major metropolitan daily. The *Red Deer Advocate*, a small daily 150 kilometres south of Edmonton, volunteered its plant — but it couldn't handle the run either. Hughes thought of combining the capacity of several smaller papers but learned that wasn't feasible because they all had different web widths and plate sizes. Copy would have to be processed and pages made up many times over to fit the different equipment.

The *Journal*'s sister paper in the Southam Newspaper Group, the *Calgary Herald*, was prepared to help, but the logistics of publishing almost three hundred kilometres to the south appeared overwhelming. The *Herald*, geared down for the holiday, had no press crews available, and, even if presses could be run, how could a hundred tons of newspapers be moved to Edmonton swiftly enough to make the effort worthwhile? In near-desperation, Hughes called an officer commanding local tactical transport squadrons of the Canadian armed forces to see whether one of the C-135 Hercules used to move tanks and artillery might be available. Red tape killed that idea. The commander had to call Ottawa for permission and on a bureaucrat's Friday night in the nation's capital that might take a long time — catastrophe in the provinces or not. Next, Hughes considered the option of chartering four Boeing 737 passenger jets but found that the available freight configurations meant they'd be able to move only forty thousand copies of the heavy Saturday paper.

At this point, publisher William Newbigging, previously isolated by the failure of telephone communications, was able to get through to Hughes and Oake on a portable cellular telephone he keeps in his four-wheel-drive Bronco. When Newbigging learned of the chaotic conditions his editor was battling, he made his way to the newsroom and established a command post in his office. Assistant circulation manager Dave Colville, assistant advertising director Gordon Lloyd, assistant production manager Bob Hill and promotions manager Dennis Skulsky joined Oake and Hughes to plan strategy. Newbigging decided to kill the whole Saturday edition, normally the biggest revenue producer of the week, and instead produce a twelve-page special disaster edition restricted to editorial content.

"It was Edmonton's tragedy," Newbigging said later about his decision. "I felt it imperative that the story be told by Edmonton's newspaper. Better that it be told in twelve pages than not at all — besides, the rest of the paper was going to be superfluous to the vast majority of Edmontonians."

It was now 10 p.m. Friday night, approaching the deadlines for the newspaper's normal midnight press run. While the managing editor had been marshalling the newsroom to produce the special, with many exhausted reporters doing double duty as copy editors, the paper's data services team had got newsroom computers up and running. They seemed tentative and fragile, but the jury-rigged computers worked and the news department was in business. Now, Newbigging chartered a fast Lear jet that the managing editor had tracked down. It left for Calgary at 2 a.m. Saturday morning, carrying page negatives, *Journal* news editor George Ward and a volunteer crew of six *Journal* pressmen headed by Dave Kealy. *Herald* production manager Ken Turner had readied his offset presses and lined up truck transportation.

By 4 a.m. the *Herald* presses had printed 150,000 copies of the *Journal's* disaster edition, wrapped in full colour with Simon's dramatic picture commanding half the front page. It was immediately loaded for the three-hour haul north to Edmonton. Meanwhile, back at the *Journal*, assistant circulation manager

Dave Colville was hard-pressed to organize his dispatch and delivery systems. The computer crash had wiped out his department's database of subscriber lists, and he was hustling to devise a contingency plan for delivery without lists. To make things worse, the power failure at the Eastgate plant had left the entire circulation department in darkness and frozen automatic doors had trapped delivery vehicles in garages.

Working through the night with flashlights and candles, Colville's circulation crews managed to pry open the jammed doors, but he had long abandoned hope of delivery to the *Journal*'s vast country circulation district, which covers the entire northern half of Alberta and extends into the Yukon and the Northwest Territories well beyond the Arctic Circle. But his problems were not over yet. They were compounded by the fact that his regular district agents were off for the long weekend and many of his regular carriers had arranged for inexperienced replacements to do their routes.

"We've always known the whole enterprise rests on the shoulders of these twelve-year-old kids," Colville said later. "When it comes down to the kids' substitutes under these conditions it gets a little hairy, I can tell you."

Normally two hundred thousand or more *Journals* are delivered by 6:30 a.m. on Saturdays, but in this case the trucks from Calgary would not arrive until 9 a.m. Colville called in his weekend drivers at 3 a.m. and asked them to start calling adult carriers where possible, warning them of the late arrival of the paper from Calgary. Perhaps not surprisingly, Colville's kids, the heart of the distribution system, rose to the crisis splendidly. In the end, the *Journal*'s special edition reached about 90 per cent of city routes and most people got their paper by early afternoon. The twelve-page special sold for the regular weekend price of fifty cents, primarily because of the difficulty of changing hundreds of vending boxes across Edmonton.

"What we hadn't counted on," said Hughes, "was the incredible demand for the paper. It was sold out in the stands and the stores within minutes. We padded our city run by twenty thousand, but in retrospect we could probably have padded it by a hundred thousand."

Alberta Member of Parliament Arnold Malone was so moved by the story it told that he ordered copies for each member of the House of Commons and arranged to deliver them in Ottawa himself. Demand for the edition remained so heavy that an updated reprint was inserted at no extra charge in the following Friday's paper. Once again, the run, this time including the regular country area, was padded by twenty thousand. It, too, sold out.

But if Edmontonians wanted to know as much about the catastrophe as possible, it was less from morbid curiosity than from a desire to help their fellow citizens. Heather Airth, the founder of a volunteer organization called Emergency Relief Services, originally intended to help destitute families following house fires, suddenly found herself operating in the big leagues. More than three hundred volunteers descended on the agency and worked around the clock co-ordinating donations from the public. On Friday afternoon, as the tornado rampaged through the city's suburbs, her twenty-five-thousand-square-foot warehouse had been virtually empty. As word of the victims' plight went out over the radio, television and news wires, a steady stream of semi-trailers, pick-up trucks, family cars, campers and people on foot began to arrive. They carried canned food, bedding, baby cribs, clothing, linens, dishes, appliances, furniture — everything conceivable that a stricken family might need. Seventh Day Adventist churches in Alberta towns as distant as Stettler and Rocky Mountain House, hundreds of kilometres to the south, dispatched three vans and a truck full of relief supplies. By 6 p.m. the following day, Heather Airth's warehouse was full to the rafters and so was a second eighty-five-thousand-square-foot warehouse loaned to the volunteers. The generosity extended even to the pets of the victims. When the Society for the Prevention of Cruelty to Animals reported it had acquired a large number of lost, frightened and homeless animals — "Their little eyes are as big as saucers," one worker said — volunteers supplied enough food that the animal shelter was able to offer indefinite homes for pets while their owners got resettled.

A year later, with the tornado fading into memory, a small political wrangle erupted in Edmonton over the right slogan for the city's tourism promoters. The bureaucrats wanted to use the term: "Official Host City For The Turn of The Century." Others, some civic-minded aldermen among them, pointed to the fact that the Edmonton Eskimos held the Grey Cup which is emblematic of professional football supremacy, while the Edmonton Oilers were holders of the Stanley Cup, making them kings of the National Hockey League. They felt the slogan should be: "City of Champions."

That was what went on the discreet green sign at the city limits, strategically placed for all visitors arriving from Calgary. Yet for many Albertans, me among them, that accolade has nothing to do with football games or the elite athletics of hockey stars. It has to do with the extraordinary things that happened the night of July 31, 1987, when a lot of ordinary people showed the stuff that makes a true city of champions.

ZERO ZERO

The consultation on the wind-swept airstrip two thousand kilometres north of Winnipeg was the one that every bush pilot dreads. It was November 8, 1972, and one of the two men huddling in the chill was under intense pressure to take a medical evacuation flight that would send him over difficult terrain and under conditions for which he had neither the flying experience nor the technical competence. Yet what was Marten Hartwell to do? The anxious young British nurse had just brought two critically ill patients from her tiny medical outpost at Spence Bay, five hundred kilometres farther out into the most isolated and inhospitable wilderness in the Western Hemisphere. Her sickest patient was only yards away at the very moment, sheltered from the biting wind in the back of a station wagon parked on the apron.

The pilot who had ferried the party in from the interior, picking his way down the stark coast of the Central Arctic to the big settlement at Cambridge Bay, now wanted Hartwell to take up the next leg of the mercy flight to Yellowknife and hospital. Ed Logozar was a senior colleague of Hartwell's at Gateway Aviation, but the next day his Twin Otter was required at Coppermine, another five hundred kilometres to the westward along Coronation Gulf.

A federal contract was in the balance and in the bureaucracy-laden North, government business was of major importance for the financial health of any struggling charter outfit. Hartwell was the junior pilot despite his forty-six years and greying hair. His anticipated night off would have to wait.

Hartwell was not anxious to go. Logozar's plane was a

sophisticated, heavily instrumented Twin Otter. Hartwell was flying an elderly Beechcraft 18 that Gateway intended to retire, and he was not yet fully familiar with the airplane. Although he had logged more than two thousand flying hours since arriving in Canada from his native Germany five years before, he had only thirty hours on the Beech. Not that more familiarity would have made him more comfortable. CF-RLD was licensed for daylight flying only and had been plagued recently with malfunctioning cockpit instruments and navigation aids that worked only intermittently or not at all. Indeed, although Logozar was unaware of the rookie pilot's limitations, Hartwell was really rated only for visual flight rules himself, which meant he was forbidden commercial night missions outside federally regulated air corridors. Also banned were flights under weather conditions where he might lose visual contact with the ground. At Cambridge Bay, 250 kilometres north of the Arctic Circle on the ice-choked south shore of Victoria Island, the window for VFR flights was getting narrower by the day.

In Canada's Central Arctic, winter arrives with an abruptness and ferocity that is difficult for the southerner to imagine. The leisurely spring and fall seasons of the forty-ninth parallel are truncated to a matter of weeks north of the sixtieth. There is a relentless mechanical precision to it. As the planet tilts its northern face farther and farther from the sun, shadows lengthen visibly from day to day, nights get blacker and longer, the stars brighten — when you can see them. Thermometers begin to plunge steadily downward, habitation fogs of glittering ice crystals settle over communities and temperature differences between sea and rapidly cooling land throw up cloud and turbulence.

By early November in Cambridge Bay, the mercury had already descended to the range most Canadians experience only in deepest winter, plunging to minus twenty-five and colder by night. Abrasive rivers of drifting snow had begun their ceaseless polishing of rock formations already rounded under glaciers and weather. The tundra, a carpet of wild flowers only a few months earlier, now was abandoned by animals and human beings alike. The only land creatures remaining for the bitter season ahead would be small herds of shaggy musk-oxen, rooting in the drifts for their sparse winter diet of moss and lichens. Occasionally, one might see the silver blur of an arctic fox or its ghost-like cousin, the barren-ground wolf, in pursuit of their timid prey, the snowshoe hare. In the settlement, school teachers and air traffic controllers alike took precise measure as the daylight hours shortened. The year slid toward aphelion and polar night. Winter solstice and the prospect of perpetual darkness were only forty-four days away.

Of greater concern to Hartwell was the weather. The coastal region was notorious for dreadful conditions on very short notice. Only the year before, the highly skilled Canadian Forces search and rescue unit from Winnipeg had lost a DC-3 with eight men aboard during a mission to the west of Cambridge Bay. They had been preparing to make an emergency supply drop to a light bush plane forced down by conditions so severe the stranded pilot radioed to beg the rescue plane to abort and come back when the weather cleared. Nobody knew why, perhaps the Canadian Forces pilot was deceived by the bizarre optical illusions that can accompany blowing snow and icing conditions. In any event, he had banked, stalled and dived straight into the ground and a fireball. The incident was still fresh in everybody's mind.

As usual along that troublesome coast, forecasts were proving chancy at best. Earlier that day, attempting a flight to a prospector's camp, Hartwell had encountered heavy cloud and poor visibility. Later, on the ground, both he and his passenger had observed the build-up of ice along the leading edges of his tail structure. If icing conditions were an ominous prospect for the most experienced northern flier, they were particularly unnerving for any pilot of a Beech 18. The aircraft had first been built more than thirty years before and was notoriously underpowered. The gallows humour of Yellowknife hangar mechanics put it succinctly: "Why does a Beech 18 have two engines? Guarantees you get to the crash scene on time. Lose one engine and the other takes you to the accident twice as quick."

For Hartwell, the ice on his tail structure signalled the risk of icing conditions any time he encountered cloud. The suspended droplets of water vapour, hovering on the verge of becoming snow, would first condense along the wings and fuselage, then freeze solid, simultaneously reducing lift, increasing drag and weighing down the already underpowered plane. And just to make things more interesting for the green pilot, CF-RLD was not equipped with de-icing boots, the inflatable rubber bladders along the leading edges designed to dislodge ice from the wings.

The Gateway pilot had already experienced one disturbing brush with changeable weather. That morning, flying a Calgary mining engineer out to a bush camp at Perry River, he'd not even been able to find the estuary. Low on fuel, he had found the Arctic coast and tracked in to the settlement of Cambridge Bay with its all-weather airstrip and its military radar base. It was while he was landing that Hartwell's radio informed him of the inbound mercy flight from Spence Bay.

Hartwell had been dubious from the moment he was asked to take the turn-around for Yellowknife, eight hundred kilometres south. It meant a three-and-a-half hour flight across barren tundra with night certain to fall before he arrived. Compounding the pilot's lack of an instrument rating was the fact that he would be operating at a latitude where the powerful fields of the North Magnetic Pole rendered his standard compass unreliable, causing it to oscillate wildly or, worse, give false headings. On the other hand, the corridor was well-travelled and there was a radio navigation beacon at Contwoyto Lake, about halfway to the distant Northwest Territories capital.

Normally, he would lock his aircraft to that beacon with his automatic direction finders, then, when the range was right, lock on to Yellowknife with its big commercial landing strip and control tower. On the surface, that procedure seemed simple enough, but Hartwell remained far from enthusiastic. For one thing, he did not completely trust his electronic navigation aids. Earlier that day, he'd lost radio contact with the Contwoyto Lake beacon, the only navigational signal in the flight corridor. In his opinion, the beacon was as much a hazard as a help, instilling false confidence in pilots who learned to their dismay that it was unreliable. He didn't count his cockpit equipment up to snuff, either. The automatic direction finders were working well enough, but the pilot's directional gyro was only adequate and the copilot's was out of service completely, as was the artificial horizon on his side of the cockpit. The radio was fine on very high frequencies, good for line-of-sight communications, but transmissions were sometimes garbled on other frequencies. He later claimed he'd asked for servicing of the instruments but, as a junior pilot with an old plane, other equipment had first call on the mechanics' priority lists. Nobody said it, but the implication was that maintenance was most important for the equipment that could generate the best revenue.

Problems or not, by the time he had taxied his old Beech 18 to the apron, the pressure to take the mercy flight was building enormously. Fourteen-year-old Davidie Peesurajak Kootook was diagnosed as an acute appendicitis case. Without the swift intervention of a surgeon in a modern operating theatre, the boy might die an agonizing death with a burst appendix and peritonitis. His aunt Neemee Nulliayuq was even more difficult. After three miscarriages, the passage from Mrs. Nulliayuq's uterus had been surgically sealed to enable her to carry to term. Now, eight months into her pregnancy, she had unexpectedly gone into premature labour. The Spence Bay nurses, skilled midwives that they were, had not been able to find and remove the sutures. The gruesome consequences of the complications seemed obvious to everyone. A premature caesarean delivery at a remote nursing station was out of the question, and a uterus ruptured in labour was too horrifying to be contemplated. Mrs. Nulliayuq had been heavily sedated with Demerol to stop the premature contractions, but she was thought so critical that when medical authorities in Yellowknife were consulted by telephone they wanted her moved out instantly. The condition of the two patients was assessed as too grave to wait even for the big, always reliable DC-3 due to arrive on a scheduled commercial flight later that evening.

Only Hartwell, if even he, knows what finally triggered his decision. For an inexperienced German immigrant attracted late in life to the romance of northern flying, the whole crushing weight of the bush pilot's mystique must have descended upon him in those final moments. Serving with the Luftwaffe during the final, cataclysmic stages of the Second World War, he had subsequently found flying work as the personal pilot for a European businessman. He'd tried being a salesman for a while when an economic recession grounded him, but after a few years he'd had it. Canada seemed to offer the greatest opportunity to do what he most wanted.

Hartwell had been in diapers when the standard for the northern mercy mission was established. A World War One ace and survivor of the last dogfight with the Red Baron, Manfred Von Richtofen, Wop May had been a barnstorming airmail pilot when he flew the freezing six hundred kilometres from Edmonton to Fort Vermilion to deliver medical supplies. He made the flight in an open cockpit biplane with temperatures plunging to minus sixty. The only heater in the aircraft, a little charcoal brazier, had to be used to prevent his cargo of precious vaccine from freezing. Resilient as they come, May suffered frostbite during the mercy mission but stayed doggedly at his controls. Overnighting in the bitter cold, he drained the oil from his crankcase and the next morning thawed it again over a farm wife's wood stove so that he could restart the engine. Conditions notwithstanding, May delivered the vaccine needed to contain an epidemic of diphtheria, always a killer in frontier Indian communities where natural resistance was low and medical resources were of the most primitive kind.

If Hartwell refused the mercy flight, it would certainly be the safe, textbook decision. It might also seem a betrayal of the romantic ideal established by Wop May and his tough winger, Vic Horner. If Hartwell accepted, it would be risky. The only public notice would come from failure, refusing to go or being forced to turn back — yet making the flight, however uneventfully, might mean greater acceptance among the bush pilots' fraternity toward which Hartwell's career seemed to be leading him. If the unseasoned flyer refused, Ed Logozar would have to divert from his own important duties because a junior pilot couldn't pull his weight. If Hartwell accepted, he would clearly be breaking the rules but, in a well-established Northerner's tradition, in the service of the greater good. It was now 3:33 p.m. Nightfall was imminent. Hartwell decided to go. It was a fateful decision. CF-RLD and its four passengers were about to become the object of the greatest Arctic rescue mission since Sir John Franklin vanished in the crushing ice of the Northwest Passage.

Occasional accidents aside, Canada's military search and rescue specialists are without question the best in the world, not by instinct but by the soldier's axiom that practice makes perfect. The search and rescue units strategically spotted across the country have dealt with more than 115 thousand incidents involving missing or overdue aircraft since Marten Hartwell's mercy flight failed to arrive. Already, they have begun to cope with this year's crop. For them, it is a matter of statistical analysis, probability factors, aircraft logistics and communications systems. It's a job they do with dispassionate thoroughness, playing the percentages by relying on proved and standard procedures rather than the legendary hunch of made-for-TV melodrama. The hunch, seasoned search masters will tell you, is usually what gets less professional pilots into difficulty in the first place.

Most of the missing aircraft incidents will be no more than a day's work for the Canadian Forces flight crews; most of them will rate scarcely a paragraph in the local northern newspapers. A great many of them will never get past the stage of jokes and joshing over coffee on a cold morning. But for the rest of the world, hemmed in by the humdrum reality of traffic jams and the daily smog index, operations of the search and rescue crews and the missing planes they hunt offer danger and high romance.

If there is one image that conjures up all the stereotypes and preconceptions of the Far North that have been laid down in the urban hearts of southerners, it is the missing bush plane and the grand wilderness challenge of tracking the survivors. Plane crashes and pilots who vanish forever in the polar night have been a fact of life across Canada's forbidding sub-Arctic wilderness since the first bush pilots penetrated the Northwest Territories in 1921. Wop May and George Gorman landed their own flimsy, fabric-covered aircraft at Fort Simpson in the spring of that year but were forced to turn back by unpredictable weather. It was another eight years before Punch Dickins, who had been the first pilot to venture into the Canadian barrens in 1928, was to make the full flight to the remote Arctic, following the Mackenzie River almost two thousand kilometres to the Hudson Bay fur-trading outpost at Aklavik.

Today, in an age of jumbo jets and inertial navigation computers, the far-flung people of the country's still-wild regions continue to rely on the little planes and the rough, irregular and inventive pilots who fly them. Starter won't work on your DC-3 and you're two days flying time from spare parts? How about a judge's baseball cap and a piece of rope to hand crank the prop? Problem with a carburettor feed? Try a wad of some local kid's well-chewed bubble gum to regulate the flow. Busted sextant? A stick and a piece of string with knots tied in it got the Polynesians to Hawaii. Loucheux kid from Fort MacPherson doesn't want to abandon his new bike while he goes to hospital in Inuvik? Boot out the pipeline economist who paid for the charter and put the bike in her seat.

There is a highway into Yellowknife now, and another pushes north from Whitehorse to Inuvik in the Mackenzie River delta. But these thin red ribbons of dirt, snaking their sixteen hundred kilometres across muskeg and ice-scoured granite, flanked by scrub spruce forest and empty tundra that rolls off the edge of the world, are tenuous links at best, hostage to the seasons and the weather. The main umbilical cords, the real psychological connections with the south and civilization, are still airborne. Indeed, the road network serves only a fraction of the northern portion of the country. The Northwest Territories alone is half the size of the continental United States. Imagine a territory enclosed by a quadrangle stretching from Chicago to Texas to San Diego to Seattle — with only two roads and two railways connecting it to the rest of the world. And inside it, only seventy-eight outposts, most of them isolated and sufficient to themselves.

Scattered across this vast expanse of tundra and taiga, united by the common bond of isolation, are sixty thousand people, about the same number as might show up at Commonwealth

Stadium to watch the Edmonton Eskimos meet the Calgary Stampeders in the annual Labour Day football game. They count on bush planes to bring in supplies ranging from the latest catalogue order of polypropylene underwear to precious cases of fresh eggs and butter, the small essentials that can be so important in coping with the basic northern problem of life in a climate that has been described as the horizonal Everest — eight months of winter and brutal weather.

Ammunition and snowmobile parts, old mail and new brassieres, short-wave radio components and Christmas tree decorations, and even the Christmas trees themselves for those who live above the treeline, just about everything that people might require and that is small enough to carry is delivered to these settlements by the bush plane. And most important, of course, people rely on the bush operators for the kind of face-to-face communication that is essential in the high-speed world of the twentieth century. They rely on bush pilots to get them "outside" to dentists that can be a full day's flight away, beyond vast and hostile expanses of sea ice, glaciers, barrens and mountains. Emerging native politicians rely on bush pilots to get them to the meetings required to conduct the business of governing, administrating, legal affairs and grappling with the political, social and economic difficulties that beset such a far-flung people of such diverse backgrounds — seven languages and an equal number of dialects at the last count.

Beat up old Dakotas and C-46s from the Second World War, decrepit Beech 18s, piston-driven Otters and turbo-charged Beavers, the tough little Cessna 185, Hercules transports, sophisticated Twin Otters and computer-assisted Lear jets — these are the aircraft that link the remote frontier settlements with each other. Their passengers are just as likely to share the cabin with the freshly skinned carcass of a hunter's caribou as with some supreme court justice taking his court to the people. On occasion, court proceedings have been conducted in the aircraft themselves, both on the runway and airborne over the Arctic Ocean; huge business deals have been signed; people have been married and people have been divorced. So it is small surprise that, in a world where people catch airplanes with the same nonchalance as a New Yorker hails a taxi-cab or a Toronto suburbanite hops the subway downtown, air crashes and missing planes are an expected part of everyday life.

At Repulse Bay on the Arctic Circle, only newcomers paid any attention to the wreckage of three aircraft splashed around the rough gravel runway. One of them was matter-of-factly bulldozed and used as fill to level off the airstrip. Farther north, at Resolute Bay in the High Arctic, twenty-eight hundred kilometres north of the U.S. border, the rolling, treeless hills of the tundra were littered with twelve wrecks the last time I descended to the runway. They ranged from Lancaster bombers pranged by Ferry Command during the war to modern turbo-props that missed the runway in whiteout conditions.

What kind of pilot does it take to fly repeatedly over the most desolate and unforgiving terrain in the world? Judging from the flyer who made Resolute Bay famous, mostly it takes a sense of humour. Weldy Phipps was inventor of the Phipps wheel, the fat balloon tires that now grace bush planes around the world. Designed to enable light aircraft to land in the open tundra, they are ideal for rough strips everywhere. Phipps has folded his wings and retired to the South, but his reputation is as sure to endure as it is certain his old air base near the North Pole will get snow every September.

Weldy was the man who opened up the farthest and most remote corner of the Arctic to modern aviation, who made a business out of flying airplanes over icy wastelands that even the bush-wise Inuit had abandoned for generations. Starting with a single-engine two-seater aircraft and an idea, Phipps parleyed his operation into internationally-famous Atlas Aviation, the airline at the top of the world. It was the only place you could buy a return excursion fare to the North Pole. And the bar at the Ministry of Transport base was the only place you could watch a pilot win a bet by drinking his scotch and soda standing on his head in the corner. Or settle an argument about the short take-off capabilities of the Twin Otter by taking off — across the runway.

Unlike many of his flying compatriots, Weldy retired with a million dollars, but none of it from the wheel which bears his name. That was his gift to aviation, a gesture guaranteed to lend substance to the endearing legends that surround him with tall tales and glitter. Take the embroidered story of bringing an exotic skydiver back from the North Pole so low on fuel that a handy bottle of brandy had to be poured into the fuel tanks. Would a turbo-prop run on liquor the human liver has a tough time metabolizing? Don't try the story on a flight engineer, but you might pitch it to a Toronto headline writer. At least one of them swallowed it. Which is why Northerners promptly christened Phipp's number one aircraft, CF-WWP, *Whisky Whisky Papa*, the alcoholic Twin Otter.

Not all the northern pilots are able to cope with the cruel

geography of Canada's North, with its blistering wind chills, long stretches of darkness, treacherous weather conditions and tricky navigational problems. Some planes simply disappear without a trace, swallowed up in the mountain fastnesses and the featureless expanse of the barrens.

Even the best pilots make mistakes. When they do, the country is unforgiving. For the incompetent, it is utterly without mercy; it is certainly without respect for status or reputation. Hale Boggs found that out when his light plane strayed from course during a flight across the twisted knot of glacier-capped mountains that form the Yukon-Alaska border. The Democratic House Leader from the U.S. House of Representatives was on a routine three-hour flight from big city Anchorage to the Alaska capital at Juneau when he vanished. N.W.T. Commissioner Stuart Hodgson was luckier. He suffered only a little bruised protocol when his own flight across the barrens from Baker Lake to Yellowknife was forced down in 1973. His pilot alertly established radio contact with the Yellowknife tower before pancaking into the pillowy snowdrifts of the nearest frozen lake whose shape he thought would be easy to find from the air. A ski-equipped rescue craft arrived a few hours later to pick up the frightened survivors. It was forty below zero with a forty-mile-an-hour wind. A forced night out might well have proved fatal.

Pilot J.W. Rutherford of Penticton and his passenger Dr. Randolph Hall of Toronto were not so lucky. Their flight plan was not closed until fifteen years after their deaths. The two men set out in 1958 across the forbidding Baffin Island wilderness from Iqaluit to Clyde River. For some reason, they were forced to set down in the shattered debris of a mountain range three hundred kilometres north of Iqaluit. Their plane was found a decade and a half later, almost intact despite the years of exposure to the elements. Of the two men, there was not a trace. All that remained was a brave, faded note in the cockpit informing whatever searchers happened along that they had stuck with the plane for a week — as survival manuals urge — and were now attempting an overland expedition to safety at a distant early warning line station seventy-five miles away. They never made it and disappeared without further trace.

Of all the incidents that texture the bush-flying lore of the Arctic, none grips the public imagination so much as the story of survival after a crash. All the metaphors for the human condition emerge from the drama of men and women battling fear, deprivation and the elements while searchers race against the clock and starvation. Some survivors make it because a little luck comes their way; others because they are skilled in the arts of survival; some because of their sheer, gritty stubbornness.

John Gaucher, a bush pilot from Inuvik, made it because he used his head — and a hand-sized mirror he carried in his survival kit. He went down in bad weather during a routine flight from the Mackenzie River delta to Old Crow, the picturesque collection of log cabins that forms the northernmost settlement in the Yukon. Landing on a frozen lake in the muskeg and spruce scrub twenty-four hundred kilometres north of Vancouver, the pilot found himself trapped by deep, drifting snow and temperatures plunging far below zero. In short order, his engine froze solid. He followed the survival textbook and stuck with his plane. After several bitter nights in the open, his patience paid off and he was able to signal a passing aircraft with his hand-sized mirror. He was rescued by a ski-equipped plane dispatched from Inuvik. That was one of the run-of-the-mill rescue stories, the kind that earns only a line in the northern weeklies and is shrugged off by most bush flyers as the kind of situation in which a pilot is simply expected to cope. There are special cases. Stories of courage and survival which earn themselves a place in the tellings and retellings of northern folklore.

Bob Gauchie was airborne on a routine flight down the same corridor from Cambridge Bay in the Arctic Islands to Yellowknife that would later claim Hartwell. It was a cruelly cold February day when his reliable old Beaver ran into a serious emergency. He had blundered into the peculiar Arctic weather condition known as the whiteout — a disorienting meteorological phenomenon in which tiny ice crystals become suspended in the atmosphere, diffusing the light until it is impossible to distinguish between ground and sky, horizon and heavens, even the difference between up and down.

Gauchie set down immediately. It was not the first time he had been down with his plane, but the previous time he had been near a settlement and was picked up within hours. Now, he was stranded in mid-winter on the open tundra far above the Arctic Circle. He made his decision. He would run for the tree line, hoping to land in a place where he could build a shelter and light a fire. He got the Beaver into the air, established radio contact and set out.

But Gauchie never made it to the trees. Somehow, his perceptions confused by the weather conditions, he wound up flying due west instead of south. He was forced down again, and this time it was bad. Although he didn't know it, he was on Samandre Lake, near to the tree line but still far from human habitation. And this time he was stuck for good. Gauchie's survival kit consisted of a few kilograms of concentrated rations and a load of raw, frozen fish he was carrying from a fishing lodge for shipment south. He had the shelter of the aircraft and a little fuel oil and hydraulic fluid to burn for heat.

For fifty-eight days, Gauchie survived, his only company a pack of howling wolves. At night, he huddled in his two sleeping bags while temperatures dropped to fifty below zero and chill factors reached ninety below and colder in the stiff winds. By day he tramped SOS signals in the snow, only to watch the tracks drift over before he had completed them. During this ordeal he lost twenty kilos in weight and suffered frostbite which ultimately cost him five toes. But he was still alive when a bright flash of light reflected from his camp attracted a plane flying between Coppermine and Yellowknife. When the rescue plane arrived at Samandre Lake, Bob Gauchie was standing beside his green and yellow Beaver with his suitcase packed, like a man going home after a weekend in the country.

Gauchie's record surpassed that of Ralph Flores and Helen Klaben, the American couple who jumped into world headlines after surviving forty-nine days on a frozen mountainside in the Yukon. Flores and his companion, a New York nurse, were on their way home from Alaska when their light plane smashed into the hills near Watson Lake in 1963. The couple built a shelter from fallen trees and claimed to have lived for six weeks on two tubes of toothpaste and melted snow.

Despite broken bones, the pilot ensured their rescue when he managed to hobble into a clearing and tramp out a large SOS in the snow. The rescue effort was almost as dramatic as the survival, with a pick-up team piggy-backing the couple down from the hillside to a dog team that carried them to a waiting aircraft and the interview that made them famous, with *Edmonton Journal* reporter Bob Hill, who had chartered the only available ambulance and was waiting to pick them up at the airport for the ride to hospital. Yet of all these survival stories, the one that remains the most dramatic is Marten Hartwell's mercy flight.

Once he had decided to fly to Yellowknife, the inexperienced pilot had accepted a race against time, weather and the strange psychology of tundra flying that he could not have anticipated. With darkness closing in, he and twenty-seven-year-old nurse Judy Hill loaded the two patients. Neemee Nulliayuq, strapped to a stretcher, lay in the back of the aircraft. There was a seat in the back of the fuselage, but Nurse Hill feared a ruptured appendix and, at her orders, Davidie Kootook lay on a sleeping bag on

the floor beside his pregnant aunt. The nurse joined Hartwell in
the cockpit, sitting in the copilot's seat. She still hadn't had time
to eat the six sandwiches her counterpart at Spence Bay had
packed for the long flight.

Hartwell nosed his Beech 18 into the wind and took off, heading southwest across the narrow neck of Dease Straits, over the
rocky shoreline and into the barrens that unfolded under his
wings like a rumpled white quilt. As CF-RLD flew southward
across the tundra, Hartwell was tracked by the radar of an electronic listening post at the distant early warning line station
called Cam Main. It lost contact as the plane passed over the low
range of hills behind the coast. The tiny blip of light disappeared
into the scattered chaff of the ground flutter that obscures and
disrupts radar close to the horizon.

Aboard Hartwell's aircraft, everything seemed fine. The
weather had been clear when he left the coast of Victoria Island.
It had begun to close in as he pressed into the barrens at four
thousand feet of altitude, but he was still able to see the ground
and his automatic direction finder was reading a strong, clear
signal from the navigational beacon at Cambridge Bay. Then,
about ninety minutes into the flight, everything went haywire.
The weather socked in seriously, and the Cambridge Bay beacon, receding behind him, suddenly faded from his instrument
reading. He had passed the point of no return. Hartwell tried
switching over to the beacon at Contwoyto Lake. It was a disaster. He got a brief, weak signal, but before he could lock on and
orient the plane his radio direction-finding equipment erupted
with the crackle of interference from the disruptive atmospher-
ics called night effect and what northern pilots call frost static.
He tried for the powerful beacon at Yellowknife, far to the south,
but after five minutes it, too, faded. He was now effectively
blind. The magnetic compass was useless, and the only way he
could locate his position was through the radio navigation beacons that he couldn't locate.

Just at that point, the barrens played their first trick. Hartwell
popped out of the dirty weather. He had three miles of visibility,
and, although night was about to fall, the interference that had
been plaguing his automatic direction finder suddenly cleared
up. He had lost Cambridge Bay and still could not locate the
Contwoyto Lake beacon or Yellowknife, but he was now picking
up strong signals from two other radio beacons. He checked the
call signs. They were beacons at Fort Reliance on the southeast
shore of Great Slave Lake and Fort Franklin, far to the northwest
near Great Bear Lake. The atmospheric conditions might be

flukey, but Hartwell was sure he was still on course for Yellowknife and had passed over the Contwoyto Beacon. He descended to one thousand feet and began to look for the familiar
landmarks that would guide him into Yellowknife.

In reality, Hartwell could not have been farther off course.
Two unconscious elements had been at work tugging him westward from his planned flight path. The first was mathematics,
the phenomenon known as precession, which is the rate at which
the earth spins beneath an aircraft holding to what appears to be
a true course established by an automatic gyro-compass. Errors
in heading can be as much as twelve degrees of the compass for
every hour of flying time. Compensating for rates of precession
is a basic element of instrument training in navigation. Hartwell
was not making the course adjustments he should have made.
The second factor was more subtle — the propensity for inexperienced pilots to move unconsciously and imperceptibly
toward the light. As night flooded into the inhospitable barrens
to the northeast, Hartwell was unconsciously chasing the
sunshine toward the southwest. He was helped along by a gentle
twenty-kilometre per-hour tailwind. Whether it was the inexor-
able laws of physics or the seductive sun that led him in a wide
arc away from his destination was really irrelevant. He was now
more than thirty degrees off his true heading.

Dark was in full descent, but Hartwell believed it was only a
matter of time before he locked on to the Yellowknife beacon.
When the beacon finally came in, clear and loud, the signal
stunned him. It was not Yellowknife. It was a place he could not
possibly be, Fort Wrigley on the Mackenzie River, 250 kilometres
west of where he thought he was.

Now, Hartwell made the first of his own mistakes. He refused
to believe what the instruments were telling him about his position. "I could not believe it," he said later. "I could not believe I
was so far off course." He flicked on the cockpit lights and, with
Nurse Hill holding the aviation charts in her lap, began a frantic
attempt to replot his position. But in his disbelief and the
urgency to confirm that he was not lost, he had forgotten the
pilot's fundamental rule — when it doubt, gain altitude. The
Arctic played its final trick. Still flying at one thousand feet,
Hartwell looked down at the map. At that precise instant CF-
RLD collided with the only hill for 120 kilometres in any direction. It was about 6 p.m.

The old Beech clipped a tree top with the right wing tip and
cartwheeled into the spruce woods. Nurse Hill was the first victim. Up and down to check on her patients throughout the flight,

her seat belt was undone and she rocketed face first into the instrument panel. When Hartwell regained consciousness in the wreckage fifteen minutes after the impact, Nurse Hill was comatose and lying across his legs. Her breathing was laboured and heavy, and she had obviously suffered severe head injuries in the crash. Miraculously, he heard voices behind him in the fuselage. Standing in the wrecked fuselage was Neemee Nulliayuq. Davidie Kootook appeared in the cockpit, apparently unhurt and attempting to help the pilot extricate himself from the wreckage. When Hartwell tried to stand, his legs collapsed. Both ankles were broken and his left knee had been smashed.

Nurse Hill was soaked in either gasoline or hydraulic fluid and Hartwell now feared fire more than the pain from his shattered limbs. With Davidie's help, Mrs. Nulliayuq was able to walk away from the wreck. Then, the boy returned, and the two of them managed to drag the nurse away from the wreckage. She stopped breathing without regaining consciousness. A fast, clean death — it was a mercy compared to what lay ahead.

Hartwell was stunned as much from a blow to the head as from the reality of what had happened. Later, his memory of the wreck and the four days following it remained hazy and he had difficulty focusing on what to do. Davidie, however, was sharp and alert. The boy rummaged through the wrecked aircraft and began building a shelter from sleeping bags, Mrs. Nulliayuq's stretcher and the tarpaulin covers for the plane's engines. Before he could finish, the pregnant woman began to moan. Two hours later, the boy told Hartwell his aunt and her unborn daughter were dead. That she had survived so long was remarkable. Her neck had been broken in the crash and her spinal cord damaged to the extent that a coroner's report later described her short walk as a medical miracle. For the other two, the ordeal was just beginning.

CF-RLD was supposed to be carrying two cases of emergency supplies — rations of bully beef, soup concentrate and raisins sufficient to feed eight people for a week — a rifle and snowshoes, wire for setting snares, fish-hooks, line, a net, a knife and an axe. For two survivors, the supplies should eke out for a month or more, and with the rifle and snowshoes they might supplement their diet with small game or, if they were lucky, even a caribou wintering in the woods. But Hartwell had not checked his survival gear before the flight. When Davidie was set to salvaging supplies there was no rifle, no snowshoes and only a single box of rations. Even they were incomplete. Instead of rations for four, the box contained only supplies for two. Their survival margin had been more than halved, and they hadn't even begun the ordeal.

The boy had managed to recover the aircraft's emergency locator beacon, designed to automatically transmit a mayday signal upon impact. The transmitter's aerial had snapped off. Hartwell struggled to repair it, got it working for five hours, only to have it quit again. In the meantime, with Hartwell instructing, Davidie had cut boughs and saplings and constructed a warmer shelter from the sleeping bags and tarpaulins. He collected firewood and piled it up. If an aircraft passed, they would burn the pile as a signal.

Back in Yellowknife, Canadian Forces Captain Keith Gathercole had deployed his search and rescue aircraft. First, an Argus from the Comox air force base on the far West Coast. Experienced in long-range patrol duties over the featureless ocean, this flight crew would start what promised to be a difficult search over the blank expanse of tundra and sea ice. Packed with sensitive electronic warfare equipment, the Argus had swept CF-RLD's planned flight path, listening for any emergency radio transmissions. When it heard nothing, a squadron of long-range Hercules transports had begun ever-widening low level sweeps. They methodically quartered across the possible crash zones from areas of greatest to lowest probability. By the time they were finished, they were to cover every square metre of more than four hundred thousand square kilometres of the Northwest Territories. Their primary search area alone was larger than Hartwell's native Germany. These military Hercules were manned by civilian spotters drawn mostly from volunteers out of Yellowknife.

Day after day, the volunteers trudged to the airport, clambered into the drafty, echoing bellies of the military transports and waited their turn to be strapped to stretchers and lowered on the rear loading ramp of the aircraft. Observers dangled in the slip-stream while the Hercs descended to five hundred feet of altitude and skimmed across the tundra in the endless repetitions of their computer-defined search patterns. Weather was lousy. In some places, winds kicked the drifting snow two thousand feet into the air. All the civilian observers were at risk of serious frostbite in the buffeting wind chills. Temperatures were now cold enough that exposed flesh would freeze in less than a minute.

It was grim, depressing, debilitating work. Flying search patterns as a spotter is like nothing else on earth, the whole mind and body poised for the sighting, yet trapped hour after hour in the absolute boredom of nothing. Eyes strain to pick out detail in the vast, empty terrain. Soon everything begins to look like a downed aircraft — and nothing does — shadows behind drifts, the glimpse of glacial debris under a cloak of snow, shapes caused by tricks of light at the edge of vision, animal tracks that resemble human messages, the glint of sunlight off wind-scoured ice that might be a signal. The whole process is subject to the most enormous psychological stress. No one wants to trouble the search master with false sightings, since each one will be checked out, diverting important resources from the main search. On the other hand, no one wants to fail to report the small vital sign that might lead to rescue. This constant dynamic of anticipation and disappointment, the flood of adrenalin followed by the drained sense of let-down, creates a hardship that is physiological as well as mental. In Yellowknife, observers coming off search missions complained that they felt as if they had been beaten with rubber hoses. They would have felt much worse if they had known that the whole process was futile. The search was being conducted 250 kilometres to the east of the hilltop where Hartwell had crashed.

On the ground, things were fast becoming desperate. The survivors had now been down for a week. Luckily, the weather at the crash site had been unseasonably mild, but the food supply was dwindling rapidly. They had stuck with the wreck for the week called for in standard survival procedures, but Hartwell was now convinced they would have to help themselves or perish. He and the boy had already written their last letters to loved ones.

Davidie pencilled a note for his mother and father in the curves and triangles of Inuktitut syllabic script:

> Few days ago we got to Cambridge Bay. We were going to go to Yellowknife. The airplane fell. When this happened Neemee died and the nurse. The pilot's legs are broken, he cannot walk. I am all right. We fell between Yellowknife and Cambridge Bay, on the hills. In a few more days, on the 14th, the pilot wants me to walk to Yellowknife so I must try and walk. I pray to God I will see you again. We eat all the time, the pilot and I. There is just two of us. We have white man's food. The food is in a box, the box is just a bit bigger than my red suitcase. The weather was bad yesterday and today is foggy. Johnny Kovalah and Lena, give them a kiss for me. We cut wood with an axe and we

make fire. There is just me and the pilot here. Neemee and
the nurse died when the airplane fell. There was four of us.
I will see you again in Spence Bay or in heaven. I try to
pray. I do not feel cold in the daytime, only at nights. We
have five thick sleeping bags. Two of them we use for a tent
and three to sleep in and another for a mattress. Today we
have been here four days. The pilot's legs are broken. I am
fine. I can walk. Give Johnny Kovalah and Lena a kiss for
me. Yellowknife is far away from here and I am going to
try and walk there. The pilot wants me to walk there. I am
finished writing now. I do not have anymore writing
paper.

Hartwell was more pessimistic. His letter was addressed to
his son Peer, serving in the West German air force, and it
amounted to a last will and testament:

When you receive this letter, I will be dead. I have had an
accident on Nov. 8, 1972, and I am still laying in the bush
with broken legs. Have no more food. Please forgive me
my sins. I love you, my only son.

Please contact Miss Susan Haley, c/o Dept. of Philosophy, U. of A., Edmonton, Alberta. She was, for the past
year-and-a-half, my closest companion. An even better address may be: Miss Susan Haley, c/o Professor Dr. Haley,
University of Wolfville, N.S., Wolfville, Nova Scotia,
Canada.

There are savings in the Imperial Bank of Commerce
here in Yellowknife and Edmonton. You should get $3,000
and Susan the rest that she may pay my debts and the
unpaid ones with the court.

I am wishing you all the best and remember me. In my
heart I was not all that bad.

Hartwell now turned to the task of persuading Davidie to try
to walk to Yellowknife. The prospect was bleak. The capital lay
three hundred kilometres to the south, and Davidie did not even
have rudimentary snowshoes. Half the remaining supplies —
four cans of corned beef, some frozen sandwiches recovered
from Nurse Hill, a handful of dehydrated beef cubes, a little coffee and some tea — went toward the expedition. The boy gathered fish-hooks, a compass, a knife, an axe and two candles. He
packed the supplies in the little red suitcase he had carried on
the plane for his stay in the hospital.

On November 16, Davidie set out to find help. The expedition lasted fifty minutes. The boy returned and reported floundering helplessly in deep snow, much of it chest high and some of it over his head. He told Hartwell that if he had to die, he wanted to do it in the camp.

It was now urgent that they supplement the food supply. Although Davidie had bravely set out eighteen wire-loop snares in the underbrush, hoping to snag a snowshoe hare or a ptarmigan, it was becoming clear that the area was devoid of small game. A small herd of caribou was wintering not far from the site, but without a rifle there was no hope of killing one. There was another possibility. From the crash site they could see a frozen lake in the distance. If Davidie could reach it, they might be able to catch fish. The boy said he knew how to fish through the ice from watching a man fishing in Spence Bay, and the survival gear had included a fish net as well as lines and hooks.

On November 21, Davidie agreed to try to make the lake. He left camp carrying an axe, knife, compass and fish-hooks and the last of the supplies — a single can of corned beef. Once again he turned back, obviously frightened. In retrospect, the fear was not unexpected for a child who had never before seen trees, let alone a forest. Hartwell noted that the boy had eaten the last can of beef. That night, as they lay in their lean-to following a supper made from one of their precious cubes of beef stock, the pilot again attempted to talk the boy into trying to reach the lake and fish. By now the stress was beginning to take its toll. Davidie responded angrily. He demanded to be paid for any fish he caught. Hartwell offered five dollars a fish and said he had a hundred dollars in his pocket, enough for twenty fish. He said that if Davidie caught more than twenty he would pay him for the rest when they got back to Yellowknife.

The next morning, the boy set out again with his little suitcase of supplies, but this time he forgot his compass. He returned in the middle of the night and said he had been wandering in circles. The following day, an aircraft flew over the site but did not respond to signals from the crash beacon indicator. Davidie agreed once more to try to reach the lake. He returned in an excited state soon after leaving and said he had found half a caribou carcass at a wolf kill. Hartwell sent him back to get meat, but the boy became lost and wandered in the woods for fifty-one hours. When he returned he had no meat and Hartwell became convinced that Davidie had seen nothing and was making excuses to avoid being alone in the forest on the trek to the lake. The pilot determined to go himself, dragging his broken legs behind him as he crawled, but the deep snow defeated him, too.

The survivors had been down for almost three weeks and the food situation was extremely critical. Already, they had been reduced to scavenging and eating drugs from Nurse Hill's medical case. Hunger outweighed the fear of side effects. They ate a candle, scraped foul-tasting lichens from trees and made watery soup. Davidie's caloric consumption had been accelerated by the heavy exercise of wading through deep snow. The boy's body weight now fell catastrophically. He was in a severe state of emaciation, having lost more than 30 per cent of his normal weight. His ribs protruded, and his abdomen had collapsed. Hunger had driven him to gnawing wood, swallowing spruce needles, bark, noxious berries and even fibrous material that appeared to be rags from the wrecked aircraft. He began to suffer severe pains in his stomach. Hartwell assumed a recurrence of the medical emergency which had led to the evacuation, and he was helpless to assist. He persuaded the boy to eat snow, which seemed to ease the pain. Later, the coroner was to find evidence not of appendicitis but of a massive stomach ulcer. Davidie fell into a deep depression.

Back in Yellowknife, after two weeks of fruitless searching, the military authorities were preparing to wind down the operation. It had been the most comprehensive and expensive in Canadian aviation history. At a cost of $2 million, their aircraft had logged 620 hours of flying time and covered the entire search zone, crawling over twenty-five thousand square kilometres of it at the dangerously low altitude of five hundred feet. Several commercial and military aircraft had reported mysterious electronic signals and blips of very short duration, but nothing had checked out. In the absence of other proposals, missions had been flown to explore predictions by psychics, the pilots looking for landmarks seen in dreams and described over the radio.

One of the most promising suggestions had come from Dominique Prinet, a French-born economist lured from Paris, like Hartwell, by the romance of the North. He had flown the same Beech 18 for Gateway Aviation while working as a bush pilot. Prinet, who went on to become a senior airline executive with Nordair and, later, Canadian Airlines International, calculated the bias of the plane's gyro compass according to rates of precession, factored in the psychological westward drift of an inexperienced pilot and predicted that Hartwell had gone down somewhere south of Great Bear Lake, perhaps on a line to Fort Wrigley. He turned out to be correct, but the Hercules dispatched to investigate Prinet's theory passed seventy-five kilometres west of the crash site and heard no signals. On November 26, while

Davidie Kootook floundered in the snow looking for carrion to eat, the search was officially suspended.

Controversy erupted immediately. While the search master believed, quite rightly it proved, that everything possible had been done to find the missing mercy flight, Hartwell's girlfriend Susan Haley did not agree. A shrewd and instinctive manipulator of public opinion and the mass media, she orchestrated a skilful campaign to bring political pressure to bear on James Richardson, the federal minister of defence. With young Yellowknife freelancer Susan Mayse telling her story under front-page headlines in the *Edmonton Journal* and the *Toronto Star*, Haley's campaign for a renewed search effort gathered momentum and won alliances. Native political organizations gave their weight, so did northern pilots who had been conducting their own unofficial and irregular search.

On December 1, although his experts in the field believed the probability of locating survivors to be exceedingly slim, Richardson caved in to public pressure and reopened the search. It was thirty below zero, the coldest day of the year. It was also the day that Davidie Kootook starved to death.

Hartwell had been awakened that night by the boy's respiratory difficulties. Suddenly, his breathing stopped. The pilot attempted artificial respiration, but there was no response. He tried to close Davidie's eyes but could not. Later, he pushed the body out of the shelter because he could not bring himself to share his bed with a dead person. He began now to contemplate the inevitability of his own death. Hartwell had been eating lichens since the eighth day. Still incapable of walking, immobilized in his camp, without Davidie to help he could no longer even collect lichens. He determined that if he were to have the remotest chance of rescue, he would have to survive until his legs healed sufficiently for him to reach the lake and catch fish. Three days later, he decided that if he were to avoid joining the dead himself, the dead must give their bodies to save his life. If it was an emotionally traumatic decision, it was not one made in isolation. The tradition of such desperation and sacrifice is a deep part of the collective consciousness of the Canadian Arctic. Dwelling in such a harsh environment, always at the brink of famine, forces people to confront the grim necessity of survival. It had happened in the previous century with Franklin's doomed men, and it had happened in the living memory of Inuit who lived through the famine the year the caribou did not come.

Marten Hartwell had chosen to live and that was enough for
Northerners.

Six days later, a Canadian Forces Hercules — not searching
but making a routine supply flight from Northern Command
headquarters in Yellowknife to Inuvik — picked up faint signals
from Hartwell's crash beacon. Another aircraft carrying a parachute team of medics was immediately diverted from the search
area and homed in on the crash site. Hartwell struggled from his
shelter and lit a red emergency flare when he heard the low-
flying plane. As he watched, Master Corporal Harvey Copeland
and Corporal Al Williams jumped into the crash zone from one
thousand feet while their Hercules circled overhead. Ninety
minutes later, Hartwell was on his way to a hospital bed in Yellowknife and a meal of baby food, pureed chicken, pureed vege-
tables and banana custard. It was all his weakened body could
tolerate. He had lost fifteen kilos.

If the ordeal by hunger was over, the ordeal by ink was about
to begin. Death, courage, fortitude, survival — the Hartwell
story appealed to every stereotype of the human condition that
is loved by the popular media and its audience. Country singer
Stompin' Tom Connors released a ballad called "The Marten
Hartwell Story" which became an overnight hit single. North of
sixty, the rescue drew hundreds of reporters, photographers,
magazine writers and broadcasters from around the world.
They came from quality newspapers like the *New York Times* to
the sleaziest of Britain's gutter tabloids. Before they were
finished, they were to spend more than $350,000 in the two
hotels and four bars that graced the territorial capital.

Susan Mayse, who had broken the story in the first place, now
wound up sleeping on the floor by the phone in her small Yellowknife apartment, fielding calls from Sweden and Japan,
Hamburg, New York and London. She took no pay for this and
was sanguine about it. The story had taken on a momentum of
its own, and she saw answering the queries from *Aftonbladet* and
Der Stern as a kind of public service for other northerners, who
seemed stunned by the frenzy. Yellowknife, a rough, casual frontier town in 1972, with a population of five thousand at its busiest, had taken on the trappings of a full-scale media circus.
Hordes of foreign reporters would stampede from hotel to hospital, from hospital to hotel, on the basis of the slightest rumour
that Hartwell was prepared to give an interview. Fleet Street
reporters paid Dogrib Indian kids to tie up pay phones at the
Yellowknife Inn so that competitors would miss deadlines. A
photographer was caught trying to climb in through a hospital

window. British and German cheque-books came out, with accompanying rumours of five-and-six-figure offers for first rights to the story. Nurses who knew nothing and had seen nothing were wined and dined in unprecedented style. Mayse recalled at one point totting up the readers represented by the reporters who had dropped over to her apartment for beer and chili and being astonished to find they numbered thirty-five million on her chesterfield alone.

By now, hints were beginning to circulate regarding what had happened at the crash site, although both the military and the police had done a remarkable job of maintaining confidentiality. It was the failure to answer questions and the refusal to discuss details that tipped reporters that something unusual had taken place. In the end, a curious sense of morality emerged that seemed to typify fundamental differences between the Canadian press and the British press. Canadian reporters and editors refused to be drawn into the hunt for the sensational, and even those who knew what had occurred insisted on awaiting the official findings of a formal inquest. The British, on the other hand, were quite prepared to speculate at the most exotic possibilities. Ultimately, it was the grottiest of British tabloids which made the issue of Hartwell's survival a matter of sensational public speculation.

The glare of publicity drove Hartwell underground, and he fled from Yellowknife to a secluded convalescence in Edmonton, refusing even to give evidence at the northern inquest. He said his presence would only intensify the distressing publicity surrounding the crash, further wounding the surviving relatives and adding to his own suffering. Quite bravely, he called a brief press conference in Edmonton, outlined the statement he had given to the RCMP to be read into the inquest record, made simple acknowledgement of the circumstances of his survival and addressed the moral imperatives faced by anyone faced with such decisions.

The coroner's jury sitting in Yellowknife included five veteran bush pilots, and they had their own view of moral imperatives. Whatever his feelings, Hartwell had an obligation as captain of his aircraft to give evidence regarding the deaths of passengers under his care, particularly since his own survival had only been possible because of them. Without the help of Davidie Kootook, the pilot would have died, said foreman Duncan Matheson, himself a northern pilot of legendary stature. The jury ruled the pilot's inexperience was a factor in the crash but, pointedly, did not condemn him for undertaking the mercy flight. They found greater fault with the condition of the instruments in his plane and the air navigation equipment under the jurisdiction of the federal government.

In the end, the pretty young nurse from Devon who had given so much, continued in death the work she had begun in life. It seems symbolic and fitting that the Judy Hill Memorial Fund should train nurses in the arts of midwifery for service in remote Arctic nursing stations. Davidie Kootook and his aunt were forgotten almost as soon as the media frenzy abated. Only two people showed up for the memorial service when they were buried in a simple ceremony at Edmonton. The lone survivor ultimately sold his story to a quality British newspaper, which published a subdued and tasteful account of his adventures. From there, he retreated into obscurity and returned to the substance of his life, still flying in the Far North, still worthy of a paragraph in the newspapers when, seventeen years later, his light plane was forced down in a minor incident of the sort that bush pilots expect and experience every day.

Susan Haley, who forced the government of Canada to yield to the power of love, turned to writing novels. So did Susan Mayse, abandoning the fictions of journalism for the truths of fiction. For Hartwell himself, perhaps everything was said when the parachute team struggled through the deep snow that had defeated Davidie so many times. When they entered the camp, the lone survivor greeted them on his knees. Safe in the arms of his rescuers, he told them it was his birthday. They asked how old he was. "Zero Zero," he said. "It's the first day of my life."

IN A CLEANSING FURY

All I wanted was sleep. I ached for it. Longed for it. Anywhere. Under any conditions. For five minutes or five hours or five days. After seventy-two hours without it, steeped in the jittery haze left by too much adrenalin and too much caffeine, my mind felt like it was beginning to separate into its constituents, different segments of myself operating independently, carrying on parallel and unrelated streams of thought, the laminations coming apart. In one layer of myself, I anticipated the vivid intensity of my final submission to the crisp white embrace of clean sheets, the pleasant sound of my wife singing to herself in another room, me going down into the sweet odour of sunshine and fresh air, a drowning man released into the blankness of not knowing and not caring. In another, I struggled to control the restless, barely acknowledged creature that moved behind the mirror of consciousness. It gnawed at the brittle foundations of reason, that flimsy house of cards we build on quicksand to convince ourselves that the world is indeed controllable. While panic stirred, however far below, sleep was denied — even if Jack had braked at that precise instant and told me to roll out the sleeping bag in the box, we were going to grab forty quick ones. Fear is the mind killer, I kept telling myself, noticing at the same time that the snot streaming out of my nostrils had turned black.

We shuddered across another set of hidden ruts and clanged off a reef of exposed granite. My skull caromed off the starred windshield and my ribs slammed into the unpadded knob of the window crank. I had ceased some time before to feel the bruises and abrasions that came from being bounced around inside the rocking, rolling cab. Other things seemed more important, although later I would curse and groan for weeks trying to get out of bed. For now, both sets of our eyes swivelled to the pressure gauge, pinned by the quivering needle.

Jack and I were friends, still are, but at that moment things were starting to unravel in the weariness and fear and confusion.

"Ya gotta watch the road," shouted Jack. "We're gonna bust an axle."

"Just fuckin' drive," I yelled back. "I can't see one fuckin' thing more than you can."

I marshalled my senses, knowing he was right, and peered again into the gathering murk, straining for a glimpse of the next boulder or jagged tangle of roots or the sudden dead fall or whatever might lie waiting to flip up over the hood and come through the windshield or, worse, through the radiator. My eyes felt like someone had poured hot sand into them, alternately streaming tears and prickling with bitter grit. One of those detached parts of me went off on an airy arabesque, analyzing this tendency to become foul-mouthed under pressure; some response, perhaps, to an early upbringing in a religious home where I once said "damn" and my mother said a prayer on my behalf while my dad took his belt to me in the wood shed. I still remember the hidden corner of the orchard where I tested the Big Word for the first time, both its sense of potency and the sudden stillness while I waited for divine wrath to descend out of the apple blossoms. Now, it seemed as bankrupt as a ju-ju amulet, an empty reflex triggered out of fright. I felt sure my mother would forgive the language and that she would certainly pray for me on other accounts.

Somewhere out in front, whipped toward us on winds gusting to fifty kilometres per hour, was a huge inferno. Already, it covered 150 square kilometres, bigger than the whole city centre of Toronto, and it was roaring toward us through stands of bone dry spruce. Behind us, at the world's biggest lead-zinc mine, the fifteen hundred people of Pine Point were poised for the single blast of the plant sirens that would signal them to abandon their possessions and flee to safety in the west. Actually, at that precise moment, we could not care less about the people of Pine Point. They, at least, had a plan and an evacuation route. We were lost and entirely uncertain about what we were doing or where we were going.

We had started out under piercing sunshine and brilliant blue skies. Then, abruptly, the wind shifted and coils of dense smoke had poured out of the sky, obscuring everything and changing a familiar landscape to something sinister and filled with evil intent. A routine trip to the forward fire line had become a nightmare. At the moment, we were blasting down what was supposed to be a road, but doubts loomed. In the smoke and gloom, it was starting to look more and more like we had strayed onto a rough firebreak hacked through the bush by some desperate D-9 Cat operator. Maybe we were shimmying and churning our way to disaster. Visibility was down to the length of the hood and the choking smoke was beginning to seep into the cab.

"We're gonna be Crispy Critters if you don't find us a way outa here," Jack muttered.

"Shut up and drive," I shouted. "I'm not your fuckin' mother."

For such a crisis, it had all started innocently enough. A week earlier, I had been far away to the north, safe on the other side of the vast, dark expanse of Great Slave Lake, a body of water larger in area than many small European countries. I was drinking the last of a precious case of southern Alberta pilsner on the outcrop behind my Yellowknife digs and watching a powerful summer storm roll across the rugged granite and its nap of stunted trees. Across the whole Northwest Territories, it had been a season of peculiar weather. The ice did not go out of the big lake until well into June, the blue pans etching a strange cast of colour along the horizon, yet by solstice, with the sun shining 18 hours a day, temperatures were high and the air had acquired a scorched, brassy tang to it. Down in Old Town, built around the outcrop they still call The Rock, and out at the Indian village of Detah, even the most aggressive sled dogs had retreated to the shade and lay panting and disinterested beneath cabins and porches. Dust devils and heat shimmers marched along the shoulders all the way out to Giant Yellowknife Mine, where gold was leeched from pulverized ore under an accompanying patina of local folklore about arsenic pollution. The poisonous tailings from the crusher and the sickly yellow seeps smouldered and bubbled in the ditches.

The deep, cold lake and the over-heated rock of the Canadian Shield triggered powerful convection currents. Thunderheads towered high into the flight paths of jet liners bound for Europe and the Orient. I sipped my beer and watched the silvery columns boil upward over their deep purple bases. I never saw a single bolt of lightning myself, although the far horizons flickered and rumbled like some distant artillery duel, the distant flashes casting a pearly hue against the flat, anvil-coloured bellies of clouds slanting into the half-light of the midnight sun.

The next morning, I did routine checks on the radio-phone to the fire control officer for the Mackenzie Forest District. He was frantic.

"It's like a nuclear war down here. Everywhere you look there are mushroom clouds along the horizon. I can't raise half my fire crews and my aircraft can't operate because of the smoke and turbulence."

The massive electrical discharges that had seemed so beautiful the night before had ignited almost three hundred major fires across the whole western sweep of the Canadian Arctic. At a rough estimate, the total area of forest in flames was about the size of Prince Edward Island or the entire state of Delaware. Short-wave frequencies chattered with reports of threatened communities and camps. Evacuations at Paradise Gardens. Emergency conditions at Hay River. Plans to abandon Pine Point. Miners fleeing their exploration camp and its two-hundred-ton cache of dynamite on Prairie Creek in the Headless Valley wilderness. Wood Buffalo National Park was at risk, and so was the last wild herd of woods bison that ranged across its drought-stricken meadows. Farther north, the fragile nesting grounds of the rare and already endangered whooping crane were in danger. A major fire was advancing on the new and stunningly beautiful Nahanni National Park. Along a thirty-kilometre front, the five-hundred-square-kilometre blaze was flashing through the dry timber and narrow smoke-filled valleys on winds gusting to forty kilometres per hour.

South of Great Slave Lake, where the forest service was head-quartered, some of the blazes had begun to take on the proportions of full-blown firestorms. One had exploded by almost fifty square kilometres in a single day, the perimeter blossoming out from eighty to 127 square kilometres and overrunning fire suppression crews in the process. The men got out by the skin of their teeth but abandoned irreplaceable equipment to the flames. At another site, six smaller fires had burned together to create one immense conflagration. To make things worse, heavy sun spot activity had severely disrupted radio communications and headquarters had lost contact with the majority of its isolated fire crews. They were well trained and relatively self-sufficient. They would have to be. If they got into serious trouble, nobody was going to know about it until it was finished.

The forest fire is one of those archetypes that reside in the Canadian psyche and make us different from Europeans and Americans, secure in their largely domesticated landscapes. It is a yearly reminder of the power of natural elements to enter our lives and disrupt the rational and the routine. Having used our systematic and scientific pacification of the wilderness within ourselves to banish the possibility of demons and the supernatural, we find a ready substitute in the wilderness without. The forest fire is the destructive, mischievous genie escaped from the bottle of civilization. It is the image of the uncontrollable with its consuming — and perhaps cleansing? — power to destroy our works. Perhaps, in a way, we welcome this evidence of Dionysian principle in our increasingly ordered, planned, scheduled existence. It confirms our impermanence in a world that seems obsessed with guarantees of everything — good health, security, material comfort, employment, education, life itself.

The ubiquitous presence of the forest fire as an icon in popular culture is evidence that it contributes to the living mythos of the country. This may be discerned in the way the mass media responds to the phenomenon. In Canadian literature, which tends to speak to professional, urban elites, the gigantic forces of the forest fire and their place in the national psyche are scarcely addressed, save for a few short stories which mostly serve to anthropomorphize courageous or suffering wilderness animals. Newspaper files, speaking on the other hand to the masses, are dense with accounts, tales, folklore and legends regarding the great Canadian adventure. Stories about forest fires in the popular press frequently exceed the coverage of foreign wars in depth and excitement. And it should not be assumed that this is some bizarre creation of public taste on the part of the press. Newspapers and television merely respond to popular demand.

The fascination with the forest fire and our collective response to it is a distinctly Canadian phenomenon, probably because of the vast forests and tiny outposts of population which may still find themselves at risk from the elements. Perhaps, however, the mythic nature of such natural disasters also finds a resonance with the anarchic current that runs beneath the surface Canadian values of order, control and good government.

Much has been made of the ordered nature of Canadian cultural evolution compared to the dishevelled and frequently violent process south of the border. And yet, much American history seems to celebrate precisely the values ascribed to Canadian society — social control and a rage for the imposition of order. Any closer examination of American national mythology finds it revolving predominantly around the process of explicit cultural and environmental imperialism. Indeed, if the history of the United States chronicles a fundamental drive for the creation of a homogeneous society, then the homogenized nature of its national mythology echoes and reaffirms this. Daniel Boone,

Paul Bunyan, Wyatt Earp, Kit Carson, the Oregon Trail, the settling of the West, all superficially invoke the unruly hero, but the
hero is always in the service of pacification and enforced submission, whether of landscape or indigenous inhabitants or dissident elements. What is the gunfight at the OK Corral but a
legendary affirmation of order? Indeed, the Civil War itself, that
fulcrum of modern American consciousness, is primarily about
this desire for order, conformity and centralized control — of the
Union over the Confederacy, of the secessionists over the slave
classes, of the urban industrial complex over the rural agrarian
hinterlands, of the federal power over individual states.

The evolution of Canadian society has been a much less
integrated process. Divided from the beginning by language,
ethnicity and class, populated by the dispossessed but governed
by distant imperial power, evolving in culturally distinct and
geographically distant regional nodes, still painfully aware of
the autonomy of the undeveloped hinterlands from the urban
matrix, Canadian mythology frequently reflects a profound
sense of isolation from, and distaste for, central authority. Simple geographic imperatives have made us much more cognizant
of the limitations of homogeneity and centralized power and
control. Where Americans celebrate their uniform dominance,
Canadians are much more aware of the fragility of place, sharing
an uneasy accommodation with, and admiration for, an environment that remains impenetrable, implacable, unpredictable and
wild. Under the apparent reserve, there is a secret glee at the
prospect of running out of control, of being immersed in forces
bigger than reason and bureaucracy. If sport offers a signal
regarding the matrix of popular values, it is not surprising that
the emergent national sport of Americans is football, with its
regimentation and patterned discipline, its reliance on the
coach's plan and the quarterback's execution. And it is less
surprising that the national sport in Canada is hockey, a fluid,
barely organized game of swift and continuous transition,
driven by individual initiative and characterized as much by the
breaking of the rules as by their observation. Nor is it surprising
that the national pastime for Canadian fans, from Montreal
Forum to Northlands Coliseum, should be the near-unanimous
baiting of the referees, who symbolize the imposition of order on
the chaos and sporadic violence of the game.

The forest fire in Canadian folklore represents the antithesis of
the growing order and control that we secretly resent. Perhaps
this is why it remains such a marginal part of American consciousness. Take, for example, the forest fire which swept

through the pine woods of Minnesota in 1894. Running before hurricane force winds, it raised the town of Hinckley and many surrounding villages. An estimated five hundred people perished in the holocaust, yet any check of reference books indicates that compared with the strictly localized Iroquois Theatre fire of Chicago, which killed about the same number of people, Hinckley remains a barely remembered incident in American history. Even the great Tillamook forest fire of 1933, which burned one thousand square kilometres in Oregon and ranks as the most severe in American history, remains small scale and largely forgotten by comparison with Canadian fires. More recently, the fires in Yellowstone National Park commanded the attention of U.S. television networks, but the story was political — as much about the miscalculations of management policy as anything else — and seemed quickly forgotten.

Ask old timers in any of the Canadian provinces, however, and you'll proudly be regaled with tales of the "great fire" of the region at hand. There have been more than fifty thousand forest fires important enough to be recorded in Canada since 1975 alone. In 1986, they were evacuating women and kids from Canal Flats, a town in the trough between the Selkirk Mountains and the Rockies. In 1987, fires threatened towns in the Maritimes. There's nothing new about any of this. In 1825, the legendary fire of the Miramichi drove the inhabitants of Newcastle and Douglastown to take shelter neck-deep in the steaming river while their townsites burned to the foundations. More than two hundred people were killed along the Miramichi by the fire, which went on to destroy an estimated one-quarter of New Brunswick's standing timber. At the other end of the country, most school children in British Columbia's interior can recount the great Fernie fire of 1908, accompanied by enthusiastically lurid details regarding the Ford family, which sought shelter in a well and was boiled alive. In ninety minutes one hellish afternoon, the blaze reduced a bustling coal-mining town of five thousand to a waste land of ash and charred machinery. Amazingly, only ten people died in the fire, but it has nevertheless passed almost completely into the landscape of legend.

The Fernie fire began somewhere in the slash — a tangle of stripped branches, shredded bark, sawdust, broken saplings and other debris left by the logging operations of the Cedar Valley Lumber Company. For some reason, whether through negligence or simple stupidity, it appears somebody had been burning the rubbish in spot fires despite the fact that it was high summer. The hot, arid Crowsnest Pass still fosters a reputation for explosive forest fires. A century ago, they constituted a menacing prospect each summer. Winds funnel down the narrow pass between tall, barren mountains, while the dry grasses and pitch-laden jack pines provide an abundance of combustible material. The coal-mining town of Michel was partially destroyed by a fire in 1902. Fernie itself fell victim to a town fire in 1904, which turned out to be ironically fortuitous, for it at least prevented the town's destruction three months later when another fire roared down and burned through the pass all the way to Alberta's rolling prairie. Crowsnest settlers were burned out at Hosmer, at Sparwood, where shaft timbers were cut for the mines, and in 1910 the fires raged north of Blairmore and Coleman while another fire threatened the towns of Passburg and Burmis. Towns in the pass were threatened by forest fires again and again in the 1920s and 1930s. Which raises the never-to-be-answered question: Why were the spot fires in the lumber company slashings left unattended in such powder-keg conditions?

On the Saturday morning of August 1, as Fernie drowsed into its hot summer weekend, a brisk wind sprang up. In a matter of minutes, as though fanned by bellows, the flames from the smouldering spot fires had jumped to the structure of the Cedar Valley sawmill itself, consumed it and raced into the heavy stands of timber that stood between the mill and the newly reconstructed Fernie townsite. The pine trees, knotty and sticky with highly flammable pitch, exploded like bombs, cascading sparks ahead of them. At West Fernie, the fire ignited six million board feet of milled timber that was stockpiled in the Elk Lumber Company's yards. Two other pincers of fire raced through dense woods to the north and south to close the circle on the townsite.

Inside the tightening noose, the intense winds of a firestorm stuttered through the lumberyard and sailed whole flaming planks into the dry shingle and tar paper of the town's rooftops. A steady rain of sparks, glowing embers, ash and other fiery debris fell across the middle of Fernie, jamming in to smoulder behind the ornate false fronts and under the board sidewalks. Photographs taken at the time capture the unforgettable image of tiny human figures transfixed before a terrifying wall of smoke and flame which rises thousands of feet in the air above church steeples and high-ceilinged saloons. The winds preceding the fire were so powerful they tore the roof off the opera house and spun it like a frisbee. It soared a full city block. Hotels, banks, the *Fernie Free Press* headquarters, more than a thousand buildings in all, erupted into flames. The heat was so intense that ore cars melted where they sat.

A deep gloom fell on Fernie as the sun first turned blood red then vanished behind a pall of black smoke. The only light was cast by burning buildings and sidewalks. In the darkness, the streets had become a scene from Goya, a bedlam of plunging horses and terrified people. Superheated air blistered skin and burned lungs as frantic mothers struggled to locate confused children and frightened husbands shouted after wives. Officials, having given up on the fire, battled instead to establish order among the citizens and contain the ripples of panic that surged through the crowds. First, the hospitals were evacuated, the nurses retreating with their patients as they were driven, building by building, before the advancing fire. Hundreds of other refugees, their lines of retreat cut off, were directed into the stone office block of the Crow's Nest Pass Coal Company, where they huddled until the fire passed. Hundreds more, many of them new immigrants unable to understand English instructions and at the verge of panic, were herded by teams of miners trained to the dangers of underground rescue work. The crowd was shunted to the railway station where people were packed into any rolling stock that could be hitched to the one locomotive in the yards. More than a thousand jammed into cattle cars, box cars, ore cars, flat cars — anything that would roll. At the last minute, the train escaped down the scorching tunnel created by houses blazing on either side of the tracks. When it was far enough from the fire, passengers dashed to safety in a nearby river.

The textbooks tell you that the fastest rate of advance for a forest fire is approximately six kilometres per hour. But experience says the mathematician's opinions were calculated in the sterile safety of a lab. W.W. Tuttle, the mayor of Fernie, said the flames advanced toward and through his town faster than a galloping race horse. Fifteen years later, at the Hudson Bay fort of Lac La Biche in northeastern Alberta, witnesses said the fire which burned their community to the ground flashed more than a mile-and-a-half in the blink of an eye.

The fire which consumed Lac La Biche in 1919 was the biggest ever recorded in Canadian history, thirty times larger than the biggest in United States records. It started in Prince Albert, Saskatchewan, 360 kilometres to the east and by the time it was finished had burned thirty thousand square kilometres of boreal forest, an area the size of modern Belgium. Constable Fred Moses of the Alberta Provincial Police strayed unknowingly into the path of the fire while in the region to investigate a murder. His entry in the day log for May 19, 1919, is succinct: "Cold. Fine. Eclipse of sun. Thunder, lightning, fires all over. Lac La Biche burnt out. Dark in the afternoon."

His laconic policeman's prose understates the story. What he thought was an eclipse was smoke so dense it blocked the sun from shining and coloured the prairie skies for thousands of kilometres around. The fire had come roaring through tinder-dry spruce and poplar, sometimes advancing at rates estimated by witnesses at one hundred kilometres per hour. It generated its own firestorm as it went. Witnesses on a relief train told of trees almost a metre in diameter snapping off like toothpicks to be hurled, already flaming, across the railway tracks to ignite the timber on the other side. Sixty-five kilometres south of Lac La Biche, the paint scorched off the railway cars in flash fires. The telegraph cables melted and molten copper trickled down the poles. Solid steel railway tracks twisted and buckled in the intense heat. At the Hudson Bay Company fort, another witness described a scene from Dante's Inferno, "black as midnight in mid-afternoon with the only illumination from the flames." As at Fernie, women and children, sick and elderly, were rushed into the nearby lake where, neck deep and covered with wet blankets, they cowered while the fire raged through homesteads, businesses and residential homes. When it had passed, only five buildings had freakishly survived, among them the Lac La Biche Inn, a doctor's summer cottage, the one-room school and the Catholic presbytery. Later, the presbytery was found to be filled with mysterious mounds of scorched pine needles. The winds had been so powerful that the needles were blasted right through the walls of the building.

I can't say that I really thought about any of this as I tried to see through the smoke that swirled around us. I was far too frightened to think about history, although part of me did muse on a story told by my father-in-law, Bill Mayse, who had been there when they fought the great fire of 1937. It had bounded eighty-five kilometres down the mountainous spine of Vancouver Island, starting in the Quinsam River watershed and threatening the towns of Bevan and Cumberland. They had no heavy equipment. No bulldozers or water bombers, or choppers with monsoon buckets pinpointing the hot spots with loads of bright red fire retardant. He said his big fire had burned hot enough to start crowning, triggering spontaneous ignition in the feathery tree tops out in front of the fire's main line of advance. The tree tops would start exploding in sheets of flame, he said.

Faster than a man could run. It could go over you before you knew it. There'd be the sound of an express train overhead, and the fire would be a mile behind you with canopies of flame above. The textbooks say a crowning fire restricts itself to the tree tops, doesn't burn down to the combustibles at ground level. He laughed at that. All that burning crud falling out of the tree tops. Of course, there's less oxygen, that's for sure. But try to lug your chain saw back through that and see what you think of theory and formula.

. The fire that Jack and I were trying to find was one of the hottest that fire boss Pete Ferguson had ever seen. He had eighteen pieces of heavy equipment and four of the forty-two water bombers in his little air force working the Pine Point fire. It was only one of a number of critical priorities. Other water bombers were concentrating on Wood Buffalo National Park, Canada's largest and one of the most environmentally important. Elite crews of highly trained smoke jumpers, spectacular and smart in their bright orange jumpsuits of flame-resistant fabric, had already dropped into the remotest area with specific orders to hold off approaching fires until the forty-three whooping cranes, already in grave danger of extinction, were able to depart on their fall migration to safer regions in the south.

It seemed a particularly Canadian set of priorities, crews of men placing the survival of endangered birds at the same level as Pine Point itself. When I asked one miner's wife about it, she shrugged, "Ah, we oughta save the birdies. You can always buy more junk." For the moment, it seemed she might be faced with just that prospect. The fire had closed X-15 pit, the most easterly working of the massive strip mine that was Pine Point's only reason for existence. I'd been through there the night before, standing safely in the barren middle of the pit at 5 a.m. and listening to the strange crackling, watching the flames dance and sizzle along the high ground on either side. Now, the fire had advanced to within ten kilometres of the townsite proper, and at his briefing the day before the fire boss had been sanguine: "If the sun comes out bright and hot and we get a stiff wind, that fire is going to go right through us and nothing is going to stop it."

Firefighters returning to the base camp were reporting a blaze too fierce for anything but bulldozer work, the big machines cutting firebreaks, then falling back to make new ones when the flames jumped their lines. There were no firefighters on the ground venturing closer than three-quarters of a mile because of the heat and the explosive speed with which the fire could move when a wind got behind it.

Sitting in the command post for the whole Mackenzie Forest District at Fort Smith two days before, I had acquired a pretty good idea of the logistical problems. The huge wall map of the Northwest Territories bristled with coloured pins — bright red for active fires, yellow for suspected but unconfirmed fires, black, appropriately, for burned out fires. I counted 263 of the red and yellow pins, and new ones were being added. On the wall next to the map were charts which indicated falling humidity and the nearly total absence of water in the environment. The radio gave voice to the basic concerns of the men on the ground. It yammered with demands:

"We need two thousand feet of hose. Pronto. That hose is a must."

"Hard hats. I gotta have four or five hard hats. There's a positive rain of shit on this wind."

"We are short of pack sacks and portable pumps."

"Send groceries."

"Send grub."

"You fat bastards ship some grub. The boys ain't ate in forty-eight hours."

"Can you find out for Jimmy on Fire Six if his baby's been born yet? Can you find out what it is? He's bugging me about it."

The fire control officer had bigger problems than supply and demand. He explained that when the electrical storms scattered the fires across his district in such numbers he had cannibalized the Yellowknife Fire District on the north side of Great Slave Lake. Now, that zone had its own outbreak of serious fires. One had cut the Mackenzie Highway, Yellowknife's only land link to the outside world, and knocked out power from the town's hydroelectric plant on the Stagg River. The territorial capital was getting by with emergency power from a diesel generator.

"Yellowknife wants its equipment back," he said. "Gotta find it for 'em."

Compounding his logistics problems, the fire threatening the new Nahanni National Park had become a major political priority just at the time the fire boss had lost three of his precious aircraft. A helicopter had gone down in the bush on the fringes of Fire Six, and two Canso water bombers had immediately dropped to circle over the wreck. They would hold over the crash until another chopper could be dispatched to pull the pilot out of the path of the advancing flames. In the dense smoke and turbulence over the fire, the water bombers collided head-on. The chopper pilot had been rescued and was already being

evacuated to Edmonton with broken legs. There were no survivors among the Canso crews. That brought the death count to
six on Fire Six. Two men on the ground had already been killed
the week before by widow-makers, dead snags dropping out of
the brittle, weakened trees.

I was beginning to think, bashing around in the cab, that Jack
and I might be about to become casualties seven and eight. And
then Jack hit the brakes. The darkness lifted as quickly as it had
descended. Around us, light filtered through a grey haze and
pale wraiths of smoke drifted among a forest of blackened trees.
They were stripped as naked as telephone poles. We opened the
doors and tested the air, flinching at the acrid odour. The
ground was still hot underfoot, and the world was muffled in a
thick blanket of ash that puffed around us with every step. It
extended to the horizon in all directions. There was no sound
and nothing alive, except two fools who had somehow, by some
divine providence, driven through the inferno that couldn't be
stopped. Cursing and swearing at one another's incompetence,
discovering the weakness and fear that breeds intolerance and
rage, we were struck dumb by the magnitude of our folly and
the desolation of the landscape. We had come to the consuming
heart of the forest fire and found it absolutely still.

When I returned years later, the fire cut was still there, suc-
cumbing to erosion and the burst of suckering aspen and brilliant northern ground cover — honeysuckles, willow, bearberry,
the pink of wild roses and fireweed. The underbrush was alive
with the cries of warblers, red-eyed vireos and oven-birds. A
pair of curious ravens swooshed past and then peeled away, rising on the thermals and then swooping down to ride them up
again.

This cycle of destruction and regeneration seems connected to
the country's vision of itself. The dark tangle of mature forests
with their choking carpet of dead needles and beards of moss
swept away in a cleansing fury of fire, to be replaced by the
riotous profusion of flowers and shrubs, the dark conifers giving
way to silver birch and the dappled light of trembling aspen.
Once, I was told by a palaeobotanist, a single forest fire moved
the whole Arctic tree line to its present position, 250 kilometres
south of where it had been. He said the smoke from that fire had
changed the climate of North America, blocking the sun's rays
and triggering colder winters and different seasonal growing
patterns. Animals moved and aboriginal cultures perished as far
south as the Missouri River basin, a stone age foreshadowing of
the nuclear winter that scientists now say will follow any war

between the superpowers that bracket Canada.

But all this was as distant from me as the burgeoning forest that lay in my own unseen future, the seeds of perception sealing themselves in my unformed awareness as deeply as the bearberry seeds that were buried under the nourishing layers of ash.

Calculating position by the bloodshot sun, we struck southwest through the pale waste behind the fire line. Vast plumes of dust trailed away among stark trees, drifted back into the tracks under flurries of delicate ash, patterned and intricate as any snowflake. When we finally reached the highway that connects the old trading post of Fort Smith and Pine Point, we headed for the mine site, counting on the efforts of fire crews to keep the one major land link to headquarters open. We were right. The glow of flames punctuated the twilight on our distant flanks, but the raw earth of firebreaks and red splashes of retardant gel marked a breach in the fire's front.

Later, at a fire control briefing, we kept silent about our strange reconnaissance. There was good news from the fire boss. The smoke jumpers in Wood Buffalo Park had saved the whooping cranes. Up on the high ridges of the Funeral Range, the fire crews operating from Dead Man's Flats had used a shift in the wind and quick thinking to starve the Nahanni blaze with backfires. There was more good news from the weatherman. A cold front moving from the west promised to damp the Pine Point fire. There might even be rain. Crews could stand down. The sleepless might sleep.

In my bunk, I could not sleep. My brain raced with images: the livid face of Jack yelling at me to watch the road; the black outline of trees silhouetted against a curtain of orange flames; the curious puffs of ash lifting over footprints, then falling again to fill them, creating indistinct dimples, softening the sharp edges we left in the landscape. I went to the canteen, drank coffee, listened to a CBC reporter bitch about overtime, yakked with the pilot of a water bomber. The whole campaign was shifting to the west. He was doing precision bombing runs on hot spots and flare-ups. It was low level stuff. Just like the old days. He'd take us along. "Yeah," I said. "Sure. Why not. Be a hell of a ride." And went to sleep.

I was still there, face down at my table in the canteen, the coffee in my styrofoam cup gone cold under a sheen of grease, when the pilot crashed his aircraft just short of the trees at the end of the runway. And that, after the fashion of Canadians, is the story of my fire.

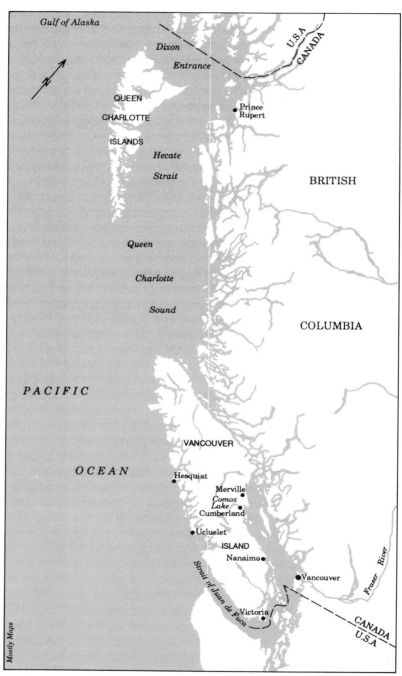

The Graveyard of the Pacific

WHERE THE BLACKFISH ROLL

Long, icy swells hissed down the sides of the *Pacific Traveller*, seethed briefly under her stern and then dwindled into the bubbling wake. The lacy arc of white curved away, vanishing into that horizonless zone where sky and ocean melt into one another. This line of froth shimmering against the slate-coloured sea was the only signal of the little boat's slow progress through a vast seascape where all seemed in motion except the watcher — the water heaving beneath, wind keen in the rigging, clouds racing, the light of heaven itself rolling over the western edge of the planet and night flooding out of the east to fill the void.

Beneath this spreading cape of darkness, Leonard Egolf watched the foaming progress of the swells as every longliner captain must when venturing into blue water. At all points of the compass, *Pacific Traveller*'s skipper saw the ceaseless march of the waves. Their tossing manes were streaked across the whole fifteen thousand kilometres that lay between him and the East China Sea. The steeds of the ocean deeps are always horses to be reckoned with, even in clear weather.

Cast up over the Ryuku Trench near Japan, these rollers drag eastward in the moon's service. As they cross the Aleutian Abyssal Plain, prevailing winds pile in behind, pushing them to huge proportions. Only the rocky coast of Canada resists, and even that is a losing battle. The towering mountains gradually succumb to an eternal pounding. First, whole faces shear away, boulders shatter into gravel, pebbles grind into sand that slides down the undertows to the continental shelf. In the end, the debris of mountains sifts into the deeps as fine silt, disappearing back into those lightless chasms where the tides are born.

At thirty-three, Egolf was skipper of his own boat, a well-maintained twelve-metre vessel sailing out of Ucluelet, a picturesque fishing village which takes its name from a Nootka word for safe harbour. The Indians, renowned among their seagoing kind as rough weather whalers, would run their great, fire-blackened dug-outs up the sheltered beaches. Some of those canoes were longer than *Pacific Traveller* herself, hollowed out of five-hundred-year-old trees. Egolf's boat was painted the traditional surgical white of the Pacific fishing fleet. Equipped with running gear and poles, Egolf's boat doubled as a salmon troller off the west coast of Vancouver Island when she wasn't longlining in the Area 2 halibut grounds of Queen Charlotte Sound and Hecate Strait. Built in 1966, *Pacific Traveller*'s wooden hull was the same sturdy design that is typical of the off-shore fleet. She had the high, flared bows that could shear through a running sea, her wheel-house perched above the foredeck to give the skipper a better line of sight in the spray and spindrift that might hide a deadhead — one of those water-soaked logs strayed from the booming grounds and drifting just beneath the surface, capable of punching through the strongest keel. Behind the bridge, *Pacific Traveller*'s gunwales swept aft with a frigate's rake, surrounding the low working decks in the stern. Here was the hatch cover and the hold where the catch would be layered into the load of fresh ice. The design of these boats has changed little in half a century and the methods of catching ground-fish scarcely at all since the days when sailing schooners would put their dories out to work the foggy halibut banks by hand.

A hundred years later, the prospect facing Captain Egolf was no different from that which challenged the long-dead windjammer crews. Miles of halibut lines waited to be baited and paid out from the platform on *Pacific Traveller*'s rear deck. Each line or skate, measuring up to fifty fathoms in length, would be equipped with gangings of two hundred or more steel hooks attached to secondary lines. The skates would settle to the muddy bottom far below, there to soak for a few hours while the voracious halibut found the baits. Flat slabs of solid muscle, the halibut would range in weight from the minimum keeper of five kilograms to fish of 250 kilos or more — the weight of a small yearling steer. Then, the power gurdies would winch the catch aboard and the hard work of dressing and stowing the cargo in ice would begin. It would be a frantic race against time, for the fishing window was a tight one.

The Pacific halibut fishery has been strictly regulated by a joint Canada-United States commission since 1924. This agreement marks a generally successful attempt to manage stocks and prevent the wasteful exploitation that threatened the survival of the early commercial fishery. Before regulations, the biggest fish might be shot in the brain with a rifle and cut loose as too troublesome to handle. Under the joint management venture, however, and in spite of the rapacious factory fleets of distant powers, the halibut stocks had actually been growing — the Area 2 grounds for which the *Pacific Traveller* was bound had produced more than four million kilos of fish in the 1984 season, double that of the previous year. And the fishery was valuable, a $100-million catch over the previous three seasons. Nevertheless, the season openings were brief and stringently regulated. There was no room for mistakes or miscalculations on the part of longliner captains. Every commercial fisherman lives on the razor's edge of disaster at the best of times. Bad weather, mechanical failure, a sick crewman, any of these might delay a boat long enough to miss the window, and mortgage payments must be met whether fish are caught or not. The short season and the proportional value of the halibut catch encourages even cautious fishermen to take calculated risks. This particular April, Captain Egolf had nine days to sprint to his fishing station, set his lines, dress his catch and run for port.

Pacific Traveller's skipper was young and hailed from The Merville. It's a dispersed community of stump ranches and dairy farms, sheep paddocks and secluded lanes strung along what the western islanders call The Inside Passage, the gentle, inland gulf which is sheltered from the dangerous Pacific by the mountainous bulk of Vancouver Island. But if Captain Egolf was young, he was not too young to know the power of the sea and the danger of the waters he was entering that spring day in 1985. History alone could tell him that. Behind him, hidden in the gathering dusk, lay the twenty-six-thousand-kilometre stretch of coastline that has been known for two centuries as the graveyard of the Pacific.

George Nicholson, on whom I've relied for details about early wrecks, spent many years in the first half of this century as coroner and wharf-master on the rough windward coast of Vancouver Island. Nicholson tallied 243 major shipwrecks for the memoir he published in 1962. He adds another seven wrecks of unknown origin. The earliest wreck in his count dates from 1803, but he compiled the list in his memoir long before divers interested in marine archaeology began talking about reports of what appeared to be the wreck of a Chinese junk. Nor does Nicholson's count include the scores of two-man seiners, trollers, gill-netters and pleasure craft whose bones also bleach in the graveyard.

On Vancouver Island's deeply indented western coast, the shoreline is part of Pacific Rim National Park. Today, it encloses one of Canada's most popular routes for experienced hikers, but it owes its present status to the half-drowned victims of the scalpel-sharp reefs and booming surf that provided Nicholson with his list of shipwrecks. Those who endured the heart-stopping cold of the ocean, who survived the powerful under-tows that sucked swimmers down beneath the kelp and the bone-smashing waves that battered them against rocky cliffs, those who did drag ashore found themselves cast away in a ghostly rain forest. Above them, dressed like priests under drip-ping robes of Spanish moss, their tops bobbed with eagle nests and hooded with rain and mist, great trees rose from impenetra-ble tangles of underbrush. Some of these trees are so old they were saplings when Drake routed the Spanish Armada. In winter, the sandy beaches would blossom with strange patterns of hoar-frost and the rocks and tree trunks glitter with lacquers of ice.

If passage was impossible by land and denied by sea, it was next to impossible even along the foreshore. Jagged cliffs and swift, deep rivers interrupt the shoreline. In some places, the rivers gush over cliff tops, their waterfalls plunging vertically into the sea. In other places, they jet through notches in the bedrock, their currents swelled by tides to create evil, sucking whirlpools. Near the Indian village of Whyack, thought by many to be the oldest point of habitation on the Pacific Coast, the Nitinat River is safe to cross only at the moment of slack water, a span of time that stretches to precisely six minutes at high tide. Miss the slack even today and you risk being swept to destruc-tion in the combers that break over the bar in the estuary. Else-where, the beaches are scoured by racing tides that can trap a walker against sheer walls of rock too slippery to climb. To make things worse, the Indian bands of the area were unpredictable at best. Long exploited by unscrupulous Yankee traders, ambitious Spanish commanders and the brutal diplomacy of Royal Navy gunboats, they were sometimes inclined not to help uninvited guests who might leave trouble in their wake.

In February of 1869, outward bound for Valparaiso, Chile, with a load of lumber, the sailing barque *John Bright* was caught by one of the howling southeasterly gales that rip in from the open Pacific. She foundered off what is now Estevan Point. It remains a mystery as to whether her crew made it to shore or was drowned in the cold waters and later mangled against the rocks by the surge. What is known is that when the schooner *Surprise* spotted the wrecked hulk of the *John Bright* and put in to look for survivors, the local Hesquiat Indians reportedly said they had seen none, although the investigating captain found on the beach the long-haired remains of a woman believed to be the lost skipper's wife. He also found the ship stripped of its equipment and supplies. After a second visit, the captain of the *Surprise* reported finding five decapitated bodies. Public sentiment in Victoria threatened an armed expedition of vigilantes to exterminate the Hesquiats, but the colonial authorities took preemptive action, dispatching the Royal Navy gunboat, H.M.S. *Sparrowhawk*.

The *Sparrowhawk*'s surgeon reported in his medical log that the injuries to the bodies looked more like the consequences of normal decomposition and battering against the rocks than deliberate mutilation by head-hunting savages, but popular myth prevailed. Under great public pressure, the Royal Navy seized seven Hesquiats, brought them back to Victoria for trial and found two of them guilty — both of them prominent leaders and therefore ideal scapegoats for a public example. This is evident from the fact that the two men were transported back to Hesquiat to be hung in their own village, where their execution was certain to make a powerful impression. Such politically expedient killings did little to endear the white man or develop his idea of justice. For years afterward, the Hesquiats protested their innocence in the *John Bright* case, convincing, among others, the missionary priest Father Brabant, who went so far as to write a formal defence which now resides in the British Columbia archives. Not that Indian protests counted for much. In the racist assumption of the day, any defenceless white in the power of Indians was immediately considered at risk.

Thus, when the occasional half-starved and nearly demented survivors did stumble out of the bush or, more frequently than legend likes to acknowledge, were brought out by passing Nootka canoes, talk was revived about the need for a life-saving trail down the west coast of Vancouver Island. By 1898, with the Klondike rush in full swing and heavy marine traffic between Seattle and Skagway, signs had been posted in strategic locations, pointing the way to the nearest lighthouse or settlement where a survivor might find relief. Emergency depots were provisioned at Carmanah Point and Cape Beale. But nothing more was done until 1906, when the iron-hulled passenger steamer *Valencia* was wrecked with a horrifying loss of life.

Of the 154 passengers and crew aboard the *Valencia*, 117 perished in the heavy surf, many of them within full view of helpless rescuers. Three other vessels, *Queen*, *Topeka* and *Salvor*, had rushed to the scene after *Valencia* fired distress rockets, but they could only stand off and watch as the ship slowly broke up. Toward the end, desperate passengers clambered up the masts as the ship foundered beneath them. Rescuers at sea and on shore watched for several days as the dwindling band of survivors, many of them women who had refused to risk the life rafts that might carry them to safety at some Indian village, fell one by one from the rigging into the boiling sea.

For those who did escape in the life rafts, things were not much better. Aboard one raft, two men were crazed with fear at the prospect of drifting into the thundering surf and jumped overboard, drowning immediately in the icy waters. Later, three more reportedly went mad and died in the raft as it washed along a beach. A seventh lost his mind on reaching shore and dashed into the woods to look for a lighthouse he was sure he had seen. It was an hallucination. Frank Connors was found the next day, clinging to the branches of a tree which he believed was the rigging of the now lost ship.

Following the wreck of the *Valencia*, a rudimentary life-saving trail was cut through the dense bush. Built in 1909, it stretched sixty kilometres, from the fishing village of Port Renfrew, a little northwest of the provincial capital at Victoria, to the lighthouse at Pachena Point on Barkley Sound. In some places as wide as a road, in others little more than a string of blazed trees, the trail fell into a long period of disuse before it became a popular hike for the experienced outdoors enthusiast. After the establishment of Pacific Rim Park in 1970, the trail was fully developed to provide an eight-day to fourteen-day walk through wild scenery that is a match for any in the world.

Today, a century after the steamer *Woodside* lost her rudder in a gale and piled onto the reefs off Pachena Point, the impassable coast has become a walker's highway. In the first five years after the trail fully opened in 1972, the Sierra Club counted more than fifty thousand people trekking the once-unthinkable route. While the hikers, clad in Goretex rain gear and packing freeze-dried meals, may enjoy the scenery ashore, a stone's throw beyond the beach it is still the graveyard of the Pacific. Many of the ghosts are new ones.

In 1975, even as the first hikers enjoyed their new park, a sudden storm swept in from the open ocean. It caught the entire Pacific herring fleet unawares, their holds laden to the hatch-covers. A day later, the grim news came to the B.C. fishing ports. The catch would be a new crop of widows and orphans — twelve ships had been lost and thirteen fishermen were drowned. The tragedy had repeated itself in October of 1984, only six months before the *Pacific Traveller* set her own course through Queen Charlotte Sound to fish for halibut. That storm had arrived with the speed and noise of a jet plane. It was twice the predicted intensity, with hurricane force winds blowing at a steady 120 kilometres per hour. In a matter of hours it had capsized eight vessels, sunk six of them outright, and thrown sixteen fishermen into the frigid water. By some miracle, only five had drowned.

The latest storm had raised a host of profound questions about federal government policy in the Pacific fishery: questions about weather forecasting abilities; questions about the seaworthiness and effectiveness of Coast Guard vessels; questions about Ottawa's commitment to marine rescue and safety. Three years earlier, the federal government had sold off its two deep-sea weather ships, the *Vancouver* and the *Quadra*. They would normally have been on patrol thousands of kilometres to the west at Weather Station Papa. This point in mid-Pacific is located precisely in the centre of the ocean alley that funnels storm systems into Canadian waters. Ottawa, faced in 1981 with mounting deficits, had opted to abandon its expensive weather ships. The annual cost of operating a ship like the *Quadra* was approaching $7 million.

Instead, the federal authorities had selected a much cheaper but reputedly more sophisticated system of space-based forecasting. It would now rely on reports from U.S. weather satellites hanging in geo-stationary orbits over the Pacific basin. The telemetry from these satellites was analyzed around the clock at Environment Canada and transmitted with religious precision on marine radio bands. Broadcasts were scheduled three times a day, at 5 a.m., noon and 8 p.m.

But that October in 1984 something had gone dreadfully wrong. Fishermen who survived the storm said that it had arrived with unprecedented speed and fury. At 9:30 p.m., the skippers were turning on their running lights and preparing for a quiet night at sea. Skies gave no hint of what lay ahead and the weather seemed fine. Ninety minutes later, the winds were hurricane force and one after another, lost in the pitch dark and the driving seas, the boats were rolling their red-painted bellies to the heavens.

What had slipped through the satellite forecasting net was

shocking even to the experienced captains of Coast Guard search and rescue vessels. One of the American satellites had not been working and the other, the one providing backup information, was too far east to properly photograph the mid-Pacific. Out there in the blind spot, the weak remains of a decaying tropical storm had undergone an explosive transformation into what one San Francisco-based meteorologist identified as a "horrendous" low pressure area of immense proportions. To make things worse, large ocean waves had developed before the gale force winds. The satellites on which Environment Canada now depended could not detect the swells as they piled into moving mountains of water. Only a human expert's gut response to the cascade of numbers had guessed the implications of the low pressure area. Far to the north, another human observer at Environment Canada ignored the San Francisco warning until the distress signals of fishermen aboard sinking boats convinced him that the computer-driven data from satellites was understating something.

Ken Datwiler, a forty-eight-year-old non-swimmer from Courtenay, B.C., was aboard his small gill-netter, the *Lady Val II*, off the west coast of Vancouver Island when the storm struck. He reported waves the size of a two-storey house crashing over his boat. When the *Lady Val II* was in the trough of the waves, their crests were higher than the top of her mast. Datwiler clambered into his neoprene survival suit, designed to keep a man alive and afloat in the ice-cold waters, and turned to fight the storm. From just before midnight, the flimsy boat rode huge, cresting waves. A big purse-seiner, the *Miss Joyce*, had stayed out in the dirty weather to assist the little gill-netter in case she sank. When she vanished from view, seiner skipper Bruce Refuse continued to search for her, braving the lightless sea and driving rain, always fearful that if the *Lady Val II* had capsized the *Miss Joyce* would collide with her or, worse, foul her own propeller or break her own rudder on the floating debris. At 4:30 a.m., the *Lady Val II* finally succumbed and rolled over in the seas. Datwiler the non-swimmer, thanking God for his survival suit, clung to the hull, knowing that beneath him, still and dark as the sea was wild, the bottom lay in maybe a hundred fathoms of water. There were no winds down there.

Datwiler rode out the storm and survived, but others were not so lucky. Stanley Szczuka of Cortez Island perished with his boat *Silver Triton*; Richard Cowlin and his girlfriend Patricia Malashewski, both of Prince Rupert, went down with their boat, the *Miss Robyn*. Meanwhile, Jack Nicol, president of the six-

thousand-member United Fishermen and Allied Workers Union, was quick to point out that search and rescue crews had watched helplessly while four fishermen drowned. Their old, decrepit rescue craft didn't dare venture into the heavy seas to rescue the drowning men. The fishermen's union was demanding two new search and rescue vessels, preferably with hulls 120 metres long, certainly with nothing less than sixty metres.

Of the Coast Guard's Pacific patrol vessels, the biggest and most modern was the *George E. Darby*, a fifty-five-metre ship commissioned in 1972. In her first incarnation, she served as an off-shore supply vessel, but she had been converted for search and rescue work. More typical was the Coast Guard cutter *Ready*, only twenty-nine metres in length and twenty-five years old. In fact, as a consequence of central Canada's failure to appreciate sovereignty issues in the million square kilometres of western ocean over which Canada claims jurisdiction, the western Coast Guard squadron had only one vessel capable of steaming the 645 kilometres it would have to sail simply to reach the outer perimeter of its Pacific patrol area.

The Coast Guard's inability to respond adequately in the midst of a crisis and Environment Canada's failure to provide appropriate warning, a failure that was specifically cited by a federal commission of inquiry, stung the government into apparent action. Environment Minister Suzanne Blais-Grenier, later to leave the cabinet and eventually the governing Conservative Party itself, in a cloud of scandal, controversy and recrimination, announced that major steps would be taken. Although she said the storm was unique and did not indicate a deterioration in federal government weather forecasting services, Ottawa would implement a $1.2-million plan to improve forecasts.

Ottawa promised a full-time, round-the-clock weather and wave forecasting position that would be established permanently in Vancouver's weather analysis office. The minister promised the fishermen five new coastal weather stations. They would be supported by a network of anchored weather buoys designed to provide automated warnings of approaching storms. The Canadian marine broadcasting system was to be improved, and so were communications between the various government services responsible for weather forecasts, fisheries patrols and search and rescue operations.

Whether any of this crossed Leonard Egolf's mind as he pushed his boat into the gathering darkness is pure speculation, even from deck-hand Randy Morrison. A year older than his skipper at age thirty-four, Morrison was brand new to the *Pacific*

Traveller, although he hailed from Comox not far from The Merville. He had signed on only a few days earlier when Captain Egolf had turned back to Port Hardy to put ashore a sick crewman. Morrison was a lucky snag for Egolf. He was an experienced fisherman, a former lifeguard, physically fit and not likely to be put off by the long hours of bone-wearying work that lay ahead.

Close to midnight, with conditions calm, Captain Egolf killed the 110 horsepower Gardiner diesel that drove *Pacific Traveller'*s single screw. He allowed the boat to wallow in the swell. He and Morrison would need the four hours sleep the night would afford. They would have to be up at the first splinter of dawn, not long after 4 a.m., if they were to get the full day's fishing they needed. Already, they had lost half of the nine-day opening the International Halibut Commission permitted over Goose Bank. By now, *Pacific Traveller* was just to the south of Hecate Strait, the body of water which separates the Queen Charlotte Islands from the mountainous coast of B.C.

Hecate Strait is named after a five-gun paddle sloop that charted the waters for the British admiralty 130 years ago. But if the strait bears the name of a warship, one might be forgiven for assuming an earlier namesake. This stretch of water, one of the most unpredictable and dangerous in North America, has all the tempestuous characteristics of Hecate herself, the Greek goddess who was a daughter to the Titans. Known as the triple goddess, goddess of magic, ghosts and witchcraft, Hecate has powers extending over heaven and hell, the earth and the sea. She certainly expresses full dominion over the strait that carries her name.

On the night that *Pacific Traveller* drifted on the swells off Goose Bank, the waters of Hecate Strait and Queen Charlotte Sound gave no hint of their turbulent nature. Windy weather was expected the next day, but as the two men took to their bunks conditions were clear and calm, the stars passed silently above and the sea was steady below. Captain Egolf and Morrison slept the dreamless sleep of the exhausted, rocked in the safe, dry cradle of their boat by the rhythm of waves that had come all the way from China.

As they slept, another storm, a storm to dwarf the one of the previous fall, was gathering strength and momentum in the central Pacific. In fact, Environment Canada had located a surface low-pressure area far to the west at about 4 a.m. the morning of April 24, but once again the speed and intensity of the disturbance had been seriously underestimated. At 4:15 a.m., the marine weather forecast for Hecate Strait and Queen Charlotte

Sound had warned of brisk winds for the next twenty-four hours, but it also called for the winds to decrease ahead of the approaching low. Almost as an oversight, tacked on as a single sentence at the end of the weather synopsis — the summary of conditions behind the forecast — was a warning that gale force winds were expected in most waters during the outlook period.

In itself, a simple gale warning would keep most fishing boat skippers alert to changing conditions but would not necessarily inhibit their fishing. Most of the Pacific off-shore trollers, seiners and longliners were designed to operate in moderately rough conditions. A gale, lowest on the level of weather warnings, is a prediction of sustained winds of anywhere from thirty-four to forty-seven knots, something to take seriously but usually well within the operating specifications of bigger boats. In any event, in the 10:15 a.m. and 12:15 p.m. marine weather broadcasts on April 24 there had been no further mention of gales. It wasn't until 5 p.m. that a formal gale warning was issued on the continuous marine weather broadcast channel, and even then the weather system was not expected to arrive before the afternoon of the following day.

On April 25, just as Captain Egolf and his deck-hand had dragged themselves out of their bunks to begin setting the skates at 4 a.m., the forecast was updated to include storm force winds. This was a more serious matter. Storms are defined as sustained winds of forty-eight knots and higher. Only hurricanes and tornadoes rate above them on the scale. However, the storm system was not expected to reach the southern end of the Queen Charlotte Islands until early Friday morning. The weather was still holding calm and clear on Goose Bank, and, while the forecast called for gale force winds of thirty knots gusting to forty, this was still well within the limits of what Egolf considered acceptable working weather for his boat. Already half way through their fishing window, the crew of *Pacific Traveller* decided to run their longlines and get in at least a good morning's fishing before dirty weather arrived. It wasn't until 10 a.m., with three longlines in the water, that Captain Egolf listened to the marine weather broadcast and heard for the first time that the forecast of gales had been upgraded to a full-blown storm warning for that afternoon — over the very waters he was fishing. Still, he looked at the chronometer. *Pacific Traveller* would shave the margin. He calculated he had time to retrieve his morning's catch and run for shelter at Spider Anchorage, thirty kilometres away, before the full force of the storm arrived on Goose Bank.

But the low-pressure system was travelling on its own

schedule, not that of Environment Canada's computers. It was accelerating steadily and at phenomenal speed along the trans-Pacific arc that would bring it to the halibut grounds. When it arrived, six hours before it was supposed to, it caught *Pacific Traveller* and most of the four-hundred-boat halibut fleet in unprotected waters. In a single terrifying afternoon, it sank seven ships, cast twenty-two seamen into the frigid waters and drowned three of them. The storm struck with such abruptness and ferocity that up-to-date storm warnings could not be broadcast because the radio bands were jammed with distress traffic.

The first mayday was recorded at 8:40 a.m. from a boat named the *Hey Dad*. She was about eighteen kilometres offshore in the upper reaches of Hecate Strait and reported she was taking water in heavy seas. With three men aboard and not much modern survival equipment, the rescue co-ordination centre headquartered at the Esquimalt naval base tasked a major response. One of the big twin-rotor search and rescue helicopters, a pair of single-rotor Coast Guard Sikorsky helicopters (one of them seconded from the U.S. Coast Guard) and two civilian helicopters, a Buffalo patrol aircraft, the big rescue ship *George E. Darby* and the Coast Guard cutter *Point Henry*, all converged on the *Hey Dad*'s last signal. She was lucky. The aircraft found her quickly and guided in the *Point Henry*, which pumped out her flooded holds and escorted her to sheltered waters.

Before the search and rescue authorities had finished with *Hey Dad*, the next mayday came in. This time it was from farther north, in the always-rough Dixon Entrance. The seventy-seven-year-old *Bethune*, her wooden hull loaded down with seventeen metric tons of halibut, had decided to run for Prince Rupert early that morning, even though the 9 a.m. weather broadcast had changed little from the previous evening. The *Bethune*'s skipper thought he had plenty of time to find shelter. But over the next ninety minutes, the wind had risen to forty knots and the seas were as high as a two-storey building. The pounding from following seas was so great that the *Bethune* was throttled back. It was now that the skipper noticed his stern was beginning to sink and his boat was listing to port. He bravely decided to bring the *Bethune* about and run across the wind, hoping to wallow down the troughs of the huge rollers toward closer shelter at Rose Spit. Fifteen minutes later, a scant eight nautical miles from safety, with his bilge alarm ringing continuously to warn that the hold was flooding, he ordered his three crewmen to abandon ship. As they went overboard into their life raft, with the seas running nearly five metres in height, its rope became entangled with the rigging of the foundering boat. Fearing that they would be dragged down with the sinking vessel, the four men leaped into the sea. Three of them wore immersion suits, designed to keep the wearer afloat and insulated from the killing cold of the water. One, however, had only a pair of flotation coveralls. His life expectancy in the frigid sea would be a matter of minutes. It was 11:55 a.m.

Sailors have long known that in shipwrecks at northern latitudes it is not drowning but hypothermia which kills first and most frequently. In this condition, the blood retreats from the body's extremities, including the brain, and vital functions become dormant. This is one reason that so many deck-hands never learn to swim. Why bother when a few minutes in the sea's icy embrace means a soft slide into oblivion and a far gentler death than drowning?

The immersion suit was invented to save the swimmer and the non-swimmer alike in wintry ocean conditions. It floats, it makes a castaway visible in the water, it seals out the bitter cold. But if the idea is a good one, it has been more difficult to realize in the real world of seamanship. People who wear immersion suits are not the stuff of laboratory experiments. They are people engaged in heavy labour in dangerous environments, from deep-sea drilling platforms to vulnerable fish boats. In the past, immersion suits have not always worked. The fabric has been holed by fish hooks or sharp pieces of equipment; the zippers have leaked; in choppy seas, the water has leaked down the neck or the glued seams have parted. In many of these cases, the wearers have died as quickly as those without suits. Still, the suits offer the best hope for survivors in the water, and intense research by the Coast Guard, oil industry and off-shore vessel operators continues the look for a system that will be durable as well as mobile, will offer thermal protection as well as dexterity and visibility as well as flotation.

For the *Bethune* crewman who went into the water without a suit five minutes before noon on April 25, all this mattered less than the fact that a quick-thinking commander in the search and rescue co-ordinating centre at the Esquimalt naval base had diverted three aircraft and a ship from the *Hey Dad* incident. A U.S. Coast Guard *Sikorsky* arrived to pluck him to safety less than five minutes later. In all, the crew had spent eight minutes in the raging sea. Their last sight before hospital was the *Bethune*, listing heavily to starboard and staggering under the waves that broke over her decks. She was never seen again.

By now, the storm had arrived in its full fury and marine

radio bands crackled with distress signals and reports from frightened skippers who had never before seen such conditions. Precisely thirty minutes after the U.S. helicopter departed to ferry the crew of the old *Bethune* to hospital, another mayday was logged from the *Miss Rachel*. At thirty tons, with a tough fibreglass hull built in 1976, the *Miss Rachel* had a powerful diesel engine and the latest navigation aids in the form of radar, depth-sounders, communications equipment and a wind velocity indicator. She was also fully equipped with survival gear for her crew of four, carrying two lifebuoys, life-jackets and a four-person inflatable life raft that had been serviced only the month before.

Like *Pacific Traveller*, the *Miss Rachel* had been fishing long hours and anchoring in the open at night to take full advantage of the halibut opening in Hecate Strait. Her skipper, too, had heard the storm warning early that morning, but it was for the west coast of the Queen Charlotte Islands. Nevertheless, by 8 a.m. the weather was deteriorating so fast that the *Miss Rachel* cut loose her remaining longline, lowered the poles which extend like outriggers and serve to stabilize a fish boat in rough seas and ran like hell for shelter.

She was making good headway when the disaster occurred. The tip of one of her stabilizer poles snagged something in the water — maybe a wave crest, maybe a deadhead — nobody saw what it was. They did, however, see the top of the pole snap off and whipsaw back toward the boat, where it wedged between rudder and rudder post, jamming the steering gear far over to starboard. The *Miss Rachel* was critically disabled. If she attempted to make headway, the jammed steering gear would force her to turn broadside to a running sea just one nautical mile off the rocks. Her skipper killed the big diesel engine and dropped anchor, prepared to ride out the gale until he could clear his rudder. With two other rescue operations going on in the area, the search and rescue commander at Esquimalt had the reports of his aircraft to judge by. Conditions were deteriorating rapidly, and the *Miss Rachel* was in an exposed and terribly precarious condition. It was clear that the weather was going to get a lot worse before it got better. Should her cable part in the violent swells, the crippled vessel would almost certainly be carried into the surf crashing over Halibut Rocks, just over one kilometre to the north. Search and rescue command diverted the Coast Guard cutter *Point Henry* to take off the stranded fish boat's crew.

Struggling through heavy seas, the *Point Henry* did not arrive until almost 4 p.m. Her captain found the *Miss Rachel* pitching and rolling at the end of her anchor cable. The Coast Guard cutter could not close with the stranded fish boat, so the skipper dispatched her inflatable rubber boat to take off the crew. The mission rapidly degenerated into a debacle, not through any fault of the rescuers but because of the almost impossible conditions. By now, the storm was at its worst, and the ships were going up and down like unco-ordinated elevators in a busy three-storey building.

In a display of courage that earned an official commendation in the federal government's marine casualty investigation, two rescue specialists from the *Point Henry* came alongside the *Miss Rachel* and managed to get two crew members into their rubber boat. The first of the rescued crew was put safely aboard the Coast Guard vessel, but as the second man attempted to scramble to safety from the bucking boat he snagged his clothing on a cleat. While he tried desperately to free himself, the inflatable boat was swamped by a breaking sea, drowning the outboard engine. It, too, now drifted before the storm, and the captain of the *Point Henry* was as powerless to aid the rescuers as he was to assist the *Miss Rachel*.

Once again, hidden beyond the curve of the horizon far to the south, making his decisions on the basis of electronic communications, the search and rescue commander had anticipated events. A twin-rotor Labrador helicopter from the Canadian Armed Forces base at Comox and two Sikorsky choppers tasked from the U.S. Coast Guard converged over the *Miss Rachel*. The Canadian Forces crew, trained in aerial rescue, immediately winched aboard the three men drifting in the inflatable boat and transferred them back to safety on the pitching deck of the *Point Henry*.

Standard Canadian procedure calls for a search and rescue technician to be placed aboard a distressed vessel to assist in the speedy aerial evacuation of crew members who are frequently frightened and almost always inexperienced in such practices. In this case, an expert was lowered from the Canadian Forces Labrador to the violently pitching deck of the *Miss Rachel*. Storm winds were now steady at seventy knots, well above the hurricane force rating of sixty-four knots on the wind scale. To make things worse, the seas were running as high as ten metres, roughly the height of a standard power pole, and the crests were exploding in the forceful gusts, creating a blinding zone of spray and rain above the ocean's surface. It was into this maelstrom that the rescue technician descended at the end of his long hoist cable. Despite the buffeting, he reached the deck and attached a guideline from the helicopter hovering above. But just as he was preparing to attach a rescue harness to the first of *Miss Rachel's* two remaining crewmen, the fish boat plunged into a wave trough. As the deck fell away beneath his feet, the rescue technician bounced at the end of his hoist cable, still attached to the helicopter above. He crunched heavily into the fish boat's rigging and spun away into space. Rescuers above winched him up and away from the flail of the ship's masts and troller poles, but just short of the aircraft the hoist cable parted and he plummeted twenty metres back into the boiling ocean. Miraculously, when he bobbed to the surface he was right beside the *Point Henry*, which took him aboard. The Coast Guard cutter's first aid specialist assessed his wounds and diagnosed internal injuries. The *Point Henry's* captain weighed the danger to him against the danger to the men still aboard *Miss Rachel* and made the hard decision — he requested immediate permission to take the injured man to hospital at the port of Prince Rupert.

At the same time, the Coast Guard was forced to respond to its own medical emergency. The Canadian Forces Labrador ran out of fuel. Its pilot had pared things to the bone in staying over the stricken fish boat. Now, his gauges were reading empty and he was in danger of crashing into the sea himself. The Labrador withdrew to the nearby shore and set down in the nearest clearing big enough to accommodate the aircraft. The tanks were dry, and the helicopter crew would wait until the Coast Guard's smaller Sikorsky could be diverted with enough fuel for the bigger craft to make it to base.

It was at precisely this moment that *Miss Rachel's* anchor cable parted. She had been fighting for her life for six hours, and once again she was drifting toward the rocky shoals of the Pacific graveyard. The skipper sent a plaintive mayday on channel sixteen of his VHF radio telephone, but there would be no help now. The *George E. Darby* had been tasked to replace the *Point Henry*, but she was faced with nine hours of steaming across hurricane-swept seas. The two men aboard *Miss Rachel* raced frantically to rig a second anchor. It dragged uselessly across the bottom as the distant line of surf grew more and more visible. Then, eighteen hours after the nightmare had begun, the dragging anchor snagged and held. The sea now did what the crew was unable to do. It ripped loose the debris which had jammed the rudder and cleared the fouled propeller. *Miss Rachel* was still in trouble, but she was no longer entirely helpless. Still, no one could assess the damage beneath the water-line. Her skipper decided it was safer to stay at anchor and test his boat's sailing capabilities only in another desperate emergency. The weary survivors settled in for a cold and fearful night awaiting the Coast Guard ship's expected arrival at 6 a.m. the next morning.

While the dramatic story of the *Miss Rachel* had been unfolding, a cascade of other incidents had stretched the resources of Canadian search and rescue teams to the breaking point. Half an hour after ships and aircraft had converged on *Miss Rachel*, the *Gibson*, disabled in shallow waters in the north end of Hecate Strait, issued her own mayday. It was followed thirty minutes later by a distress signal from *Gotstad*, also foundering in heavy seas. By now the search and rescue commander was running out of aircraft and ships.

The *Gotstad*, burdened with almost seven metric tons of halibut and a ton-and-a-half of ice, was another boat that had begun fishing that morning in flat calm conditions and had been surprised by the suddenness and power of a storm for which the marine weather broadcasts had not been sufficiently clear. At 1 p.m. on April 25, her skipper had looked at the freshening wind, ordered the crew to cut the halibut skates that were still out and run for safe harbour. Forty-five minutes later, the *Gotstad* was hove-to and trying to survive the hurricane. Three times over the next two hours, the hold of the boat was to flood. On the first two occasions, the crew pumped the bilges dry to the planks. The third time, the pumps could not cope, and the skipper ordered his two deck-hands to put on their life-saving gear and prepare the life raft. This they partially inflated and secured alongside the vessel in preparation for quick access in the event they had to abandon ship.

The departure, when it came, was far quicker than the *Gotstad*'s crew could have anticipated. By now, the boat's stern was sinking rapidly as water poured into the hold from an unfound breach in the hull. The skipper later told marine casualty investigators that he kicked in the *Gotstad*'s engine and increased speed in the hope that the flooding could be slowed enough for the bilge pumps to cope with the excess water. The tactic failed and, to complicate things, the half-inflated life raft broke loose and began drifting away to the stern. At this point, the skipper decided his boat was lost and that the life raft offered a better chance of survival. He used the time he might have spent climbing into his own immersion suit to stay at the wheel, bringing the crew as close as possible to the drifting life raft.

By the time he abandoned ship, the *Gotstad*'s stern was submerged and water was pouring into the wheel-house. But the crew would have only a few feet to swim to the raft. They leaped into the six-metre swells, dragged the shivering skipper into the raft with them and stuffed him into the immersion suit to which he was still clinging. Behind them, the *Gotstad* rolled on her side, her engine choked and finally died and she vanished under a huge breaker. An hour later, a Buffalo from 442 Squadron at Comox had located the bobbing raft, marked it with a smoke flare and guided a U.S. Coast Guard helicopter to the scene to winch the survivors aboard. The skipper had been in the water without his immersion suit for a matter of seconds, but already he was showing symptoms of hypothermia.

In the storm below, the eighty-year-old *Gibson*, a wooden hull built in Tacoma, Washington, in 1915, was also taking water. She was carrying two metric tons of halibut and five tons of ice when the storm caught her in exposed and shallow waters. Her skipper, too, had listened assiduously to the marine weather forecasts and had been deceived by what he heard. He also had twenty years experience on the fishing grounds, seven of them as a captain, and, unlike many of his colleagues, he held a master's certificate of competence. He watched the weather build and his instincts told him that what he was seeing and what he was hearing on the radio were poles apart. He ordered the crew to batten down for severe weather and turned to run for Skidegate on the Queen Charlotte Islands.

By 1 p.m., the seas were breaking over the *Gibson*'s decks and the pounding was taking its toll. A fuel tank welded to an iron stanchion on the boat's port side had broken loose and had begun to move with the rhythm of the sea and the sloshing liquid within. Although there were less than six centimetres of play in the broken tank, it was enough to cripple the *Gibson*. As the vessel yawed and wallowed in the towering seas, the filling pipe from the moving fuel tank pried apart the planking of the main deck. Soon, the sea was pouring through on to the batteries immediately below. When the batteries shorted out, the boat lost power to all her navigation and communications equipment. She was now deaf, dumb and blind. The crew managed to seal the leak in the decking, dry the batteries, get the bilge pumps working and restore electrical power long enough for the skipper to let marine authorities at Prince Rupert know of his difficulties.

But by 2:30 p.m. the boat was beginning to come apart in the pounding seas. An eye bolt restraining one of the long trolling masts sheared off, and the fourteen-metre pole on the starboard side began catching in the wave tops, bending like a bow and then flailing wildly as it sprang free. The *Gibson*'s crew struggled to secure the thrashing mast before its rigging fouled the propeller. They succeeded, but the boat was now without its starboard stabilizer. She was only four nautical miles from the rocky shore, dead in the water and drifting before a wind that was gusting to eighty knots and pushing eleven-metre seas. The water here was too shallow for the *George E. Darby*, but a helicopter equipped with power winches and a recovery basket was hovering overhead. With night about to fall, the skipper decided to abandon the ship. One by one, wearing their immersion suits, the crew stepped over the stern and into the wild sea, where they were hoisted to the U.S. Coast Guard chopper.

A little to the south, a boat called the *Dee-Jay* had suffered the same fate. She too had listened to the marine forecast and put her skates in the water, only to chop them loose at noon and run northeast before the storm. Ninety minutes later, the winds were blowing at a steady seventy knots and the *Dee-Jay* was overtaken by a series of giant waves. One after the other, they broke over her stern, stripping away the fishing gear stowed there and smashing a metal davit. The skipper brought his boat about, pointed the bow into the wind and hove-to to wait out the bad weather. It was a fruitless attempt. The seas grew even bigger. At about 2:30 p.m., a tremendous roller curled over the foredeck and smashed the main window of the wheel-house. The sea poured down the hatches into the engine room, soaking the batteries and killing the *Dee-Jay*'s electronics. Now, the skipper turned again and let her run with the sea, but twenty minutes later he was convinced that to save the lives of his men he would have to abandon ship before dark. The *Dee-Jay* was listing forty-five degrees to port and rolling violently as water in the bilges began to affect her trim. He turned her broadside to the wind and attempted to run down the trough of the waves toward the *George E. Darby*.

With unsecured trolling poles lashing the decks and visibility down to almost zero in the violent seas, the search and rescue crews decided it was impossible to winch the survivors from the pitching deck. Nor could the rescue ship approach the rolling fish boat in such heavy seas. The next alternative was the men abandoning the *Dee-Jay* for their inflatable life raft, which would at least provide a clean platform. But the life raft was punctured by something during launching and deflated almost immediately. Now, the men were faced with stepping into the sea and taking their chances. Not one of them had an immersion suit. They put on their key-hole life preservers and jumped over the stern rail into the freezing water.

One could not have asked for a more professional rescue from the crew of the U.S. Coast Guard *Sikorsky*. With hypothermia a critical factor, the chopper crew from Sitka, Alaska, secured and winched aboard one survivor every three minutes, saving all four men and whisking them to Prince Rupert. By now, the U.S. Coast Guard flight crew had saved fourteen Canadian seamen from four boats, and they were approaching their mandatory rest period. Instead, the pilot requested and received permission to continue flying whatever rescue missions were required by the Canadian search and rescue command.

When Leonard Egolf and Randy Morrison had decided to run for shelter, they must have been aware of the perilous nature of their position. By mid afternoon, the marine radio bands were alive with distress signals and reports of severe weather. Some of the messages were coming from another Ucluelet boat, the *Galleon*, about eighteen kilometres to the south behind *Pacific Traveller*. The storm reached her first, and *Galleon*'s signals must have alerted Egolf to the monster that was gaining on him and his little boat. What finally happened to the *Galleon* remains a mystery. Her fate can be partially pieced together from radio distress calls, the last one recorded at 9:02 p.m. It was a report that she was hove-to with her decks awash and rolling heavily. The next clue comes from the dead crew itself, skipper Neil Swan and deckhand Pierre Bernier. They were found floating in their immersion suits, but the suits had filled with water through rips in the midriff and thigh, tears that seemed consistent with chafing against a sharp object. Presumably, the *Galleon* capsized and the two men clung to the hull until their suits chafed through and the cold finished them off.

For the crew of *Pacific Traveller*, however, the nightmare was just beginning. Half way through her run for shelter at Spider Anchorage, the chain which transmits power to her steering gear suddenly parted. Access to the chain, which resembles a motor-cycle chain and rides on a pair of sprocket wheels, is through a cockpit hatch on the rear deck. It was into this hatch that Egolf was forced to descend to repair the broken chain. While he was below decks, with the weather worsening by the minute, *Pacific Traveller* drifted five nautical miles to the north of her course. Egolf returned to his wheel-house to find winds exceeding forty knots, heavy seas and almost no visibility in the pouring rain and spray. By now, the safety of Spider Anchorage was beyond hope. The skipper decided to run before the storm for shelter behind Cape Mark to the north.

One after the other, following seas were surging over *Pacific*

Traveller's low stern. Morrison decided he had better have a look. What he saw was horrifying. The hatch that covered the rear cockpit was torn away, and water was pouring in with every wave. At that moment, a massive breaker crashed over the stern and the rudder jammed fast. *Pacific Traveller* wallowed in the tempest. Morrison raced to the cabin below to retrieve the two immersion suits he was certain they would need. When he returned, there was nobody in the wheel-house. Egolf had gone aft — in the words of the marine casualty report, "with complete disregard for his own safety" — in a vain attempt to repair the steering gear and nail a temporary plywood cover over the cockpit.

The captain was too late and the plywood wasn't big enough to cover the opening. When Morrison looked out the window, he saw only the green prism of a wave so big it had buried the whole boat. He struggled into his survival suit. As the engine room began to flood, Egolf made his way back to the wheel-house, not for his immersion suit but to get off a last desperate mayday and *Pacific Traveller*'s position before the electronics went out. It was 7:05 p.m.

With her holds flooded, the boat rolled violently to starboard and lay on her side, throwing Egolf and Morrison out of the wheel-house. They clung to the rigging and then Morrison realized that his skipper's immersion suit was still inside. Egolf hauled himself up the sloping deck but couldn't find the survival suit among the flotsam and debris. He didn't have time to stay and look, as *Pacific Traveller* was foundering beneath him. The captain clambered back out and sat on the capsized vessel's side. He tried to lash himself to the rail, but, although he had been in the water only a few minutes, he was already too cold and numb to tie secure knots. "I can't hang on much longer," he told Morrison, then a wave came and he was gone. He yelled something as he went, but Morrison couldn't make it out in the screaming of the wind and spray. Another wave came and Morrison, too, was torn from the *Pacific Traveller*. For a few seconds, he caught the white flicker of the boat's hull about forty metres away, then he was absolutely alone on the dark sea.

Around him in the night were only the restless manes of the sea's conquering horses and the endless hiss of rain and spray. Carried on the seventy-knot wind, it spiked into his face with the force of driven nails. And the cold. Even with the insulation of his immersion suit, the ocean seemed as cold as death. He remembered his life-guard training: stay alert, stay upright, keep your face out of the water, keep moving, but slowly, slowly, to conserve energy, go with the wind and the currents. He swallowed salt water deliberately, used his body to heat it, then pissed back into his suit to raise the temperature of the thermal layer between him and the sea. It was a calculated risk. If he wasn't found soon, keeping the water in his suit warm wouldn't save him from a worse death by thirst and dehydration.

Above him, even the Canadian Forces' specialized surveillance plane, scanning Hecate Strait with all the sixth and seventh senses of black-box electronic warfare, even the long-range *Aurora*, named for the magical displays of northern skies, even she had turned back to shore for the night. Randy Morrison, raised up on the waves like an offering to the sky and then sucked back down to lie in the belly of the sea, was as alone as any human being can be.

He had been drifting for five hours, his legs gone numb from the constant immersion, the sound of the wind and the sea subsiding into a kind of cosmic white noise, his spirits sunk to the point where he had contemplated simply opening his survival suit and letting the cold take him. How could he expect rescue, so small a figure in such a vast and empty seascape? It was then that he saw the light, a brilliant white light circling him on the dark sea. What it was he can't guess to this day. Some mysterious natural phenomenon, some kind of luminescent sea creature churned up from the deeps, a ghost boat, hallucination, a glimpse through the doors into whatever comes after life? All he knows, he said later, is that the light renewed his hope of rescue. He knew he did not want to die at night, alone on the dark sea. He prayed.

Close to dawn, he saw the rescuers he'd been praying for. He saw them clearly. They were aboard an old wooden boat, a long one, like the schooners that once plied the western halibut grounds. "Old guys in long, grey coats," he recalled from his hospital bed for a *Vancouver Sun* reporter. "They beckoned me and said, 'Come on, get aboard.' They were calling to me to come to them. I reached out to them, and my arms went through the side of their boat."

When dawn did come, it was not the dawn he had expected, but the milky white haze of blindness. The sea salt had leached the moisture out of his eyes, leaving them the pale and gelid as hard-boiled eggs. Whatever he had seen the night before, it had been with vision of another kind. He had now been in the water for twelve hours, still treading slowly with his senseless legs, still keeping his blind face out of the water, trying to keep the sense of up and down in his near weightless condition. The dawn he could not see flooded across the western sky, the sun rising behind the snowy peaks of the Coast Range to shoot its brief arrows of gold beneath the scudding clouds of the storm.

At 7:05 a.m. the wreck of the *Galleon* was found, with the bodies of her crew drifting beside her. Not far away was the wreck of the *Pacific Traveller*. There were no signs of life. An hour later, a sharp-eyed watch on the Coast Guard cutter *Racer* spotted a fleck of orange against the grey sea. It was Morrison, still moving weakly, still treading water. He did not respond to their signal at first because he couldn't see them. Then they hailed him. The voice yelled out of the grey haze, "Grab this." But this time when he reached out, his arms did not go through the sides, they struck the hard, real circle of life — a ring thrown from the deck of the Coast Guard cutter. He grabbed it, clung to it as they pulled him back into this world from wherever he had been.

Of his skipper Leonard Egolf, we only knew that he vanished into the graveyard of the Pacific and not a trace was ever found. And as for the miracle of Randy Morrison, what did he plan to do with the rest of the life that had been handed back to him? After a time, he recovered his vision and finally escaped the boredom of hospital beds and solicitous nurses. A *Vancouver Sun* reporter caught him heading for the docks and asked him what he planned to do with the mysterious gift of his life. He explained with plain eloquence the elemental imperatives that govern lives lived at the edge of the world. "I'm going back fishing," he said. "I have to."

A Certain Slant of Light

"The light enters into the darkness
that we may see it not only with
our two eyes, but with the one eye,
which is the heart . . . "

Black Elk

THE HEARTWOOD OF OUR PRESENT

If the making of history is a conscious act of men and women, a decision to establish a sequence of priorities in their collective experience, then the accurate documentation of historical events is critical in providing shape to the social and cultural process from which the present state of Canada emerges. This rendering of some sense of human permanence in the flux of time and vast landscapes, this act of making history in the mind, is the loom on which we weave the cultural fabric of the nation. If the fabric today seems somewhat threadbare, it is because our politicians, in large measure, appear to think that they alone are of historic value and their simple presence is sufficient for posterity.

Evidence of the neglect attendant upon this attitude is found both in the cavalier approach displayed by our legislatures toward history that does not involve their own immediate place in it and in the generally sorry state of archival and documentary resources across the country. In Alberta, one of Canada's wealthiest regions, where cabinet ministers found more than $50 million to improve the grounds outside their windows, the relatively impoverished provincial archives has been forced to rely heavily on non-professional volunteers to conduct its business. Tens of millions of dollars have been made available for the construction of interpretative centres at buffalo jumps and dinosaur beds, but this is less from a commitment to the province's history than to an enhancement of the tourist industry. While visitors flood the interpretive centres, small budgets restrict access to Alberta's archives to those hours when most members of the general public are at work and cannot use the facility.

Frequently, it turns out, the archives are not much help to

serious researchers in any case. A 1988 investigation by the province's independent audit office discovered that more than 90 per cent of the documents directed to the archives had been neither sorted, nor evaluated, nor even recorded in an itemized inventory. Tons of records of great historical significance and monetary value had been simply dumped in warehouses without regard to the environmental controls essential to the preservation of fragile papers. Rolled maps and film reels were found to have no protective coverings, and documents themselves were stored in already damaged boxes. "Historical records in the custody of the provincial archives are not adequately protected against loss or damage," the auditor concluded.

The consequences of such shoddy practice are most immediately evident in the jurisdiction of Alberta's western neighbour. In British Columbia, the invaluable early records of the B.C. Provincial Police sat in a leaking warehouse until water damage had rendered illegible much of the irreplaceable personal and official correspondence dealing with the early administration of justice on the western frontier. More recently, the preservation of an astonishing and important collection of glass plate photographs recording the social life of the pioneer Asian community in a West Coast coal-mining town had to be underwritten for the local Canadian museum by a Japanese department store company. This is a shameful state of affairs, although we must all bear responsibility for the election to public office of the cultural illiterates who force us to beg wealthy foreigners to fund the preservation of our own remembrance of history.

As individuals, we are nothing more or less than an accumulation of memories. It is this matrix of remembered events that provides a context in past experience for our awareness of the present, and it is this remembered past that enables us to move into the future. Those of us who have witnessed the ravages of Alzheimer's disease, which systematically eradicates memory from the human brain and in so doing irreversibly alters the mind, are aware of how the ebbing of memory is also the ebbing of much of what it is to be human in the first place.

Societies, being nothing more or less than the grouping of individual consciousness and the expression of sets of values that evolve out of shared experience, undergo the same kind of process. Those rendered incapable of transmitting the memory of their collective experience are doomed societies, doomed to fragmentation of cultural values, doomed to a pathetic inability to understand what is happening to them. So, politicians notwithstanding, accurate, easily accessible knowledge of history and of our collective cultural origins is of paramount importance to a Canadian society that is determined to survive in the world.

Many centuries ago, at a time when the people of Ireland were being converted to Christianity, much as the Indian people of Canada were converted by men such as Father Brébeuf and Father Lacombe, the missionaries from the Church of Rome persuaded the high Irish king that he should banish the poets from his court. These poets, with their bronze-strung harps, were certainly wild and undisciplined men by contemporary Christian standards. Their beliefs and traditions were deeply rooted in the pagan religion of which the ancient Druids had been priests. They bore a definite enmity toward the new Christian religion, which they sensibly feared would displace them and the traditions they represented. These poets sang in the king's hall, and their songs represent the oldest extant work in the native literary heritage of the British Isles. Their work provides the ancient trunk from which grows one of the main branches of our own intellectual culture. In their own time, they served a powerful social function. Their poems contained the most ancient history of the Celtic peoples. They kept detailed genealogies in their mental filing cabinets. They told the mythology of their nations, kept track of the lineage of royal families and served as living libraries for the laws of the society in an illiterate age. In a way, travelling around the country from household to household, they were like CBC's "Morningside" and the Canadian Press, transmitting gossip and news from one region of the kingdom to another.

The Irish king had been persuaded by his Christian priests that these troublesome heathens should be banished from Ireland. But one native Irish priest named Columba, who had the advantage of being of royal descent himself, intervened with the king and urged him to reconsider. Columba argued that to banish the poets, troublesome as they were, would be to amputate Ireland's understanding of itself. These men, with their heads full of visions from the past, these men alone, and not all the gold in the king's treasury, were the true wealth of the nation. To banish them would be to banish the past. To banish the past would be the destruction of Ireland and its people.

Columba prevailed in his wisdom and was later sainted for his work in Ireland. What he told that ancient king is equally important today. It was not accident centuries later, when the English were still trying to conquer Ireland, that one of their major objectives was the eradication of the Irish language and with it the whole body of myth, legend and historical tradition that made the Irish people feel unique and connected to one another through a common past. The English almost succeeded, but in the end they failed and the Irish have embarked upon a program to reclaim their language and everything contained in it. They understand that they will find their future in their past.

For this reason, we should sympathize with the struggles of our native peoples and other minority groups to preserve their cultural and linguistic distinctiveness in the face of our own dominant cultures. Ultimately, it is in all our best interests to ensure that the survival of Cree, Dogrib, Ukrainian, French or Kwakiutl be secured in our community. In the end, it is the same for all of us. To find out where we think we are going in this confusing world with its murky possibilities, we must first attempt to discern where it is we think we have come from.

Our own national ability to learn the past and map the future for Canada is far more tentative and uncertain than we might like to think. As yet, we have no Columba to intercede on behalf of Canada's fledgling cultural resources. We do have powerful political interests that see no merit in the continuation of a distinct national identity if it should stand in the way of greater economic gain. We have business interests quite prepared to submerge Canada's unique cultural voice in that of the United States in pursuit of greater profits. We have politicians who see no value in either the aesthetic of natural landscape or the integrity of urban landscape as an archival record of our heritage, no value in the importance of native religions and languages, no value in the preservation of history at a local and regional level, no value in the significance of traditional place names. So we develop a literature that is hostage to a process whereby the majority of decisions regarding which Canadian authors will be published, and which Canadian books will deal with what subjects, are made either in the United States and Britain or by the local proxies of those foreign interests. We develop a broadcast industry in which Americanized programs and programming values saturate prime viewing periods — even on the so-called national network — and in which critical film distribution decisions are made elsewhere. Canadian cities are denied sports teams in the National Hockey League on the basis of decisions by American owners. Slavish pursuit of high-demand American markets by Canada's world-class pulp and paper industry limits the supply, and artificially inflates the cost, of paper for publishing ventures serving Canadian communities large and small.

Canada's future lies in the understanding of its past and the coalescing of a national vision around the events in that past which establish the icons of our moral landscape. Yet, which of those events are the important ones? The politicians and many of our academic historians are obsessed with political and economic posterity. The documentation of this posterity, the politician's justification of the exercise of power and the academic's validation of insight, is structurally based in the bureaucratic process itself. It is based in the process of government, which is designed as much for the industrial production and circulation of documents as it is for the making and implementing of decisions, and it is based in the increasingly specialized and compartmentalized university, which, as it moves farther from its original shape, comes more and more to resemble the government to which it is financially beholden. But experience tells us that the bloodless abstracts of political life are frequently of less importance in determining the truth than the experiences of the inarticulate and the dispossessed. Often, the event dismissed in its own time as insignificant later proves of the greatest moment. Conversely, seemingly momentous events often prove of little actual impact on the course of history.

Our perception of true insight is always flawed, and the structure of factual data on which we build our understanding of present events is always fragile. It is the intangible, the insubstantial, the essentially human elements in the equation that demand our attention. The understanding of events is not fully possible in their absence.

Human culture resembles a coral reef in many ways. The human part of the process is soft, difficult to measure, composed of emotions, passions, beliefs, commitments, concepts — all things that we have difficulty defining, even with the sophisticated tools of language and science. Around those components of the human condition, we build a crust of supporting facts and data which we use to quantify our daily actions. Remove the human pulp from the coral and we are left only with a brittle structure of shells which serves to define the absence of what we wish to study — but not necessarily the thing itself.

Perhaps a better analogy is the excavation of the entombed people of Pompeii and Herculaneum. They were buried when the volcano Vesuvius erupted and buried thousands of victims under mud and lava. The bodies decayed, but over the intervening millennia the outlines remained intact. Thus we learned a great deal about the ancient lives of the Romans by examining the space they left in the stone that surrounded them.

Much of the documentary study of history is based on the

same principle. We learn things not only by what is there but, frequently, by what is not there. This interplay between what is absent and what is present generates the uncertainties and ambiguities which characterize our ability to find the truth in the past — even the highly documented past. I have had a good deal of experience in precisely this uncertainty myself, researching historical events in which one of the key elements revolves around the shooting of a left-wing politician by a policeman during World War One.

The details of the incident are not important here, but one would think that this should be a relatively straightforward matter. This is an event in which the entire apparatus of the state came to play a part. There are police reports, a coroner's report, a preliminary hearing before a provincial magistrate, a grand jury hearing and elaborate newspaper accounts. What is more, this was an event that occurred within living memory. There were men and women alive at the time of the research who knew both the slain man and the slayer at the time of the occurrence. But what I found was that, despite this wealth of documentary and eyewitness material, the circumstances of the event are confused and destined to become murkier yet. The documents themselves offer no nuance or subtle sense of the human beings they record. Indeed, they seem as brittle in their meaning as the empty shells of that metaphorical coral reef. And the people who lived through those times? Their memories are transformed by the substance of their own souls. Their perceptions are constrained by anger and hate, expanded by love and admiration and corrupted by their unconscious desires to remake the pattern and meaning of events to reflect their own perceptions of what occurred. Even in the community of people who were there, I learned, the name of the slain man had begun a transmutation in the mouths of their own children, borne into another name with another spelling and with the trappings of wholly mythical events. The truth of what happened on that sunny afternoon the better part of a century ago was known to only two men. When they died, one at that instant and the other forty years later, the truth died with them. All the documentary evidence in the world will not resurrect that truth, it will only give us indications, a glimmer of possibilities.

So even with the best documentary evidence and oral sources, history is as insubstantial as mist on the river on a summer morning. From one generation to the next, we forget things that seem unforgettable, things so entrenched in our daily lives that we cannot conceive that our grandchildren might not know them. The cultural landscape of Canada is littered with the evidence of such forgetting.

Across the road from my house in the heart of Edmonton there is a park. A pleasant path winds through a small series of rolling, tree-covered hillocks. How many of my neighbours today know that these little hills under their dappled canopy of trembling aspen and wild roses are all that remain of a great coal mine? That the trail is the grade for the coal cars? That my house itself is built on the right-of-way for a line to the mine's power station, and that if you plunge into the poplar thickets to look you can still find the huge concrete footings of that powerhouse? The concrete is mostly corroded and what remains is disintegrating, so rotten you can pick it apart with your fingers. One more generation and it will be completely gone, as much from Edmonton's memory as from the landscape it once occupied.

This process of generations forgetting the immediate past is a reminder of the ephemeral nature of the events of our contemporary experience, which are already beginning to recede from us to become the obscure stuff of our great-grandchildren's history. This is why it is important that we create instruments by which we can remember. These instruments are not merely the formal machineries of archives, libraries, newspapers — no society could afford to construct an archive big enough for everything of conceivable importance. They include the simple equipment of our daily lives, the mnemonics of place names in our communities, the vigorous marking of historic sites, a commitment to the integrity of our past. If we do not take these steps at the local and regional level, we will surely lose our soul as a country.

What we find in the past are only signposts pointing us in a general direction, but all the signposts to the future do lie in the past. Too often we permit those signposts to be torn down in the name of progress, destroying the past in the name of the very future to which it gives birth.

Red Campbell's farm is the site of a shopping mall today. It is not right that his place in history should be forgotten simply because of the press of commerce. Red Campbell and his brothers were successful entrepreneurs, storekeepers and farmers who did a thriving business. During a great coal strike at the beginning of this century, Red Campbell turned his farm over to the starving strikers who had been evicted from their company houses, so that they might keep their little gardens on his land and feed their children. And he let the strikers run credit at his store because he believed they were right and the tycoons of the collieries were wrong. The miners' credit at his store ran to ninety thousand dollars that bitter winter of 1912, and it nearly bankrupted him.

All that remained of Red Campbell seventy-five years later was a blue ceramic tile that set his name into the old sidewalk running past the site of his vanished store. Civic authorities, consumed with the spirit of progress, tore it up to lay a nice new stretch of sidewalk. It is utterly featureless, its main distinction being that it differs in not a single respect from the countless miles of sidewalk that homogenize our streetscapes from Halifax to Victoria.

In Edmonton, the city revved up its chain saws to mow down trees planted by Frank Oliver, the pioneer publisher and politician who helped bring Alberta into Confederation and create the form of Canada as we know it today. The trees were cut to make way for construction of a Heritage Trail celebrating the city's pioneer roots.

It is one thing, of course, to allow the signposts of our past to be torn down by accident or error. This is in the nature of the human condition. And it is in the nature of necessity that sometimes these signposts must be torn down to make way for the new. Old buildings deteriorate and cease to be adequate to the needs of the modern work place. The health and safety of the living must take precedence over the artefacts of the dead. It is quite another thing, however, to have our history wilfully rewritten to reflect the prejudice of people who are less concerned with the preservation of our vanishing past than with serving the venal needs of the present. Examples of cold-blooded betrayal of cultural stewardship occur across Canada and every community has its horror story, but perhaps the sharpest examples are to be found in Alberta.

Back at the turn of the century, the progressive merchants of Medicine Hat decided that the town deserved a name more representative of their energy and industry. The existing name was based on an Indian legend which descended from a great and bloody battle between the Blackfoot and the Cree. But Medicine Hat's commercial interests wanted a name that would ring in the minds of other businessmen. A name that would represent the enthusiasm of the citizens. A name that would attract industry and enterprise. Not Medicine Hat, but . . . Gasburg. This shameless prostitution of history enraged no less than the Nobel Laureate himself. Rudyard Kipling had paid a visit to the town and came away impressed by the romance of its history and the beauty of its location amid the coulees and short-grass prairie above the South Saskatchewan River. The town had been more or less founded in 1883, when an enterprising wrangler from the interior of British Columbia drove a herd of horses eastward through the supposedly impassable Rocky Mountains in anticipation of the CPR railhead arriving at the south fork of the Saskatchewan River. When Kipling was informed of the business community's intent to rename the town with something more appropriate, he entered the debate with a furious letter to the *Medicine Hat News*.

The name Medicine Hat, he said,

has the qualities of uniqueness, individuality, assertion and power. Above all, it is the lawful, original, sweat-and-dust-won name of the city and to change it would be to risk the luck of the city to disgust and dishearten old timers, not in the city alone, but the world over, and to advertise the city's lack of faith in itself. Men do not think much of a family which has risen in the world, changing its name for social reasons. They think still less of a man who because he is successful repudiates the wife who stood by him in early struggles. I do not know what I should say, but I have the clearest notion of what I should think of a town that went back on itself. What, then should a city be re-christened that has sold its name? Judasville.

Seventy years later, Alberta's ruling politicians had learned nothing from Kipling's sermon on the importance of traditional place names. When Premier Don Getty assumed the mantle of departing Premier Peter Lougheed, he rushed with unseemly haste to establish himself as a reverent disciple and to pay homage to his mentor by renaming Kananaskis Park after the retired politician. There is no doubt that most Albertans respect and admire Peter Lougheed as a politician and a statesman, and most would agree that he deserves to have his name established as a legacy for future generations. But to ransack what Kipling would have described as the true and honest history of the province, to rewrite it in the service of toadying political posterity, that was an act of disgraceful cultural theft.

"What's in a name?" some might ask. "Why make a fuss about a couple of syllables?" We make a fuss because historic and traditional place names are as much a part of our collection of signposts to the future as artefacts and monuments. They show reverence for the people upon whose shoulders we stand, and, for those who take the time to search them out, they evoke the human substance in history that is the heartwood of our present.

The kinds of things one finds in a simple name can amaze and illuminate and attach us to a seemingly shadowy and inchoate past. At one point, after spending most of my adult life away, I returned to the region of Vancouver Island where I had spent much of my childhood. I took a break from the writing and research that took me there and went for a walk through the woods to a beach where I once went to fish for cutthroat trout. In those days, I would hike through the dripping rain forest, clambering over slippery deadfalls and getting soaked in the wet underbrush. There's no surer way to break the tip of one's fly rod than bushwhacking through the salal and willows that grow into dense tangles beneath the towering cedar and Douglas fir. I was pleased to find that the area had been made into a little community park and that, while the integrity of the rain forest had been left intact, some trails had been cleared — even one for fishermen.

One of these trails was named McIver's Trail. Now, I'd never heard of McIver, so I set about finding out. I found nothing in the history books, not even the local histories that are seldom circulated outside the immediate community. I found McIver in people's memories — the memories of old people, and the more accessible memories of people like my wife and her father, who had himself grown up in the area more than half a century before.

Jaimie McIver, I was told, came to the place in question by accident. He was sailing his schooner single-handed to the Klondike gold-fields in 1898 when he ran her on to the bars off the estuary of the Oyster River in the teeth of one of those vicious southeasters that come storming three hundred kilometres up the Straits of Georgia from the American border. His schooner foundered and McIver came ashore in the wilderness, clinging to his mast and having salvaged an axe from the wreck.

He had nothing with which to make a fire, so he walked twenty kilometres in the rain until he came across a man who was homesteading. The man gave him two matches, and he walked back to where his ship was wrecked and used one of those matches to light a fire, which he was forced to keep fed and burning all the time. Then, he went into the timber with his axe and made a clearing. In the clearing, he built a log cabin. He set the mast of his lost schooner up in front of the cabin, a signpost of remembrance from his own past, and set about clearing the land to make himself a farm.

When pioneer settlers of that region finally got around to building a road through to the outside world, Jaimie McIver is said to have come down to help with the building of a bridge across the Oyster River. Oldtimers who were there tell me that McIver was paid double wages for his work on the bridge because he did the work of two men. They told me that when another sailing ship ran aground on those treacherous bars off the Oyster mouth, Jaimie McIver went into that freezing, pounding surf to bring survivors ashore. When he was finished, he lashed the bodies of drowned sailors to his shoulders, two at a time, and carried the bodies nearly twenty-five kilometres so that they might have a decent burial in a churchyard. He made four trips like that and thought the last one easy because he had to carry only one sailor. The gravestone of those seven French sailors can be found near the town of Courtenay.

A seventy-year-old woman told me with great fondness how, when she was a pretty young girl, Jaimie McIver, still speaking with the rolling burr of his Scottish Highlands, approached her father and offered to buy her. Only later, with some anthropology courses under her belt, did my mother-in-law recognize that her father was being offered a bride price in a ritual that was as ancient as the remote Scottish clans McIver was descended from.

So what's in a name? Today, McIver's farm is lost, absorbed into an experimental dairy operation run by scientists and technocrats from the University of British Columbia. All that remains of McIver and his strange and wonderful life is a name on a trail through the dripping gloom of an island rain forest. And, of course, the memories of people who knew him. And now the memories of people like you and me. That is what resides in a name.

How about Kananaskis? What's in that name? The name comes to us from illustrious sources. We have it from John Palliser, who passed through the glorious country of the Sarcee and Stoney Indians in 1858. They lay claim of first right to the name Kananaskis. The premier of Alberta thought it was his name to dispose of at his pleasure. He thought so, presumably, because his government developed the countryside with money that was provided by the people of Alberta — money that was earned on the very same land seized from the Indian people in generations long past. But Alberta's politicians, like those in other provinces, think that historic names are just commodities to be used and discarded like styrofoam coffee cups in the smoky back rooms of politics. To them, historic names are currency to be spent when expedience dictates.

Castle Mountain, one of the most spectacular peaks in the Rockies, was renamed Mount Eisenhower in the euphoria after

World War Two and reverted to Castle Mountain when American presidents fell from favour. In Blairmore, a Crowsnest Pass coal-mining town with a strong tradition of militant labour, the main street was named in honour of the outlawed founder of the Canadian Communist Party, imprisoned in the 1930s for his political views. This bit of history was later sanitized by more conservative municipal authorities. Only the retired miners sunning in front of the seniors' home know that the secret name of Main Street is Tim Buck Boulevard.

Renfrew Park, a name with its roots in the origins of the city of Edmonton itself, is arbitrarily renamed John Ducey Park so that municipal politicians may reap the benefit of publicly paying their debt to a much-loved sports figure. And in one consummate irony, a park, originally named by a mayor who was, not once, but twice removed from office by judicial order, is ordered renamed in his honour by his successors, bearing for posterity the name of the departed mayor who had named it something else in the first place. Yet, while the politicians act as though the historic names of their communities are mere largesse to be bestowed as favours — a kind of posthumous patronage — the politicians are wrong, both morally and ethically.

The name Kananaskis does not belong to politicians. It belongs to the people. Most of all, it belongs to history, not just our history but the history of the Indian people before their culture arrived at its fateful confluence with the current of our own. The name Kananaskis refers to a legendary figure from the oral history of the Indian people, a history that has been mightily abused in Canada, and one to which our obligations are no smaller than to our own history.

Kananaskis is said to be the name of a warrior who was struck down by an axe and who miraculously recovered from his grievous head wound and rose up again to become a great leader among his people. This is no trivial name to be discarded at the whim of a politician seeking to ingratiate himself with the party faithful. The counter argument is that there are plenty of other places named Kananaskis. There are plenty of places named Edmonton, too, but that gives no politician the right to change the name to Gettysburg, or Brampton to Davistown, or Ottawa to Mulroneyville.

It is important that citizens themselves — the stuff of their own history — recognize that place names and historic artefacts, these signposts rooted in the past, are the landmarks of Canada's culturally distinct future and not baubles to be heedlessly dispensed with in the name of political expedience and commercial progress.

These are the true riches of our patrimony, the riches that Columba recognized so long ago. It is the important task of ordinary citizens to take ownership of these treasures, not abandon them to the custody of political officials. By making history part of our lives, however small a part, we make ourselves part of the fabric of Canada itself. And when the politicians talk of cultural sovereignty and all that it entails, we can go to bed at night and sleep securely, knowing that, whatever they may say, defence of the sovereignty of Canada rests not in the shallow expedience of their rhetoric but in our own true memories and steadfast hearts.

CHEATING AT THE FACE

They called the place Union, and the real story of Labour Day is written here in a sun-drenched meadow, drowsy with bees and splashed with wild flowers. It is a story written in tears, coal dust, fury and blood. A story to remember that first Monday in each September. For this sunny meadow, high on the northern shoulder of Vancouver Island, browning out in the dry rain shadow of Forbidden Plateau, this sunny meadow is a graveyard. A graveyard of the working class, of the crushed, the burned, the gassed, the blasted and the shot. It is the burial ground of the oppressed, and it hovers as a pale spectre haunting the dark zone of the Canadian conscience.

Like the men who peopled it, like the town of Union itself, the story has become dream, mystery, enigma — scattered nuggets of fact to be sifted out of brittle documents and the collapsing memories of the old. The first clues start up from the blaze of fireweed and goldenrod, rooted among vines that yield tiny, fragrant strawberries. They explode into a tangy red sweetness in the mouth. A kind of Bolshevik communion, the earth exchanging this exquisite beauty for the payment of their poor bodies.

I come to it bored at first, assisting another writer, my wife, by taking on a share of the drudgery of documentary research. Then, I am seduced by the unknown and the never-to-be-known. The clues will lead deep into a maze of mysteries within mysteries, the stuff of romance and legend and myth. Like others before me, I will delve into sheafs of official correspondence in the provincial archives, discover bundles of personal letters still bound after sixty years in faded blue ribbons tied by an unknown lover. I will read the secret reports of police spies, informers, coded intelligence cables, the feverish political landscape of fear and lies, the bizarre sense of eavesdropping on half a fragmentary conversation in the distant room of an echoing hotel. But for now, the clues show only as faded Chinese characters, branded with hot irons into wooden posts, disappearing under a century of weather; some as bundles of burnt incense sticks and bleached prayer papers, ephemeral, white, fluttering among the soft halo of milkweed and black-eyed Susans, a curious counterpoint to the brilliant shout of plastic carnations left in rusting tobacco cans on broken cement slabs.

Still other clues emerge from Japanese elegance, chiselled into stones that crumble back into red earth beneath a whispering stand of pines; curlicues of florid Italian script sweep across stained sandstone pillars; the stolid capitals of Scottish names, their no-nonsense alphabets a strange betrayal of the sweet Victorian sentiments obscured by moss and the accumulation of half a century of dirt on the Presbyterian granite. Some clues are simply cryptic — initials scrawled on a painted rock; rust stains where something was stamped through the galvanized surface of a metal plate; a tattered list in the stylish calligraphy of a hand that predates typewriters.

They don't call the town Union now, they call it Cumberland. It was renamed by a coal baron after the memory of his lost British childhood, an attempt, perhaps, to retreat from the grim source of his present wealth. So Union is vanished into memory like the men who made it, the men who boozed at the Bucket of Blood and lounged outside Shorty's Pool Room and the Vendome Hotel; the gambling men of the fan-tan houses; the whores who worked upstairs at the Halfway, paying their protection money to the provincial constables; the men of Chinatown, Japtown, Coontown. The desperate men who promised never to strike in exchange for a pittance; the steadfast men who raised their kids in tents that whole bitter winter of 1913, the men of Striker's Beach.

Most of this story is names. The names of men who died in the dark, lying on their backs in the two-foot seams, narrow as coffins and tight as the womb, cutting coal from the world's most dangerous mines. The names of men who fought the coal tycoons to bring the miners justice. And the five-day week. And the eight-hour day. And holidays like Labour Day.

There are 289 of these names in this sunny country cemetery. The 288 dead by disaster and Ginger Goodwin, "A worker's friend," slain by a government bullet in 1918. For the most part, they are immigrant names, the muscle and sinew and blood of this country. The Scots, first, refugees from the great diaspora of the Highland Clearances, driven out to make way for sheep and the greed of wool magnates. Then, the Welsh, the Chinese flotsam of the railways, Yorkshire labour organizers gone to ground, Finns on the run from the Czar's secret police, Italian agitators, Irish, Japanese, Ukrainian, American blacks, French and Québécois. Men without names or nationalities or pasts.

They worked hard and they died hard. Here are the words of Hjalmar Bergen, logger, early labour organizer and now a disembodied voice preserved for us by the British Columbia archives Sound Heritage collection, saved for the historical cult of personality that his movement scorned: "Until the union was established, if somebody got killed, that didn't stop anybody from working. No, you'd just throw them to the side and keep on working. You took them out when you had time. That's the way it was, production came first."

At Union, the mines were wet and filled with explosive gas. The miners' lights were the flames of open lamps burning fish oil. Down pit you learned quickly to carry your lamp chest high — too low and it winked out, smothered by the choking gas called black damp; too high and the methane flared with a roar.

Some miners were paid by the ton. It was pick and shovel work, contract work — the more coal you cut, the more you got paid. But you lived in a company town, and there never seemed to be enough to go round.

Poor men take risks. You used a technique called pillar and stall, holding the mine roof up with columns of coal, cutting in the chambers between and leaving just enough strength in the pillars to keep you alive. Sometimes, with another birth coming, or a sickness in the family, you'd cheat a little at the face, shave the margins to get your easy tonnage up.

Here's Ben Horbury, Cumberland miner and another of those voices from the Sound Heritage collection, quoted by Patricia Wejr and Howie Smith in a booklet compiled for the archives:

> After you got to the end of your boundary, they'd come back and take the pillars out, one at a time. And then the roof would start to talk. . . . During that time, you cleared all your equipment out. The section would collapse and then you'd go back in. I've been knocked down by the puff of air when it collapsed because I waited too long getting out. When the roof was coming down, there was also pressure on the face coal and the coal came easy. You could

take it with a pick and pull it down in big chunks. Well, if
you got greedy, if you were loading coal fast and the empty
cars were coming in to you, you stayed until the last
minute, and then ran.

And if you didn't run fast enough, got caught by a blow out or a
rock hurtling out of the face, they laid your body to the side and
you went to the pithead at the end of shift or on the first full coal
car bound for the surface, whichever came first.

The gravestones show miners began dying for the privilege of
work almost as soon as they went below ground. At Union, the
first miner was killed in 1888. Fatal accidents and disasters are
recorded almost annually for the seventy-five-year span of the
mines.

Take as one example, February 15, 1901, 10:40 a.m. — a whole
sixty-four-man shift gone in a single blast down Number Six pit.
The memories of that morning come in bits and pieces, glinting
on the gathering dark like flakes of mica in the washer creeks.
Jimmy Halliday was whistling as the swaying cage took him
down eight hundred feet to his drift. He told the boys above
ground he'd just had word his wife and child were bound westward from Nova Scotia. William Sneddon was silent and drawn.
He was just going underground to collect his tools before heading south to Nanaimo to bury his child. Georgie Turnbull was
just married. Joseph Allison was apprehensive as anybody on
his first shift, anxious to prove his right to a good place at the
face. When it came, the force of the blast threw men to the
ground almost two kilometres away.

"The scene on the top floor of Number Six baffled all attempts
at description with its chaos of twisted pipe, scraps of iron and
wood, splinters from several pounds weight down to sawdust,
some being blown clear from the bottom of the shaft and everything within a radius half-a-mile from the shafthead being
covered with a deposit of the infernal black dust to a depth of
several inches — an appropriate pall for the death-desolated village," wrote an exhausted *Vancouver Province* reporter who hiked
sixty miles over the muddy ruts of a forestry trail to get his
story.

Below ground, the mine rippled with aftershocks; cave-ins
filled stalls with rubble and dense curtains of smoke seethed
with flame. Where there wasn't fire, invisible pockets of deadly
gas collected to asphyxiate survivors lost in the ruin of lightless
tunnels and blocked ventilation shafts.

An hour after the first explosion, mine manager John

Mathews, fire boss William Johnson and two miners Dick McGregor and Charles Webber went down the main shaft. A continuous stream of ice-cold water was drawn from the frozen creek and poured over their descending cage to protect them from gouts of flame and to suppress the smoke and poisonous afterdamp. Two hours later, with McGregor, Webber and Johnson unconscious from breathing gas and smoke, the gritty manager struggled through a landscape that must have seemed like hell itself, dragging his rescue team back to the main shaft, loading them one by one into the cage for the slow trip back to daylight and life.

Far underground, a pit boss named Walker assembled another team for a desperate attempt at cutting through from the undamaged drift of an adjacent second mine. Three of the men trapped in Number Six bore the name Walker, explaining, perhaps, his willingness to break through to the wounded heart of the mine and face the risk that opening a new source of oxygen would suck the inferno down upon the rescuers. Were they father? Brothers? Sons? It seems likely. Kin often went down pit together, working their place as a unit, blood being trusted over strangers in the dangerous conditions. When they died, they died together and whole networks of women and children would be widowed and orphaned at the same instant. In any event, assisted by fellow miners Kesley, Strang, McArthur and Coomb, Walker tried to cut through from a neighbouring shaft. It was a failure.

By next morning, the owners had decided there were no survivors and took the hard decision to protect their considerable investment. They ordered Number Six flooded to prevent fire spreading from burning timbers to the high-quality coking coal of the main seam itself. The Puntledge River, a dappled stretch of trout and salmon water that many of the miners worked with the same skill and precision as their gentlemen bosses, was diverted down an eight-inch main and into the smoking shaft. The horrified *Province* reporter was left speculating on the possibility of survivors in their underground tomb, slowly drowning in the friendly waters that had known the long coil of their casts, split-cane rods dipping and nodding under the jade-green vaults of maple and dogwood.

James Strang, the fearless man who went with Walker on the dangerous attempt to cut a rescue drift to Number Six, soon joined the dead himself. He was killed in an accident a week before Christmas in 1904: "Having finished life's July, he now sweetly rests." He was fifty-four, a veteran of many years in the

pit, and his death was not unexpected. Dying below ground at
Union was commonplace, as it was in all the coal-fields of Vancouver Island. In 1887, 150 men in a 157-man crew perished in a
single accident at Nanaimo. The following year, seventy-seven
men died on the same day at Robert Dunsmuir's Wellington
mine. Miner John Brown remembered the 1923 explosion at
Cumberland that killed thirty-three men: "At the pithead, the
dead men were laid out in rows, like the fingers on your hand."

At first, the miners hauled coal from below ground by bucket.
Robert Dunsmuir paid them just over one dollar for each ton
hauled, then marked it up 800 per cent and sold it in San Francisco. When he decided to undercut competition, he took the
difference out of the men's wages. The profits went to maintain
the magnificent sea-front estate of Hatley Castle near Victoria,
now preserved as Royal Roads military academy, and to buy a
second twenty-acre estate in Victoria for the building of a Scottish castle, Craigdarroch, complete with Italian glass, hardwoods
and thirty-five fire-places. His son James bought a newspaper,
the *Colonist*, founded ironically enough by a radical named
Amor de Cosmos as a platform for his fulminations against the
British establishment. The younger Dunsmuir remade it to serve
the interests of that same establishment and used the *Colonist* to
launch himself into a political career distinguished largely by
corruption, scandals and incompetence. Surrounded by controversy, James Dunsmuir became the only man in British Columbia history to serve as both premier and lieutenant-governor —
and to resign from both posts before completing his term.

His father Robert had been a miner himself, arriving in 1851
from Scotland to work for the Hudson Bay Company. He
discovered a rich coal seam north of Nanaimo, soon to become a
key coaling station for the Royal Navy's operations in the Pacific.
Following some fancy footwork with a scandal-dogged Royal
Navy officer of aristocratic pedigree and good connections, he
wound up proprietor of a new colliery. Dunsmuir was a tireless
worker, a shrewd entrepreneur and a ruthless capitalist who
kept his labour costs low by becoming a fierce and successful
union buster on every front. His antagonism to organized labour
was wedded to a disregard for mine safety that remains legendary in union ranks today. He dismissed and blacklisted those
fire bosses with the temerity to report gas in mines notorious for
being among the gassiest on the continent.

For those forced to accept the conditions, Dunsmuir drove
down their already marginal wages by hiring cheap Chinese
labour from among the desperate multitudes thrown out of

work on completion of the Canadian Pacific Railway through Hell's Gate and the Rocky Mountains. At the turn of the century, these exploited Asian workers, denied their civil and political rights by the most shamefully racist legislation in Canadian history, outnumbered embittered whites in Cumberland by a ratio of three to one and the whites of the town lamented the largest Chinese community in North America outside San Francisco. Across the straits in Vancouver, the racism took more tangible form. On September 8, 1907, whipped up by the demagogues of the Asiatic Exclusion League, fifteen thousand whites rioted, sacking Chinatown and fighting pitched battles with broken bottles and stones against the more militant inhabitants of Japtown.

These differences between the men going into the cemeteries and the men for whom they worked were what radical reformers like Albert Goodwin set out to fight. Ginger Goodwin is today an ideological icon of Canada's labour left — a conveniently red-headed saint murdered in cold blood by the black forces of capitalist conspiracy, his hand-hewn gravestone an artefact copied for the national archives, his name adorning leftist magazines and eulogized by working-class poets. But a search for the flesh and blood remains elusive. Old timers remember him as an unhealthy wisp of a man, mouth full of rotten teeth, but one hell of a soccer player. We know where he was born, in 1887 in a South Yorkshire mining village that remains the heartland of labour militancy in Britain a century later. There is a brief line in the steamship passenger manifests of 1905 listing an A. Goodwin bound for Stellarton, Nova Scotia, aboard the S.S. *Sicilian* out of Liverpool, but whether it is the legendary Ginger is just a guess, and a poor one at that. We have tangible evidence he spent some time in the coal-fields of the Crowsnest Pass and that the memories of his soccer playing abilities were accurate. A medal he once treasured commemorates the Crowsnest championship of 1911 and is a testament to both.

Newspaper accounts of the day confirm his presence as a prominent and articulate socialist who campaigned in the election of 1916. The *Victoria Times*, dismissed by the *Rossland Miner* as a pompous, boot-licking organ of the Liberal establishment, in turn dismissed the budding politician as a well-intentioned neophyte: "Albert Goodwin is a young man, full of the vague and irrational sort of half-baked thinking which passes muster for reason." The *Vancouver Sun* was even closer to the Liberal party, to the profound disgust of its own founding editor, J.P. McConnell, who denounced his wayward offspring as "the harlot of Canadian newspapers. Absolutely shameless in its painted prostitution, it flaunts its rags of deceptions and lies and peddles its spurious wares, its tattered virtue to the Liberal Party and the public." It is worth noting that the paper generally considered closest to the scandal-ridden Liberals of the day was the most strident in its condemnation of Goodwin. In a sharp personal attack, it ridiculed his physical characteristics, complaining that "in a near falsetto voice he reeled off yards of the usual twaddle and economic fallacies of his type of speaker."

Goodwin was anything but popular with the establishment — both in the realm of politics and within the labour movement itself. He was an ardent pacifist in a day when pacifism was scorned as cowardice and a tough and fearless labour organizer despite his ill health. In 1917, as secretary of the Smelter Workers' Union at Trail, Goodwin organized a major strike that was opposed by the union's own international wing. Goodwin was fighting for the eight-hour day in the mines and factories, but the Great War raged in France and the Allies were at their nadir, bled white by the endless slaughters of the Somme and Verdun, faced with the collapse of their Russian ally into the Bolshevik revolution. Canada had just lost sixteen thousand men at Passchendaele, and British Columbia battalions were averaging casualty rates that claimed one out of every two men who had enlisted. The smelters at Trail produced vast quantities of metals essential for the manufacture of British and American bullets to kill Germans in Flanders. To rigid military authorities, the distinction between Bolshevik revolution and the agitations of an outspoken socialist to disrupt the war effort must have seemed a fine one.

In the middle of the five-week strike, Goodwin was reclassified as fit for active military service. He had been classed as unfit before, because of poor health and a lung condition. Suddenly, his health was no longer a factor. The local exemption tribunal, headed up by a friend and social equal of the smelter manager, aimed to send Goodwin to France. Many still believe the plausible argument that he was drafted to muzzle his labour voice. Local legend speaks of a letter from the mine manager to the exemption tribunal asking that Goodwin be reclassified as fit for service, although there is no record that such a document exists or ever existed. But Goodwin did report to the draft board, appealed their decision and, when it was turned down, fled back to Cumberland where he was remembered for his role in a widespread Vancouver Island strike crushed by the army and militia just before war broke out in 1914.

The industrial abattoir of island coal-fields made fertile

ground for labour action marked by union violence, countered by company brutality and characterized by networks of professional spies. The sophisticated secret service apparatus that ran these operations was a chilling foretaste of the shadowy unofficial world of informers, intelligence agents, espionage and counter-espionage that was to herald the full arrival of the twentieth century.

In Cumberland, Goodwin found friends to support him and refuges deep in the gloomy tangles of Douglas fir and hemlock. These forests make the rugged country below Forbidden Plateau some of the most inaccessible terrain in Canada. The government, acting under the powerful authority of the Military Service Act, dispatched a special posse to hunt down the labour leader. The posse was under the jurisdiction of the Dominion Police, a national agency directed by Arthur Percy Sherwood, later knighted for his effectiveness as midwife at the birth of Canada's secret service. The Dominion Police were subsumed by the RCMP in 1919 and, not surprisingly, documentary records of their activities are limited, although there are oblique references in some RCMP correspondence regarding the need to dispose of a certain former Dominion Police operative. No reasons are given, save the inference that his true loyalties may lie elsewhere — with British military intelligence, perhaps?

The Dominion Police team searching for Goodwin was headed by William J. Devitt, a dashing former North-West Mounted Policeman who had served as both chief of police and town clerk at Trail and Rossland when they were rip-roaring frontier boom towns. Devitt had arrived in Canada as a fifteen-year-old immigrant from Ireland and rapidly made a mark for himself with the Mounties. His letter of application to the British Columbia Provincial Police in 1896 offers personal references from none other than legendary Superintendent Sam Steele of Fort Macleod. In that letter, Devitt describes himself as a robust twenty-eight-year-old man, obviously proud of his looks, "fairly well-educated," with light brown hair, blue eyes and a forty-three-inch chest. His sense of patriotic flair impressed the townsfolk of Trail when he led the Dominion Day celebration in 1901, prancing at the head of the parade on a grey charger, flanked by four returned troopers from the South African campaign. When he died, just before Christmas in 1937, at the age of sixty-eight, his obituary noted that Devitt had always been a crack shot with a revolver, winning a gun duel with two escaped bandits as the chief of police for Burnaby in 1931.

During the years before the Great War, Devitt had a habit of showing up on the same hotel guest lists as Malcolm J. Reid, a dominion immigration officer from Vancouver. The son of a coal miner, Reid was an imposing man of military bearing and proud of his association with the Seaforth Highlanders. He is perhaps best known for his role in the sordid Komagata Maru incident of 1914, in which Sikh immigrants were denied entry to Canada. Archival correspondence suggests that Reid worked for Sherwood as an intelligence officer during the war. At one point, Reid is recorded as demanding, and receiving, from the superintendent of the British Columbia Provincial Police, a full accounting of the location of every policeman in the province. None of this was surprising. Reid's connection with intelligence services was revealed in the assassination of his immediate subordinate. Immigration inspector William Charles Hopkinson was an agent of the British India Office charged with spying on Asian activities in B.C. and reporting to the Canadian deputy minister of the interior.

Was Inspector Devitt also involved in intelligence work, Kipling's Great Game of Empire, before the war? Who knows? What is certain is that a number of the police authorities involved had careers that ran in curious proximity to known intelligence operatives. A.T. Stephenson, the chief constable for Nanaimo who was called in to investigate the aftermath of the Goodwin manhunt, was one of them. Before the war, Stephenson had been stationed both in Vancouver, where he worked as a detective on Malcolm Reid's waterfront, and in Cumberland, where he served at the same time that Goodwin was present and where he must have been in contact with the Pinkerton-run spy networks set up to infiltrate the turbulent labour movement.

Devitt also swore in a special agent named Dan Campbell, a forty-six-year-old hotel-keeper with an unsavoury reputation as a bounty hunter and a chequered past in police work. The son of a highly respected policeman, Campbell had himself been cashiered out of the B.C. police in 1905, not long after his father's death. Deeply in debt to the owner of a local gun shop, Campbell was caught supplementing his pay packet with an extortion scheme which shook down Victoria prostitutes. He was dismissed by personal directive from Frederick Hussey, an incorruptible and iron-handed superintendent. From police work, Campbell went to run the Colwood Inn, a local way house and tavern. Victoria police day-books yield a glimpse into his character. Records show the cashiered policeman who forced kickbacks from prostitutes next harassing his former colleagues with mean-spirited complaints about the public sexual conduct of his neighbours' livestock.

Campbell was not atypical of the men recruited for special service with the Dominion Police. In August of 1918, Constable Arthur Arden was arraigned on charges of extorting the equivalent of a month's wages from Giuseppi Tombosso in exchange for not pressing charges. Arden, too, was a former B.C. provincial policeman who resigned to go overseas and was invalided home to a position in the Dominion Police. Court was informed of a mitigating circumstance, that Arden had volunteered for the Siberian Expedition that was to put Canadian troops in the field against Trotsky's Red Army.

The cavalier approach of both Dominion Police and military intelligence toward due process in the enforcement of the Military Service Act clearly caused friction between the federal agencies and the B.C. Provincial Police, who appear to have believed that the normal rules of evidence and arrest had not been suspended simply because there was a war in Europe. Bristling exchanges of correspondence between these authorities and Superintendent Colin Campbell, whose personal mentor had been the highly principled Hussey himself, reveal the intensity of the strained relations. It comes as no surprise to discover Campbell suddenly relieved of his police duties late in 1917 and shuffled off to the obscurity of Oakalla Prison Farm, where he remained warden until retirement.

The western air was tainted by military paranoia about Bolsheviks. Socialists and trade union activists were frequently assumed to be revolutionary traitors by association. Official dispatches of the period are laced with references to the Bolshevik menace, the labour threat, the infiltration of socialist agitators. In Fernie, several Ukrainian miners are arrested for owning an edition of Karl Marx. They had come under suspicion for painting their house with red paint. The Social Democratic Party is banned, as is the Social Labour Party, the Ukrainian Social Democratic Party, the Russian Workers' Union, the Chinese National League and the International Workers of the World. In Vancouver, the chief press censor orders the B.C. Federation of Labour to dismiss the editorial staff of its newspaper, the *Federationist*, and replace them with people sympathetic to government aims.

But by 1917, public sympathy indicates little of the enthusiasm shared in 1914. By now, forty-three thousand men have left British Columbia to fight in France, ten thousand of them have been killed or wounded and eight thousand are declared unfit for further service. The Methodist Church of Canada is calling for the overthrow of capitalism and blames World War One on the economic system. The files of official correspondence are dominated by letters from informers and military cables regarding the suspected whereabouts of draft dodgers, enemy aliens and suspected insurrectionists. At Nanaimo, a holding facility is established. It is officially designated a concentration camp.

Goodwin, in the meantime, had been leading authorities a merry chase. He was exceptionally popular with women and would slip into Cumberland for dances and socials, then vanish like a wraith into the woods. The local people say to this day that Cumberland constable Robert Rushford never had it in his heart to catch Ginger anyway, that like the rest of his friends and neighbours he had an open admiration for the man's principles and convictions. It's said that when Rushford, who doubled as the town's game warden, did encounter Goodwin or any of the other scattered draft evaders living in the woods, he'd shoot his rifle in the air to warn them he was coming. When Campbell came to Cumberland, that atmosphere changed.

Testifying before a Victoria court, Peter McNiven swore that Campbell said to him: "Mac, we are here to get these men dead or alive." Four Italian miners made their way to Victoria at their own expense to corroborate the testimony. Rasie Gievanni told the court that Campbell was open in saying that, where Rushford had been reluctant to shoot Goodwin, he would have shot and intended to bring the draft evader in — "dead or alive." Carlos Cavaliero, himself to die in the mine explosion of 1923, told the court he heard Campbell making the same boast.

On July 26, 1918, Campbell did confront Goodwin near Cruikshank Creek where it rushes toward Comox Lake through the rugged notch between Alone Mountain and the peaks of Rough and Tumble ridge. He shot him in the throat with a soft-nosed bullet, the kind of flat-nosed slug still outlawed for warfare by the Hague conference because it maims so horribly. Campbell said it was self-defence, that Goodwin had pointed a .22-calibre rifle at him. Others believe that Campbell shot Goodwin from ambush, a paid government bushwhacker hiding in the trees. Some evidence suggests that Goodwin's hand had been raised in surrender, that the mushrooming bullet had ricocheted off his forearm and into his neck, blowing apart his spinal cord and killing him instantly. Another witness, Bill Pritchard, reported powder burns more consistent with an execution than a chance encounter. These powder burns are confirmed in evidence given at both the inquest and the preliminary hearing, but why are the burns only around what was

supposed to be the second wound in the neck? How would the
first wound be free of powder burns? And why were police ini-
tially intent upon burying Goodwin's body where it lay in the
bush, until it was retrieved two days later by appalled citizens
from Cumberland who believed, rightly, that a coroner's inquest
was required by law? And what ultimately happened to
Goodwin's gun and personal effects?

Campbell was returned to Victoria under the guard of B.C.
Provincial Police Sergeant F.R. Murray, the same policeman
whose investigation had led to Campbell's dismissal from the
force thirteen years before. Bail was set at ten thousand dollars
with a personal security bond of five thousand. During the preliminary hearing, court heard the official view of Goodwin
summed up by defence lawyer W.C. Moresby: "As to the use of a
soft-nosed bullet, Campbell would have been justified in using a
bomb in self-defence." Strangely, nobody asked why such a
powerful force was mobilized to track down a single draft
evader, particularly since a general amnesty for all deserters and
draft dodgers had been imposed by parliament. Ginger
Goodwin had nearly a month before he was compelled to turn
himself in to the authorities.

The court decided that a *prima facie* case of murder could be
brought against Campbell and referred him to a special Grand
Jury of the Fall Assizes. That tribunal, hearing the case in secret
with Mr. Justice Denis Murphy presiding, dealt in less than
forty-five minutes with a matter that had occupied the Victoria
court for days. Campbell was acquitted, but if he was innocent in
the eyes of the authorities he was guilty in the minds of the
working class. In Vancouver, between the coroner's inquest and
the preliminary hearing of the murder charges, trade unionists
had shut down the city with a general strike. Returned war
veterans mobbed the Labour Temple, destroying furniture and
documents. When they tried the same thing at another hall the
next day, the longshoremen fought them off in a pitched battle.
In Cumberland, the whole community turned out to march
Ginger Goodwin's coffin through the streets to the little
cemetery where he lies today, surrounded by his comrades from
the mines.

Ben Horbury again, from the B.C. archives Sound Heritage
collections: "The casket was packed shoulder high right through
Cumberland. When one bunch of men got too tired, another
bunch went in. He was so highly thought of, you know. A man
has to be highly thought of when he's accused of a crime and
killed as a criminal and yet the whole town turns out for the

funeral and he's packed shoulder high through the town."

Only a month after Goodwin's funeral, sixteen miners are killed at Protection Island near Nanaimo when the cable for the Western Fuels Company cage breaks and drops the men six thousand feet down the main shaft. In the mines of Cumberland in 1918, there are seventeen disasters yet to happen and seventy-nine graves yet to be filled.

A lifetime after all that, somebody still carefully tends Goodwin's grave, with its rough-hewn piece of rock for a head-stone and the hand-carved hammer and sickle. And who is the woman who still lays down red roses in the snow? And who under a winter moon leaves midnight footprints around the grave?

The mysteries deepen with time. The old men, who knew, now join the legend one by one under grass and wild flowers. Was Ginger Goodwin assassinated by his government? Were the miners that surround him murdered too, in their own way, by the system Goodwin fought to change? It depends on your point of view. Whatever that view is, they deserve remembering. And since Labour Day is their day, that is the day to raise them a toast. Remember them well. When the Union miners go from your memories, they are gone forever.

1888 — G. Feodamard; Kilpatrick.

1889 — Yeut Ah.

1890 — Yon Yun; Huey.

1891 — John McAllister; John Cushon; Chue Ah; Yung Won.

1893 — Coon Ah; David Thomas; I. Thew; R. Gibson.

1894 — Ah Tuck.

1895 — Wong Ching; Ah Wing; John Jess; John Rowe.

1896 — A. Leland; Wm. Moore; Ah Yum; Suen Tai; Chung Chu He.

1897 — Ah Lun; T. Taniguchi.

1898 — Okading; Ah Moy Chin; He Da; Alf Whittle.

1899 — Sen Mah; T. Torrence; Thos. B. Jones; Bernard Zucca.

1900 — Gus Ruffings; Clue; Takematsu; L.C. McDonald; Kin Mar; J.J. O'Neill; John Barkley; Ah Duck.

1901 — Joe Allison; Avo Chisosa; Chas. Bono; P. Bardessona; Chow Bing; Boo Wong Hik; Joe Crosetti; Mah Chung; Der Chow; Lung Chung; Fook Chung; Lam Chung; Mah Chow; Wong Chow; D.M. Davis; Lam Dina; Twa Dam; Ah Dan; Robert Flack; Dang Foy; Hong Gan; Jas. Halliday; Woo Hae;

Wong Hong; Mah Hoy; I. Ikegami; Art Jang; Mah Jug; Yee Jung; I. Kinchite; T. Kukutam; S. Kurshima; Chong Keep; Mah Kune; Thomas Lord; Lue Lam; Dune Munro; A. Mafaddo; E. Murra; Yee Moo; G. Monkawa; Lanpe Oku; Sky One Mah; E. Okatani; C. Pun Wong; Robert Steele; Louis Simondi; Andy Smith; Tom Sneddon; Wong Sing; Woo Sang; Geo. Turnbull; Quong Tai Mai; Gee Tan; W. Walker; Wm. Walker; Geo. Walker; John Whyte; Mah Wing; Mah Yong; Hoq Yee; Chan Yan; Tye; Ah Gow; Urig; Thos. Nicol; Song; Mow; Sing.

1902 — Mah Shing; Ham Fong; John Caulerly; Joe Caulerly; On How.

1903 — Lim Fin; Ah Sing; Yuen Chung; Wong Foo; Jung Bing; Jung Bow; Chong Chi; Mah Ching; Chong; Mah Dow; Chong Doo; Jung How; Mah Lee; Mah Lee; Mah See; Wong Tong; Ting Tah; Wong Yuen; Chuen.

1904 — Wong Chong; Mah Jung; Tong Hing; Jas. Strang; McInnis; A. Clarkson; Jas. Watson; Thos. Neilson; Mah Way; G. Yun Lun; Stamima; Wong Chong; S. Tanaka.

1906 — Yoon Fong Jun; Chin Gat; Ot Okura; Mayeda; Joy Chung Lung.

1907 — Chung Dang; Chas. Bardrick; Tomao Ruihi; Hing Jung.

1908 — Chung Jung Sing; Hoy Lew; Quong Lee Lung.

1909 — Wm. DeLacy; Fung Quock; Wong Joe; Jen Juji; M. Robinson; W. York.

1910 — Fugi; Dick Wong; M. Danus; B. Kosllowski; Joe Bardoni; Wong Chung; Y. Ovona; John Prince; Aisoka.

1911 — Jas. Lanze; Biffo Rositti.

1912 — Chee Wee; W. Logan; Alec Borski; Sing Mah Fung.

1913 — Lee Yung; Yup Ma See; Chuck Yuan; G. Continenzo; Elias Dorvin; Thomas Smith; Chow Ping; Austin Harper; Wm. Styles; Wm. Carwell; Hing Dong.

1915 — Sune Young; Chun Chin; Chee Yee.

1916 — Sam Mah; Ging Mah; Wang Hin; Kee Lung.

1917 — Uno Sanzio; Sing Low; Joe Bertram; John Brugh; Frank Bobba; Louis Murdoch; Ed Towers; Thos. Lumsden.

1918 — T. Kinura; Peter Bobba.

1919 — Sung Wung; Len Mah; Tan Chin.

1922 — Chun Looy; R.K. Dunsue; John Gibson; Hon Leung; John Johnston; H. Kajiyani; Man Leung; Noon Wee; Nam China; C. Sanano; S. Shigenni; G. Suyama; Kay Yee; Wing Mah;

M. Watanaba; Yim Wong; R. Yoshido.

1923 — A. Bonora; C. Cavellero; A. Charleston; Dong Fong; Ding Jung; J. Freeloni; Goon Lee; Jung Hing; Kit Jew Hung; Kept Jung; Kay Jung Gas; Long Louise; G. Martinella; W. Mitchell; P. Manicora; Bing Jung; Quee Sick; Alec Robertson; Sing Leung Toy; R. Smith; Don Sommerville; Wah Jung; Woy Jung; Wm. Whitehouse; T. Williams; Chung Wong; Lung Mah; How Wo Weel; Hah Jung; Norman Huby; Wong Toy; Tow Jung; J. Turner.

1924 — Wm. Jones; John Kirkbride; Tai How; T. Tatishi.

1929 — Ken Chow Gah; H. Yamamaka.

1930 — A. Guy.

1931 — Mow Yung.

1932 — Ye Yong.

1934 — Tom Millar.

1935 — Y. Kawaguchi; Thos. Robertson; Jas. Walker.

1937 — Mike Zenovitch; Paul Toth; Andrew Frew; Wm. Waugh; J. Thorburn.

1946 — J. Warren; John Watson; M. Broderick.

1950 — Fred Semister.

1951 — Robert Robertson.

1956 — Harvey Ellison; Frank Dixon.

1959 — Albert Brown.

1964 — Thos. J. Bates.

INTO THE WOODS ALONE

In my only surviving photograph of William George Morrow, he kneels in waist-deep snow with his prized .30-.30 Winchester cradled in one arm. The other is draped over the antlers of a trophy-sized bull caribou. According to the calendar of the Northern Indians, we are in the season of the Dog Barks Moon. It is the day after a storm, and the spruce trees are still laden with caps of snow that resemble chefs' hats or soft bonnets from some medieval passion play. The wind has swept away all traces of itself and only the hunter's tracks mar a dazzling landscape, save for the shocking crimson splatter around the muzzle of the slain animal. A fierce sun throws shadows into the crumpled trail leading to the kill, and the sky is an acute, painful blue. It is the telltale rime, hoar-frost, obscuring his face that betrays the stabbing cold.

Icicles hang from his eyebrows, unshaven stubble glints with crystals, his spectacles are glazed with the frozen mist of his breath. The temperature is only minus twenty, but with a brisk wind the chill factor makes it as dangerous as fifty below. Exposed flesh can freeze in less than a minute under these conditions. The press-ganged photographer, dropping parka hood to record the hunter with his own camera, has already developed the numb, waxy whiteness of seriously frozen ears — an injury not yet perceived, but one that will trouble me every winter for a decade afterward.

I know this picture is the one that Bill Morrow wanted me to hold in my memory. He gave it to me because it spoke so powerfully to his vanity, his pride that a soaring intellectual life should include this elemental capacity. Looking at the picture again, so many years after, I'm tempted to speculate that he treasured this moment of expression above more abstract victories, the bushwise hunter with his kill, the austere purity and absolute finality of the decision rendered by his weapon. This skill, with its ability to deliver precise, irrevocable conclusions, appealed to his sense of inner rather than public self as much as any of the judicial triumphs with which he altered the landscape of Canadian jurisprudence. Yet, there is a brittle quality to the portrait, a clearly evident vulnerability that belies the posturing, as though this bravado already masks some wound as mortal as the one just delivered.

For all his desires and dreams, the legend Morrow wished to create in his own mind and thrust upon the world, this is not the image that most occupies my recollection. My strongest memory is an image for which there is no record save the one in my brain. In my picture of Bill Morrow, the judge is on his way to court at Igloolik, one of the most ancient Inuit communities in Canada. The tiny settlement of 750 souls is snuggled into the naked granite of a small island just off the Melville Peninsula. The treacherous gut of Fury and Hecla Strait and the bountiful walrus and sealing grounds of Foxe Basin separate it from the bleak uplands of Baffin Island. This place has been continuously occupied by the Iglulikmiut and their ancestors for at least four thousand years. It is old even by the standards of European settlement. The first white man visited the area in 1613, but it remains so remote that even the ubiquitous Hudson's Bay Company did not establish a trading post until the Second World War.

At Igloolik, the judge is in a hurry because the weather is closing in rapidly and he wants to wrap the hearing up, get back to his plane and get away. He has an important adoption hearing at a village farther to the north. If the weather deteriorates and his pilot refuses to fly, the entire court party might be stranded here for days, putting his circuit of the Eastern Arctic behind schedule. Out in the settlements, where people sometimes travel days from distant tundra camps, Morrow's court may surrender its pomp but it is always punctilious. To speed things, the judge has dressed in the cramped tail of the DC-3, struggling among cargo nets and baggage to get into his black robes with the imposing scarlet sash of the Northwest Territories court.

But the plane is early and nobody has informed the RCMP. The constable is out on the land somewhere, patrolling hunting camps. He is not expected back until late afternoon, and there is no transport up to the schoolhouse where court is to convene.

The judge has commandeered his transportation from the hamlet council. All it can provide is the village garbage truck. He insists that any ladies present squeeze into the cab while he, the crown prosecutor, defence lawyers, court clerk and court reporter clamber into the greasy box for the rough ride in from the airstrip.

And that is my enduring picture of Bill Morrow, an awkward, slightly stuffy figure, his normally ruddy face turned brick red in the chill, leaning forward over the cab of a garbage truck and laughing like a mischievous schoolboy at the ridiculous spectacle of public protocol held hostage to necessity. His dark robes gather around him like a raven's wings, flapping in a breeze rich with the scent of decaying potato peels and rancid fat, and the judge of the Northwest Territories rides in a garbage truck to preside over important constitutional questions in a school kitchen.

Mr. Justice William Morrow was sixty-three when he died, surrounded by the unfamiliar and ultimately useless high technology of a University of Alberta cardiac unit, but he left a powerful legacy for the empty, snow-blown Arctic that he loved. He left the law. More than the law, he left a legacy of uncommon justice for the little people of Canada's North. "We go where we can go and when we get there, we do what we can, as best we can, with what we've got," he once said. What the judge of the Far North did, with few resources other than his courage and imagination, was change the legal landscape for all Canadians.

Morrow travelled his circuit with a pistol and a case of rye whisky. The pistol was part of his survival kit for the long, lonely flights over glaciers and barrens. So was the rye, although his own drinking was necessarily temperate, a rarity on a frontier where hard drinking was often held up as proof of toughness. Privately, he would express dismay at the occasional irony of members of the court party nursing hangovers in the back benches while an alcohol-related offence was tried. Still, if the judge frowned on the failure of self-discipline he associated with excess, the drinks were there when they were needed, and so was his dry sense of humour.

On one occasion, flying back to Yellowknife from the High Arctic in a crowded Lear jet, the aircraft lost an engine and a great deal of altitude. There had been a bang, and the cramped cabin stuttered and yawed as the pilots fought for control. Unlike the old DC-3 which the judge usually insisted carry his circuits, there was no hope of crash-landing the Lear jet somewhere in the barrens. If the second engine failed, the stubby-winged craft would have the glide path of a grand piano. The fear was palpable. Morrow simply asked for his camera. Since this was a test flight for the twin-engine jet, its demise might be the otherwise uninteresting passengers' only chance to make the pages of *Life* magazine, he deadpanned. The others were not amused. "Then maybe now is the time to bring out the V.O.," he said. It was one time that he passed no comment on levels of consumption, although one passenger later confessed she was so frightened that for the rest of the flight she was unable to get the spirits to her lips without spilling them.

Morrow was that rarity, an original Edmontonian. He was proud of his prairie roots, especially his family's origins in a sod hut, and throughout a career in the upper altitudes of legal philosophy he never lost his sense of connection with the land. He kept his father's eighty acres of land north of Edmonton and by the time he died he had planted eight hundred trees by hand. His father, William Morrow, Sr., bootstrapped his way out of a homesteader's poverty in Manitoba to found a law firm in Edmonton that proved sound enough to survive the depression. Morrow joined his father after graduating from the University of Alberta with distinction in 1939. Like so many prairie boys, he left almost immediately for a commission in the Royal Canadian Navy, where the young sub-lieutenant was mentioned in dispatches after the H.M.C.S. *Georgian* cut the first mine off the beaches of Normandy on D-Day. And like many another dry-lander, he was simultaneously developing an overpowering romantic attachment to the sea. Morrow would save up his meagre junior officer's pay to commission oil paintings of his beloved ships. Years later, giving a speech, he told his audience: "The only time my soul is at rest is when I'm at sea." This prompted his wife Genevieve, struggling at home with four young children, to fire off a starchy telegram suggesting: "Why don't you go to sea now and put your soul at rest permanently." It was the kind of vigorous, self-confident rejoinder that he loved to tell about, making himself the foil of his wife's wit.

When Morrow returned from the war on the Atlantic, it was to launch a career in law distinguished by a prescient anticipation of the great issues of national jurisprudence that were to emerge over the next forty years. The growing awareness of native concepts of cultural sovereignty, aboriginal land claims, Canadian sovereignty in the Arctic, constitutional guarantees protecting individual rights from the power of the state, the second-class colonial status of northern citizens, the development of autonomous institutions of northern government —

Morrow grappled judicially with all these ideas long before they had taken their pre-eminent places on our present national agenda. His enthusiasm for the difficult and thorny questions, his willingness to risk his reputation with daring and innovative judgments, his big, encompassing, brave vision of the law as a defender of the weak, the powerless and the voiceless, all earned the resentment of more timid and conventional colleagues who preferred that the law should serve the comfortable, the powerful and, above all, the interests of the state.

Morrow first went to the North in 1960, regularly abandoning his lucrative duties as a senior partner with what was to become one of Edmonton's most prestigious law firms in order to defend obscure legal aid cases for ten dollars a day. His interest in legal aid as a mechanism for assuring justice to the poor and disenfranchised was original and profound. As a young lawyer, he was a seminal influence in the setting up of a legal aid program, the first in Canada, which became a model for other jurisdictions. Indeed, he had returned to his father's firm after the war only on the guarantee that he could pursue any case he believed in, regardless of cost, as far as possible and at the firm's expense.

Whatever his vision as a young man, his beginnings as a lawyer had not been auspicious. After losing thirteen cases in a row, he seriously considered returning to the navy, which said it would be happy to have him back. But then a couple of his lost causes were appealed to the Supreme Court of Canada and the rulings overturned. From that point, he never looked back. As a lawyer, he appeared before the Supreme Court of Canada twenty-five times, not including applications, and he frequently did so without payment from his clients. Morrow's cold logic, an inability to tolerate fools or dullards in the law and his uncompromising intellectual honesty soon earned him a reputation for legal snobbery and even arrogance among some of his less-talented colleagues. But even his worst enemies conceded he was a brilliant court-room tactician and legal strategist, usually because they bore the scars to prove it. More important than his consummate skill, he revealed a sweeping and lofty comprehension of the constitutional implications of what to others seemed to be minor cases appearing before the backwater court of Judge J.H. Sissons.

Jack Sissons had been the first judge appointed to the Territorial Court of the Northwest Territories. It was a lonely and awesome post, making him the only one dispensing justice in a region of 1.5 million square kilometres. A member of parliament for a northern Alberta riding during the war, Sissons served as a district court judge in southern Alberta and was chief judge when he was asked to establish the northern court in Yellowknife. Prior to that, southern judges had been parachuted into the North to conduct their courts, or, as in the celebrated trials of Sinnisiak and Uluksuk in 1917, the year Morrow was born, the accused had been brought "outside" for justice. It must have been an experience, Morrow later observed, that seemed like travelling to another planet to face procedures one didn't understand, conducted by people one had never seen before, in a language one couldn't comprehend. Imagine a pair of Zulu warriors arriving on Bay Street, arresting a Harold Ballard or an Allan Eagleson, then whisking them away to face a trial in Africa for violating tribal taboo. He saw this as a fundamental injustice that characterized the assumptions of paternal racism, however benevolent, which suffused Canadian social values.

The social and ethical consequences of this Kafkaesque approach to the administration of justice in the North has been ably outlined by R.G. Moyles in his fine book *British Law and Arctic Men*, a specific study of the trials of Sinnisiak and Uluksuk. These were two hunters from the Coppermine area, one of them a powerful shaman. They had killed two Roman Catholic priests near Bloody Falls, ironically the long-remembered site of a massacre of Inuit by Chipewyan Indians which was recorded in grisly detail by Samuel Hearne a century and a half earlier. Arrested in 1916, having seen only four white men in their entire lives, the accused Inuit were transported from their ice-bound coast to Edmonton. Their trial took place during a summer heat-wave that caused corsetted ladies to swoon and turned the court house into an unbearable oven. They pleaded self-defence and evidence was introduced which indicated one of the priests had been threatening and abusive, harnessing the men to his dog sled and pointing a rifle to force them to pull it. When the Edmonton jury stunned the court by ignoring the judge's charge and finding the two men not guilty, the accused were dragged off to Calgary to be tried and there convicted on a second count. Their death sentences were commuted to life imprisonment in a northern Indian community. Sinnisiak and Uluksuk were eventually released on parole, but not before the experience had confirmed for many Inuit the belief that white society was quite crazy. Shamans explained that the *kadlunaaq*, as the hairy, pale-fleshed strangers were called, were descended from the frenzied mating of a sled dog with the moon — and usually behaved like it. The argument had some justification, the judge would reflect, citing the horrific story of a native child's body, returned to its parents from a southern autopsy with its dismembered remains packed in plastic baggies in an empty beer case.

Morrow would muse for hours over the morality of such incidents and the structure of underlying attitudes they revealed. He always liked to tell of the shock he himself felt when his own court interpreter explained the difficulty of translating the terms "guilty" and "not guilty" because these words did not exist in the dialect of the accused. The interpreter had been asking the accused, "Did you do it or didn't you do it?," a simplification that grossly distorted the intent of the plea, which is based not on the physical act but the knowing intent. Technically, Morrow pointed out, the Christian-based concept of guilt which lies at the heart of British common law did not exist in this mind. The specifics of the criminal code might be clear, but how does one resolve the ethical problem of comprehension?

On the question of how an alien law should be applied to aboriginal cultures, the North's new judge was as forceful in his written judgments as he was in private conversation. He denounced the Crown's authorities for stooping to legal technicalities, particularly in the blocking of appeals where minor errors had been made by RCMP officers or prison authorities attempting to assist the frequently illiterate accused: "I refuse to allow the right hand of the government, the prosecution, to take advantage of the mistake and error, albeit well-meaning, of the left hand of government." Procedural rules, Morrow argued, should never become the instrument of a denial of justice, and, while the Crown's approach was "ill-advised and cowardly, and contrary to the best tradition in our jurisprudence," its greatest evil was that it caused a substantial denial of justice to native communities and, in so doing, brought the whole administration of justice into disrepute.

In other decisions, the judge argued that sentences must take into consideration the shorter life expectancy of native people. He elaborated on this reasoning in a surprisingly candid 1971 interview with Ben Tierney of the Southam News Service: "An Eskimo's life expectancy is 53 per cent that of a white man's. What does that mean? Well, I say it means that when you send an Eskimo to jail for two years you are actually giving him the equivalent of four years for a white man."

Furthermore, it was the practice of the Crown to seek sentences that would routinely require transportation to southern prisons. Convicting people to long sentences outside their own country, even for serious offences, amounted to cruel and unusual punishment and usually served to destroy individuals instead of attempting rehabilitation. Morrow said:

> He may be a hunter. He may have spent all his life in a community that is 700 miles from the next community. He doesn't know anything about the white man. Suddenly he finds himself in a place where there are nothing but white men. He's surrounded by them in an environment that is totally different from what he's used to. He doesn't speak English. He has no one to speak to even. The prison psychiatrist can't speak to him. Even if the Eskimo speaks English, the psychiatrist won't know a thing about Eskimos ... how they think, why they do certain things. He can't be expected to know. The result is that the Eskimo suffers terribly. They withdraw. They wither up.

In court, he was no less passionate in his defiance of what he believed was an evil policy. "So long as the government of this country does not provide for penitentiaries within the territories, I will resist sending these people outside," he said in the manslaughter case of Adamee Onalik, whom he sentenced to two years less a day so that he might serve his sentence in a northern correctional institution.

Morrow was no stickler for protocol, permitting defence counsel to wear mukluks under their lawyer's gowns on more than one occasion, on others skipping the afternoon to go fishing — and taking the whole court with him. He also believed the awesome majesty of the law must be seen everywhere in the North if it was to be present in guiding everyday lives. He would tolerate no behaviour among court officials that diminished his dignity. On one occasion when his wife was sitting in the back of the courtroom waiting for the conclusion of a long, boring case and whispering with a friend, somebody giggled. The judge instructed the RCMP sergeant at arms to approach his wife and "tell that woman in the parka that if there is any more laughing she will be evicted from this court." Afterwards, he lectured her on the dignity of the accused, an Inuit man who spoke no English. "What if he were to think you were laughing at him?" he asked.

Like his predecessor on the northern bench, when people could not come to the court, he took the court to the people, flying endless hours across the vast northern territory, frequently to places that had never seen a court. His itinerary for first appearances is impressive: Snowdrift, Gjoa Haven, Igloolik,

Alert, Eureka, Bay Chimo, Paulatuk, Belcher Islands and a dozen more. One winter, he travelled five thousand kilometres to hear an Inuit divorce case and, when it seemed a reconciliation might be possible, adjourned it for another hearing and another weary five thousand kilometres in the spring. He averaged more than fifty thousand kilometres a year on his circuits, and of his decade in the North he spent approximately one year of it airborne, cooped up in a tight metal cell that Amnesty International would protest for any political prisoner.

If getting his court to the people meant setting up court rooms in cook shacks with bottles of mustard and ketchup still gracing the tables, that was fine by the judge. As a defence counsel, he had once interviewed his client in a two-holer, sitting beside him in the outhouse that offered the only private place in the settlement. As a judge, he took evidence in his pyjamas at 5 a.m. and once held court in a room shared with the flying dentist, who continued to work on one of the witnesses during proceedings.

Morrow's courts were convened in the bedrooms of log cabins, sitting on forty-five-gallon oil drums by the side of the Mackenzie River, aboard his swaying DC-3 above ice-choked Arctic seas and, more than once, when no other facilities were available, inside the freezing airplane cabin while parked at the end of a rough, snow-ploughed strip. He accepted the elements and he adapted to culture. When Chief Paul Baton of the Fort Norman band was called to testify in a land claims case in 1973, the chief spoke Slavey and Dogrib but no English. The court's interpreter, Joe Tobie, a native language announcer borrowed from CBC Northern Service, spoke English, Chipewyan and Dogrib but no Slavey. So Chief Baton translated from Slavey to Dogrib, Joe translated from Dogrib to English and the judge translated the easy-going bush jargon into proper legalese. "It was a three-way circuit," Morrow pointed out, "but it worked just fine." He was arguably happier discussing intricate constitutional points of law over a slab of dried Arctic char at some stained frontier table than he had been travelling to London on the very last Canadian case to be heard before the Queen's Privy Council.

Even the polished oak and walnut of the Privy Council's chambers now seems a foreshadowing of the curious combination of formality and familiarity adopted by Morrow for his own court. On that occasion, his wife recalls, the sweltering summer heat had been cruel. The Canadian lawyers were told that it was too hot in the airless chambers and that the Privy Council, in acknowledging the conditions, would — on this occasion only —

permit them to take off the powered wigs that British protocol demanded. Morrow demurred: "I've waited all my life to wear a wig. I'm not taking it off now." It was no act of deference. Morrow was both an ardent Canadian patriot and an avowed enemy of colonial assumptions. It was, however, a chance for a little preening over the historic ceremony, even if the sweat trickled off his chin throughout. And what could be more Canadian than sweat on the brow of a farmer's son? Later, his populist colours showed and he rounded up the clerks, or ushers as they are called in such elevated chambers. They were burdened with reference tomes for the Law Lords, but he marshalled them in the courtyard for his tourist's snapshot. "They blustered and complained and protested loudly that this sort of indecorous behaviour simply wasn't proper," Genevieve says, "but really they loved it that somebody should pay attention to them. They never forgot Bill and his damned camera."

To help cover the personal expense of his appearance before the Privy Council he had a gift of five thousand dollars from his father. It is a measure of Morrow's vision that he used it to cover the cost of taking with him the junior partner from his firm, Bill Stevenson, putting his party up in the relative splendour of The Savoy for the historic occasion. His justification for bringing the young lawyer was as elegant a wedding of form to function as the stock of one of his rifles. The event heralded the closing of his country's colonial relationship with Britain. If it was the penultimate milestone in the development of our national sovereignty, to be followed he was sure by the bringing home of the Constitution itself, then Morrow believed the coming generation of lawyers and judges — in whose stewardship that sovereign power would reside — must bear witness to its birth. Morrow lost his case before the Privy Council, but he proved as astute in this judgment of its symbolic importance as he had in other cases. And losing the argument was no dishonour. Of the four Canadian lawyers arguing the case, all were to advance to the highest ranks in the judicial system: Morrow as judge of the Territorial Court of the Northwest Territories and later as a justice of the appellate division of the Supreme Court of Alberta; Stevenson as a justice with the Alberta Court of Appeal. On the winning side, J.H. Laycraft became Chief Justice of Alberta and J.V.H. Milvain became Chief Justice of the Alberta Supreme Court's trial division.

This strong sense of the evolution of jurisprudence, indeed, the movement of all social and political life toward the final emergence of a true and distinct national culture for which

Canadian law provided a common thread, soon drew this prairie lawyer to the attention of like minds in Ottawa. Morrow, steeped in the rock-ribbed values of his native Alberta, had been a staunch Progressive Conservative early in his career but resigned from the party when some of its members spoke against admitting Newfoundland to Confederation. He seemed the ideal man to test the feasibility of creating the autonomous territorial judicial system that the Northwest Territories would need if it were ever to disengage from the colonial status in which it had stagnated for half a century.

The federal commission that Morrow headed up in 1967 brought down almost a hundred recommendations for setting up an independent court system in the Northwest Territories. He was called to Ottawa to present it in person and summoned to Lester B. Pearson's office.

"If this were England I'd be knighting you Sir William," Pearson said. "But since this is Canada, I'm simply going to table this in the House of Commons. How would you like to sit in my box and watch it happen?" It is significant that even with the troubled minority governments of the day, virtually all Morrow's recommendations were eventually adopted. In 1966, with a weary Jack Sissons looking forward to his retirement — he was to die less than three years later — Morrow had already begun to do the very things he believed could and should be done. Leaving his wife and four children behind in Edmonton, he moved to Yellowknife, sleeping in the basement suite provided by Anglican Bishop Henry Cook and commuting south every weekend. This he did for two years until he could provide what he considered a proper home in a town bursting at the seams with the arrival of Stuart Hodgson's new territorial government, recently removed from Ottawa to the new capital at Yellowknife on the north shore of Great Slave Lake. A first he stayed, like so many other newcomers, in one of the houses provided by the government, but he refused the subsidies that were standard with such housing. Morrow was determined that he should be subject to no influence, however indirect, from the territorial administration and eventually built himself a residence at his own expense.

Hodgson and Morrow were charged with the same task, but they were cut from wholly different bolts of cloth. Both were navy men, but where Morrow had been an officer on the bridge, Hodgson had been an able seaman in the forecastle. Morrow was an ardent hunter who prided himself on the accuracy of his shooting and his ability to make the clean kill; Hodgson confessed in private conversations that he had killed a man during the war and would never kill anything needlessly again. The precise, intellectually rigorous Morrow, his legal ego coupled to the public stiffness that masked a deep underlying shyness, was determined that the new court system would be an independent custodian of the law north of the sixtieth parallel. He intended to shape it to the needs of its people and not the assumptions of some political bureaucracy. Hodgson, bluff, boisterous and pragmatic as an axe handle, was equally determined that the court system, however independent, should be integrated into his master plan for the birth of fully responsible democratic government. This difference of opinion was a source of great contentiousness during the early years of the two administrations, although, ultimately, the two men edged into a grudging, if wary, respect for one another. Even then there was never any love lost between them. When Morrow took the territorial council to task for drafting ordinances which contradicted and nullified one another, not entirely unexpected from a collection of amateur legislators, he soon found his own judgments assailed from the privileged impunity of the council chamber.

The judge was no stranger to criticism of this sort, seemed even to enjoy it. He pointed out gleefully that the feistiness of the council was increasing in inverse proportion to the decline in appointed members. An occasional tone of immaturity in the rhetoric of elected councillors might be irritating, but it also represented the maturing of the political process — something even its victims should celebrate. The judge could, however, be swift and vigorous with any criticism that impugned the integrity of the judicial process itself. In 1975, he pressed a contempt of court citation that publicly humiliated the publisher of the Yellowknife newspaper, the *News of The North*. The controversy had arisen when a senior official of the territorial government had been convicted and sentenced on a charge of impaired driving. The official had appeared before the judge, sitting as a magistrate, at 9 a.m., one hour earlier than is the normal starting time for Canadian courts. The newspaper accused the judge of a double standard of justice for government mandarins. Privately, Morrow expressed a deep sense of dismay at the proceedings because he had always prided himself on good relations with the press. In court, however, the evidence on behalf of the judge was devastating. The court had indeed heard the case an hour early, but his court regularly sat early because of the heavy workload — in this case, twelve of the previous thirty-two sittings had been scheduled for 9 a.m. and Morrow had shoehorned this case into his schedule because of the gravity of a criminal charge against a senior official and because he was about to leave on an extended circuit the next day. The fine he levied had been heavier than normal because of the accused's position of public trust. Even when the presiding judge upheld the contempt citation, Morrow did not press the *News of The North* for an apology and said he was content that the court's reputation had been cleared. The paper published one voluntarily.

Although the confrontation with the traditionally rowdy Yellowknife newspaper distressed him, Morrow had no doubts about the necessity of his action. With political maturity must come responsibility, he said. That maturity was a goal to which Morrow was no less committed than his sometime foe in the commissioner's office. He saw an independent and self-confident North, distinct in the cultural substance of its own regional identity, as a vital necessity for the sovereignty that Canada claimed and would have to be equipped to justify.

Again and again, frequently in what seemed on the surface to be routine cases, Morrow's written judgments addressed with eloquence and power this issue of Canada's jurisdiction in the Arctic. In the case of *Regina v. Tootalik E4-321*, an Inuit hunter charged with unlawfully killing a female polar bear with young, he ruled that the jurisdiction of the territorial court extended not only over the land, but "also in the areas of sea and sea ice lying off such land . . . including the sea and sea ice in all that part of Canada north of the Sixtieth Parallel of North Latitude" through the full sector north to the Pole. He presided over the calling of two federal justice ministers to the Northwest Territories bar at remote settlements in the High Arctic — John Turner at Pond Inlet on the north end of Baffin Island and Ron Basford at Eureka, a tiny federal weather station even farther north on the desolate western side of Ellesmere Island, an area the size of Great Britain and occupied by fewer than 250 people.

Many of the court activities that less thoughtful observers dismissed as the eccentricities of a wild romantic may, in retrospect, be seen as the carefully laid framework for future claims of sovereignty that he believed might eventually be argued before the World Court, particularly since the United States has steadfastly refused to acknowledge full Canadian authority. He landed his plane on the sea ice at forty below zero and formally convened his court, establishing a precedent for the physical presence of his jurisdiction over the waters of the Northwest Passage. Twenty years ago, the story was carried by southern newspapers as an oddity. Today, it stands as a shrewd forewarning of the questions that would be raised a generation later when the United States challenged Canadian claims to sovereignty by steaming an armed vessel through the passage without seeking prior permission. Morrow, in fact, was not above challenging the American presence in Canada's North himself. In 1970, slyly inviting along a *New York Times* reporter, he convened a court at the Bar Four Radar Station of the distant early warning line. The case itself was a straightforward civil suit between two trappers, but it was the first time a Canadian court had been held at a distant early warning line site and offered the judge an opportunity to once again extend his jurisdiction — this time over a quasi-military base adjacent to the strategic Beaufort Sea. In his decade on the northern bench, Canadian courts were to convene at American-run distant early warning line bases from the western Arctic to Baffin Island in the east.

Morrow believed that Canadian sovereignty over its Arctic regions would always be an empty claim so long as it relied solely on the technical precedents he used to establish official jurisdictions. True sovereignty, he said, lay in the sinew and bone of the aboriginal people who inhabited the North. Any argument that they represented an extension of Canadian society into those regions also demanded full acceptance of their cultural values as a living part of the Canadian commonwealth. If the expansion of an evolving British common law had been based on principles of inclusiveness that permitted it to flourish in cultures as disparate as India, Australia, the United States and even South Africa, then the Canadian version should be flexible enough to learn from and absorb native cultures. Some of Morrow's most important decisions served to incorporate the traditional laws of Inuit communities as unquestionably legitimate elements of Canadian civil law.

He had still been a lawyer when Judge Sissons railed at the refusal of federal authorities to accept the legality of traditionally contracted Inuit marriages. The specific case involved the rights of a widow and daughter to inherit the estate of a dead husband and father. Federal authorities in the department of Indian and Northern Affairs ruled that because the marriage had occurred in the customary way, without the benefit of either state or clergy, the widow was merely a concubine and the daughter was illegitimate. The estate, said the bureaucrats, must go to the dead man's brothers and sisters.

"Crass, cruel, smug and sly," Sissons said of the attempt to force Inuit communities to accept the imperial imposition of the white man's own traditional Christian values. "No Ottawa bastard is going to tell me ten thousand Eskimos are bastards." Morrow, the precise intellectual, finding remarkably similar precedents in ancient Scottish custom and English common law, provided Sissons with the arguments that permitted the tough old judge to find traditional Inuit marriages as powerful and binding as any contracted in the rest of Canada.

In the Sikyea duck trial, Morrow argued before Sissons that the ancient, aboriginal right of native people to take sustenance off the land took precedence even over international conventions — in this case, the Migratory Birds Act, a piece of southern legislation designed to protect southern interests. It established hunting seasons for migratory waterfowl which effectively prohibited Inuit and Dene people from their traditional hunting during the only season ducks and geese were in the North. They were legally permitted to hunt, ironically, only at a time of year when the ducks and geese had all returned to the south. This law effectively converted a traditional northern food source into a luxury recreation for southern duck hunters, an objective, Morrow observed, which was completely contrary to his idea of natural justice. It was an argument that Morrow finally lost when southern courts ruled that, while Indian hunting rights under the British North America Act might have been breached, the other legislation took precedence. Nevertheless, the moral force of Morrow's position today remains germane to much of the debate regarding the dominant culture's obligations to its aboriginal minorities.

When he became a judge himself, Morrow continued this campaign to stitch Inuit and Indian values into the fabric of Canadian law. He hounded counsel that appeared before him until, in 1967 at Aklavik, in the Mackenzie River Delta, they selected an all-native jury. For the first time in history, an accused native person would be judged by his true peers, selected from his own community. This was not to be the last of Morrow's firsts in establishing jury precedents. Across the male-dominated Arctic, he pushed for the inclusion of women in juries. At Spence Bay, Hay River and, finally, Yellowknife, he achieved success. In 1968 at Snowdrift, he swore in the first all-Indian jury, following with the first all-Inuit jury at Rankin Inlet in 1971.

Another landmark decision by Morrow came in 1972, when he ruled that traditional verbal arrangements to give or accept children for adoption according to ancient Inuit custom had full force in the civil law. Custom adoptions and exchanges of children — a second son exchanged for a friend's second daughter, a fourth or fifth child offered to a childless couple or grandparents — were prevalent and were always founded on verbal agreements. Before Morrow, Canadian law refused to acknowledge the deep importance attached to these adoptions and failed to address the issue of their legality. "This custom or method of handling surplus children was obviously born of necessity," the judge wrote. "I would say this is the most out-standing characteristic of their culture and appears to outrank marriage and hunting rights. In my opinion, the white culture could learn a lot from these customs."

His own court certainly seemed prepared to learn. At least two hundred times, the judge brought his court to remote points to hear petitions from people seeking some formal documenta-tion of their custom adoptions. Although he had made the tradi-tional verbal arrangements fully part of the law, numerous fami-lies, mistrustful of intentions in Ottawa, still sought technical sanction for their arrangements. Morrow cheerfully provided what was no longer necessary, believing that if adoptive parents felt secure, then children would also feel secure. This matter-of-fact premise that courts have an obligation to serve their consti-tuents, as well as provide guidance and punishment, character-ized Morrow's tenure as the senior judge in the Northwest Terri-tories.

The images of that service are as vivid to me a decade after his death as they were at the moment. At Pelly Bay, a community 250 kilometres north of the Arctic Circle which did not see its first white man until the 1930s, one mother stands up in the mid-dle of proceedings and marches to the back of the court to retrieve a small daughter clattering among pots of poster paints. While Morrow leans forward patiently, a little girl in a Mother Hubbard parka and rubber boots that are too big clumps up to the bench and peers gravely at the speed of the court reporter's shorthand. The court clerk catches her attention with a wink, then has to abandon his flirtation to hold the naked, squirming baby handed him by another mother who wants hands free to sign papers. It's the same story of informality at Igloolik, where mothers bare their breasts to silence squealing babies, suckling the hungry while the judge gravely takes depositions. In fact, if anything can be said to exemplify these adoption courts, presided over by this starchy, constitutional judge who else-where is the terror of officious bureaucrats, it is the babies. Babies laughing, crying, gurgling, wailing, sleeping, wetting themselves and getting informally changed on the judge's table while the law provides its swaddling for their little lives.

Morrow often said that these custom adoption courts, introducing the unruly flesh-and-blood reality of northern life into the staid chambers of the law itself, were his favourite sessions. Undoubtedly, in some sense they were, yet it was also true that he was never happier than when he was wrestling with some great, difficult issue of principle.

In his own mind, the high point of his career as a jurist was the Drybones case in which the clarity, eloquence and power of his written judgment compelled the Supreme Court of Canada not only to deal for the first time with John Diefenbaker's Bill of Rights but to uphold its supremacy over other federal legislation. This was no mere footnote to the country's legal history but an important milestone in the evolution of constitutional democracy, in the development of individual rights and, not the least, in charting a more activist direction for the highest court itself.

Canada's Bill of Rights, passed by Parliament in 1960, has been largely superceded by the authority of the Canadian Charter of Rights and Freedoms which came into force in 1982. A generation earlier, Diefenbaker's bill had been a trail-blazing attempt to define and entrench those basic individual rights that deserved protection from the arbitrary actions of the state. The bill guarantees equality before the law, ensures the individual's right to legal defence and a fair trial and protects fundamental freedoms of speech, assembly, religion, personal security, enjoyment of property and an unencumbered press. Unfortunately, the prime minister's inability to marshal provincial support left his legislation only partially effective — it applies only to federal laws and federal jurisdictions — and the act carries a notwithstanding clause which permits Parliament to override the provisions of the bill as it deems fit. Canada's judiciary had further rendered the statute toothless by virtually denying its express power, restricting the concepts it embodied to the narrowest interpretations. For more than a decade, if it was referred to at all, the Bill of Rights languished as a kind of secondary instrument to be used in interpreting the intentions of other laws. In 1967, Morrow was to change all that, and, in doing so, he was to change the course of judicial history.

Once again, the facts of the case were simple, straightforward and utterly routine. Joseph Drybones, a forty-year-old Dogrib trapper, had acquired a skinful in a Yellowknife bar called the Old Stope and had been arrested by the RCMP. He was routinely charged under Section 94 (b) of the then-current Indian Act, convicted of the offence of being intoxicated while off an Indian Reserve and fined ten dollars. It was a scenario that had been played out countless times in the North and elsewhere. But Morrow, with that incisive intellect and broad vision, saw vast implications for the workings of Canadian justice in a case that others might have dismissed as just another drunken Indian. The prospect fascinated and excited him. At home that night, staring at the ceiling while he turned it over in his mind, he told his wife: "I'm going to write this judgment so that once and for all the Supreme Court of Canada has to deal with the Bill of Rights." It was an ironic position for a man who had argued strenuously against any need for such a bill in the first place, taking the conservative view that the listing of one's rights in a document created a dangerous tendency in government to presume that what was not formally specified was, *ipso facto*, not a right. He confided to his wife that he was rapidly coming to the conclusion that his early position had been wrong, and that, even in the Canadian form of democracy that he loved, powerful protections for the individual were necessary.

What Morrow had seen in the Drybones case was two-fold. First was the intolerable discrimination inherent in a justice system which applied different laws with different penalties to different Canadians solely on the basis of race. Other Canadians arrested for liquor infractions in Yellowknife would be charged under the Territorial Liquor Ordinance. Joseph Drybones was charged under the Indian Act. Compounding the injustice was the fact that there were no Indian Reserves in the Northwest Territories. Technically, people of Indian ancestry who wished to over-indulge legally, as scores of others did every night, would be forced to travel to Alberta to find an Indian Reserve on which to drink. The converse was an absurdity. Every native person north of the sixtieth parallel who had one drink too many, however unobtrusively, was committing an offence.

The second and more abstract element that seized his imagination was the unreasonable infringement by the Indian Act upon rights which were clearly specified in the Bill of Rights. One of the statutes must prevail, Morrow reasoned, and for both logical and ethical reasons it should be the Bill of Rights. For the better part of a decade, Canadian judges had evaded the invocation of the Bill of Rights, the more conservative among them perpetuating the argument that laws should be judged only on the issue of whether federal or provincial governments had exceeded their powers under the British North America Act.

Morrow's decision to overturn the Drybones conviction and cite the Bill of Rights as his authority went off like a bomb-shell in Canadian jurisprudence. Three years later, the Supreme Court of Canada upheld his decision, striking down whole sections of the Indian Act based on the Bill of Rights guarantee of equality before the law. Unless Parliament were to specifically apply the notwithstanding provisions in each case, then federal legislation must bow to the superior intent of the Bill of Rights. Almost twenty years after, with a powerful new charter and a Supreme Court that is activist to an extent not dreamed of in Morrow's day, the Drybones case is still referred to by many eminent legal scholars as the decision of the century for Canadian constitutional law. It certainly marked the dramatic emergence of Canada's superior courts as truly national institutions, beginning the process that political scientist David Milne believes will make them pivotal in unifying values around the Charter of Rights and Freedoms.

"By aggregating the interests of individuals and groups from across the country on such matters as the scope of police powers, abortion, pornography, affirmative action, compulsory retirement and labour rights, the new Charter will redirect political attention from the old regional and provincial-federal controversies," Milne argues in his essay "The New Canadian Constitution," written for the scholarly collection *Canadian Politics in the 1980s.*

> The highest court will also set uniform national standards in place of the diverse array of provincial measures in areas like film censorship and employment practices. Provinces seeking to escape those national standards by using the notwithstanding clause against a Supreme Court judgment will find themselves in new and politically difficult circumstances where the rhetoric of regionalism is unlikely to be as successful as it might once have been. In all of these ways the nation-building potential of the Charter, as well as the critical role of the courts in shaping a new political alignment between themselves and the Canadian people, should become increasingly evident in the years ahead.

The Morrow ruling of 1967, written to force the Supreme Court to a decision, seems in hindsight to offer a kind of constitutional déja vu to all that now unfolds.

If the Drybones case was Morrow's high-water mark as a far-sighted jurist, his lowest ebb came during the first emergence of land claims by the Indian Brotherhood of the Northwest Territories, later to name themselves by their own tongue, the Dene Nation. This native organization, led by Dogrib James Wah-shee and represented by a young graduate of the University of Alberta law school named Gerry Sutton, was mobilizing to block the plans of a multinational consortium to build a natural gas pipeline down the Mackenzie River Valley. Sutton devised the ingenious strategy of approaching the matter as any ordinary citizen would approach a neighbourhood dispute over property rights. He went to the land titles office and asked permission to file a standard caveat declaring that his clients had an interest in the property in question and that their interest should be satisfied one way or the other before development plans proceeded. There was one difference. He had filed the caveat on behalf of seven thousand status Indians against all the unsurveyed Crown land in the western half of the Northwest Territories — a region amounting to 575 thousand square kilometres. The registrar of land titles referred the matter to court. Could the Dene nation file a caveat against all the Crown land in the Mackenzie River drainage basin?

The Indians of the western Arctic had signed two treaties with the federal government, Treaty 8 in 1899 and Treaty 11 in 1921, but those treaties had never been settled and no reserves had been established. Now, the Indians said they had compelling evidence that the treaties had been signed under duress and that there had never been an intention to surrender aboriginal title to their lands. Morrow permitted the filing of the caveat on an interim basis and granted them a temporary freeze on land transactions in the disputed area, although he made it clear that in any cases of individual or municipal hardship he intended to grant immediate exemptions from the freeze. The Native Brotherhood agreed. It was not their intention to disrupt the lives of their northern neighbours, only to assert a principle they felt would be essential in future negotiations of land claims with the federal government. Morrow prepared to hear the Indians' case and determine whether the caveat should remain in force until the issue of aboriginal rights was decided by the courts.

Ottawa moved swiftly and without any pretence. The federal justice department claimed that Morrow, the sole judge of the Northwest Territories, had no jurisdiction to rule on the Indians' case and flew in trouble-shooter Ivan Whitehall to take charge. Morrow was at first dumbfounded at the arrogance and then enraged at the stupidity. The federal justice department was openly attempting to reassert the paternal colonialism that both he and Hodgson had been struggling to shed. He was also deeply wounded, less by what amounted to a public expression of non-confidence by Justice Minister Otto Lang and Indian and

Northern Affairs Minister Jean Chretien, than by Ottawa's betrayal of all that Morrow believed regarding judicial independence and the dismantling of colonialism in the North.

Speaking for the Crown, Whitehall argued that Morrow's jurisdiction was limited to the decision as to whether a caveat filed against the disputed land could properly be registered with the land titles office. The strategy of the federal government was clear. It wanted the judge to rule on the application alone, avoiding the broader and vastly more complex issues of aboriginal rights which were fundamental to the Indians' arguments. Those issues, Ottawa said, were properly heard in a superior court — in this case, the federal government's own court, the Federal Court of Canada, founded only three years before. Whitehall sat back and waited for the Northwest Territories judge to either rule that he had no jurisdiction or refer the matter to the federal court. But Morrow's reputation as a court-room strategist was not an empty one. The pistol-packing judge was more than a match for the justice department's top lawyer. He lobbed a judicial grenade of his own. He reserved his decision, adjourned the court for two months and ordered the lawyers to be prepared to present him with all the evidence involved in the case. The judge of the Supreme Court of the Northwest Territories could not render an intelligent decision regarding his jurisdiction until he had heard all the evidence, he said.

"I have heard argument based on references to aboriginal rights, Crown title, Hudson's Bay land, the manner of the handing of patents and land grants, transfers of land involving the two governments — none of which is before me in concrete form as evidence. There has been very little agreement as to the true nature of these things," he pointed out. The Crown lawyer seemed stunned. He rose to object that Morrow was entering into the merits of the case. "I agree that I am entering on the merits of the case," Morrow grinned. "I appreciate your position entirely. At the same time, whether rightly or wrongly, I think these proceedings should be completed. I do not feel disposed at this time to decide on jurisdiction alone. I may be doing the completely wrong thing in law and I may be subject to criticism from a higher judge — that's the risk of being a judge."

The federal government, having failed to intimidate the judge in his own court, then sought the blunter expedient of simply ousting him from the case. It applied to its own Federal Court of Canada for a writ of prohibition preventing Morrow from continuing and ordering the case removed from his court to be heard by a federal judge. It ordered a special sitting of the federal court in Yellowknife to decide whether Morrow could be stopped. This was an unprecedented step and violated a long-standing tradition in both British and Canadian law that one judge of equal status does not attack another judge. The normal procedure is that if one superior court justice finds himself in dispute with another he waits until a decision has been made and then deals with the matter in an appeal. Morrow was clearly a judge of equal status. He was appointed by the federal government and had the same rank and salary as a federal court judge and, although his court was that of the Northwest Territories, he was appointed under the same provisions of the British North America Act as other federal judges.

If Morrow had been angry before, now he was appalled and deeply disturbed. That night, his wife recalls, he lay sleepless, wrestling with the moral dimensions of the issue. "I don't know what to do," he told her. "This is so unbelievable. . . . "

She turned on the pillow in the dark, sensing his hurt. "Do you love your country?," she asked.

"Of course," he replied. "That's why I'm up here."

"Well, then, fight 'em," she said.

The federal government's attempt to seek the writ of prohibition before the presiding judge had even rendered a decision was a grotesque interference in a case already in progress. Furthermore, it sought to discredit the superior court judge of the Northwest Territories with a precedent that would radically alter the traditional structure of all Canadian courts, creating a parallel authority belonging solely to the federal government.

Morrow countered with an unexpected and devastating thirty-page judgment of his own. On the technicality, he ruled that his court did have jurisdiction. Then he added a withering lesson in constitutional etiquette for the politicians in Ottawa that he was convinced were seeking to interfere on behalf of the huge northern development lobby. Anyone prepared to diminish the autonomy of the northern justice system in order to satisfy a political lobby was beneath contempt, he suggested privately. Publicly, he was more restrained, but only marginally.

"To me this represents a policy decision by the government which can only be interpreted as an affront to my court and to me as the judge of that court," Morrow wrote. He said the federal move sought to subject him not to the proper discipline of the Northwest Territories Court of Appeal, "which discipline I respect and am constitutionally bound to adhere to," but to another judge of equal rank.

"I am certain that it is the first time in the history of Canadian jurisprudence, the first time since Confederation, when one superior court judge has been placed under attack by another superior court judge of equal status.... By having the Federal Court appear in Yellowknife, not only does this executive act threaten the very integrity and independence of this court, but, by the same token, it runs the risk of throwing a cloud on the reputation of the Federal Court." The process begun by Ottawa put before the public the impression that the Federal Court was a creature of the federal government, ready to jump whenever asked by federal bureaucrats. This, he argued, disgraced the principle of independence for judges first won by the British parliament in 1701 and now entrenched in the Canadian constitution.

I suppose it can be said that if a judge of the Federal Court can hear application for such things as writs of prohibition against me, then there is nothing to prevent a similar application being made to me for relief against a Federal Court judge. This surely must not be the way in which jurisprudence in this country is now to develop. It seems to me that if I can be entrusted to adjudicate on cases involving the liberty of the subjects of the Territories permitting me to put them in jail, I should be capable of adjudicating on questions involving their property, unless, of course, property including land is placed on a higher plane.

Morrow went on to explain that his interim judgment would have been better issued after his scheduled hearings, but that he was yielding to government pressure: "I am moved to do this against my normal inclination to not back down, because I feel it is my constitutional duty to let the people within my jurisdiction and their Parliament know what is happening and so they will have their judge's side of the sorry story. I would be derelict in my duty if I did not rise to this challenge."

Then, like Sir Edward Coke, the Chief Justice of England who defied the arbitrary will of King James I in 1616, establishing thereafter the moral authority for an independent judiciary, Morrow withdrew from the fray and left his judgment to make the arguments. Three weeks later, Federal Court Judge Frank Collier was sitting in Morrow's chair and reflecting on the evidence in Morrow's office. On July 6, 1973, Judge Collier categorically dismissed every aspect of the federal government's attempt to remove the Northwest Territories only judge from the case. As soon as Judge Collier had left the bench, the Indian Brotherhood's lawyers let out a war-whoop and produced a bottle of champagne. It was the kind of informality on which Morrow would have frowned, but he was at home preparing for the hearings into aboriginal claims that he intended to conduct throughout the Mackenzie Valley. Two days later, the federal government's high-powered team of lawyers had fled the Northwest Territories capital, leaving to the local prosecutor, Orville Troy, the unpleasant business of informing the judge that Ottawa had withdrawn from the case in a final, petty attempt to disrupt the proceedings. Commissioner Hodgson was having none of that. When Morrow appointed Yellowknife lawyer Dieter Brandt to act as "friend of the court," Hodgson's territorial officials were instructed to assist further in carrying out the procedures Morrow would normally expect from the Crown. The judge ordered his staff to prepare for moveable proceedings. Once more, the judge was in his element, going to the people with his court.

The hearings that followed produced remarkable evidence from old men, some of whom testified from near death, regarding the nature of the two treaties signed in their distant youth. In Hay River, the judge found Jimmy Sibbeston, a hundred years old and the only living man who had travelled to every settlement with the official party for Treaty 11. Sitting at his kitchen table with the judge, Sibbeston explained that in Fort Simpson, after three days of failed negotiations, he was sent by the government agent to ask the chief why he wouldn't sign. And what was the chief's answer? "He didn't want to let his land go," Sibbeston told the court. Oblate Father René Fumoleau said his analysis of signatures on Treaty 8 led him to believe that at least three of them were forgeries. He pointed out that prior to 1867 the Anglican and Roman Catholic churches and the Hudson's Bay Company had cared for Indians in times of hardship. After the formation of a national government, the Indians were pressured to sign treaties in exchange for federal assistance. To obtain what was the moral right of every Canadian citizen, the native people were expected to surrender their most fundamental property rights. Vital Bonnetrouge, the seventy-six-year-old chief of the Fort Providence band said there had been no mention of land surrender in discussions with the federal agent: "It was a peace treaty. They took the treaty on that condition, not for the land."

In the end, Morrow ruled that the Indians of the Mackenzie Valley did have a profound interest in the land of the western Arctic and what happened to it. He hardly seemed surprised when his decision was appealed to the Northwest Territories court of appeal, where Morrow had said it should properly go from the very beginning. It was as though he had decided his time was over in the North. The attempt by Ottawa to remove him from his case, to subject him to the authority of a fellow judge, all that seemed a hinge in his career. "I felt that partly killed him," his wife told me years afterward.

A tribunal of five southern judges from Alberta heard the appeal of the famous Indian caveat case. Deciding the case on the narrow technical issue of whether a caveat could be filed against Crown land, they overturned Morrow's decision with one dissenting voice, Mr. Justice Arnold Moir, who said that the Indians did indeed hold the rights expressed by the northern court: "It is the right to use, to farm, to hunt, to fish, to trap, to pick berries on the land. A right to live on the land as their fore-fathers did and to win from it a living by hunting, trapping, fishing, farming and generally using the land."

Those were the values cherished by Bill Morrow and expressed by the photograph he gave me. That day in the bare, rattling bush, 150 kilometres out of Yellowknife, with not the slightest thought that death was already stalking him, we surprised our caribou crossing an ice-covered lake. The judge stood up suddenly, froze the startled animals and dropped his trophy with one quick shot. I hesitated a split second, hit mine on the bound and wounded it. It was a clumsy gut shot. I tracked that animal three-and-a-half kilometres through the waist-deep snow to finish the ugly thing I had started. It was a scrawny, underweight animal, hardly worth the bother. I regret-ted shooting it, but it seemed a sin to do what I had seen others do — hike back out and claim a clean miss. I harnessed myself to the caribou and skidded it back through the heavy snow, anx-ious not to be caught by dark. The judge watched while I dressed it. Before we left, he asked me to take a picture of him while the sun was still bright. Later, the judge presented me with a fat, prime hindquarter from his own kill. And a photograph. He looked at me with his head cocked, as though he were fixing me in a frame somewhere in that complex memory: "It's hard to go into the bush alone to finish what you've started. Sometimes you wonder if it was worth it. It always is."

IT IS IN MY MIND THAT THIS IS MY HOME

I had first looked out across the confusing tangle of blind channels, oxbows and saucer lakes that make up the Mackenzie
River's northern delta almost twenty years before. Now, once
again, the whole glittering prospect spread from horizon to horizon before me, a vast, jewelled fan suddenly unfolding under
the wing tips. Nostalgia for that lost instant of discovery crashed
in with the force of the great, coffee-coloured river itself.

Behind us, nearly twelve kilometres wide in some places,
pouring two billion cubic feet of water an hour into the Beaufort
Sea, the Mackenzie reached back 4,250 kilometres into the heart
of the continent. It reached back through the tight bed-rock gut
of The Palisades, past the roller coaster haystacks of the Sans
Sault Rapids and past the drying racks of the Boots brothers in
their little meadow at Willow River. At Fort Simpson, it boiled
through its mean confluence with the wild and perilous Liard,
the tributary a kingly river in its own right, thundering down
from the snow-clad Pelly massif in the distant Yukon. Back,
beyond the curve of the earth, the Mackenzie reached past the
bluffs of Fort Providence and into the lightless canyons of its
source in the deeps of Great Slave Lake, itself nourished by
glacier-fed tributaries rising in the Rocky Mountains of central
Alberta, another thousand kilometres to the southwest.

To encounter the natural enormity of the physical world in
this form is to confront the pressure-laden consciousness we
have evolved to deal with our final decades in the twentieth century. The tyranny of calendars, schedules and programs permeates civilized life. These instruments, however sophisticated
and complex in form, represent only our most primitive

instincts. Through them we seek to attenuate time, as though we might stretch our little allotments by the process of its efficient segmentation, slicing it ever finer, from months to minutes to the microsecond agendas of particle physics and computer electronics. But time on the Mackenzie seems to run in reverse, the careful compartments opening outward, the contents merging with the organic pulse of the river.

At first, you feel the days, then the weeks, then the months slough away like scales, and once you've eaten the slab-sided fish that the voyageurs called Inconnu, "the unknown," and the Dene netminders call simply "Coney," or laid down your bedroll among the ashes of campsites occupied for nine thousand years, sensing all those bodies before yours, snugging down into the same hollows you've spooned out for your own bony hips, you feel the templates click into your DNA. The experience of place locks into memory at some mysterious, cellular level, waiting to blossom into vivid images and the recurrent sense of something moving just at the edge of wakefulness. What moves just beyond the thickets of sleep is the river, always the river, that slow rippling of iron-hard force under the perfect skin of a huge, tireless animal. Even the Oblate priests go strange, their Christian devotions mingling with the subtle rhythms of an ancient animism. Time alters its dimensions. Soon, the river seems its own epiphany, T.S. Eliot's strong brown god, coiled for release, containing everything changeless, eternal, beyond the limits of knowledge and the impermanent heart.

And yet the last time I had been here, the river was a torrent of change. The northern oil play seethed through the whole lopsided pentangle sketched between the settlements of the lower Mackenzie. Biggest among them was the new government town of Inuvik, all raw red earth and prefab housing like a kid's Tinker Toy construction set, the buildings connected by the engineers' answer to permafrost — the above-ground umbilical cords called utilidors, each one carrying water, power and heat. A hundred kilometres east, at the old Hudson's Bay Company trading post of Aklavik, a dispersed jumble of weathered log cabins on the flat, delta flood plain, up-scale indoor plumbing still consisted of a bare room with a plastic-lined garbage can and a toilet seat. Down-scale was a rough piece of plywood with a hole cut with a jigsaw. The coastal Inuit settlement of Tuktoyaktuk, where families still carry the jack-tar surnames left by American whalers and Scottish traders, was a bewildering frenzy of large-scale marine activity.

Farther south were the Hare and Loucheux Indian villages of

Arctic Red River and Fort McPherson, the former a key staging point for canoe travel on the Mackenzie, the latter descended from a famous NWMP post at the mouth of the Mackenzie River's great northern tributary, the Peel. In the days when Mounties still bred prized dog teams on Herschel Island and patrolled the outback with paddle and sled, this country had been considered the most remote on the continent, so far north that — well, Inuvik is farther from San Francisco than Seattle is from the state of New York. A typical winter patrol, at temperatures of forty below zero and colder, would cover distances equivalent to those between Detroit and Atlanta or, in European terms, between London and Geneva. That quintessentially Canadian invention, the bush plane, arguably the most important technology in the country's national evolution, had slashed distances and travel times. The RCMP abandoned their Malamutes and Huskies for Norseman, Beaver and Otter.

By the early 1970s, bush planes came and went in such numbers that landing strips in Yellowknife and Inuvik were among the busiest in North America, ranking with Chicago, Dallas and Los Angeles for daily aircraft movements. Through hastily built airport lounges flooded a steady, jostling stream: toolpushes in from Indonesia and Venezuela, sun-burnt geologists from the North African desert, seismic crews with five-star sleeping bags good for sixty below zero perched on their shoulders, helicopter cowboys back from Vietnam with their long-billed baseball hats, mirrored aviator's shades and T-shirts blazoned with Stamp Out Fixed-Wing Aircraft. Subsumed in this, waiting to snag a flight to some place the choppers never went, leaning on their packs and chewing the ubiquitous spearmint-flavoured toothpicks of delta hash houses, were prospectors, native muskrat trappers, smoke-cured summer firefighters, deadheading Cessna 185 pilots — all the bemused folks who had been in the delta before the boom and planned to be there when it ebbed.

"Oh yes, my great-great-grandad met Alexander Mackenzie," one leather-faced Loucheux trapper told me as he restrung a pair of long, wide-bodied snow-shoes for his nephew. The footprint of these snow-shoes has stamped a unique winter seal on the delta bush since at least Mackenzie's time. "He went. These roughnecks, they'll go. You'll go. But us, we're not gonna go. We'll be here as long as this river." An anthropologist once described this trapper's culture, dwelling at the fringes of the sparse boreal forest, as a people of astonishing genius who had developed this ability to live in absolute austerity, surviving with not much more than a string of animal sinew and the resourceful ideas of their fountaining imaginations. Yet, now their capacity to adapt, in itself a testament to the spirit of human ingenuity, was being tested as never before.

Less visible than the flood of rig workers and scientists, whispering in on Lear jets and Challengers that set their own flight schedules, came calculating mandarins from Ottawa and Yellowknife and flint-eyed oil executives from Dallas, Houston and Calgary. If the risk-driven oil industry was born in the speculation of wildcatters, it will always demand that nerveless combination of killer instinct and a gambler's sense of timing. In the oil business, cash flows are huge, up-front costs are enormous, lead times to production are long, prices are volatile. When you're ready to cash out, there's always some populist demagogue who wants to step in, after you've borne the costs, and take a big piece of the profits in the name of the people. The commodity is globally strategic and the stakes are for hundreds of billions of dollars, often for national security itself. Dividing up the energy pot is a geopolitical poker round that has become, outside of warfare, the biggest game that modern civilization has yet devised. Oil companies trim the risks as best they can, lobbying the politicians, harnessing the research and analytical skills of scientists to an extent not seen outside superpower military projects, but ultimately the decisions are gut-based speculations on the odds, made by people with courage hot enough, and blood cold enough, to play their best instincts despite those odds. That much of the exploration in the Canadian Arctic was driven by public incentives and government subsidies makes for an irony that was not lost on the wheeler dealers who took advantage of the programs.

None of which altered the basic fact: Drilling a hole in the wrong place in the Arctic is like shovelling millions into the corporate shredder; drilling one in the right place just changes the game. Does a hit mean a commercially viable formation? Even if it does, do you have the resources to exploit whatever window of opportunity it affords? Misreading the drill core data and leasing the wrong holdings or miscalculating the pay-back schedule on discoveries — a single slip in the lab or the finance department can mean a sudden slide into obscurity or, worse, the public humiliation of take over and forced merger with a competitor, as Smiling Jack Gallagher discovered. His company, Dome Petroleum, had been the fastest rising bullet in the oil patch, one of the first Canada-bred private sector giants. A decade and $4 billion later it was on the auction block to an American multinational.

Oil exploration in Canada's Arctic began back in 1959, although the federal geological survey of 1947 had alerted earth scientists to the possibilities of the region. The sedimentary formations were huge, and they resembled those in the three other great oil producing zones on the planet. Possibilities are one thing, money and production are another. In a decade of exploration, all the geologists had for their efforts were three dry holes. Then, in 1967, while Canada celebrated its one hundredth birthday, a joint drilling venture by the Atlantic Richfield Company and Humble Oil punched through into a Triassic formation that flowed great quantities of crude and even more natural gas. The name of the place was Prudhoe Bay. It was located on the marshy coastal plain where the rugged Brooks Range slopes down to the Arctic Ocean. The discovery well sat smack in the middle of what looked like the largest oil field ever discovered in North America. By 1968, the rush was on, and on September 10, 1969, the State of Alaska sold the oil rights to four hundred thousand acres of the North Slope. The price was $900 million, the biggest payment in history for a single sale of oil and gas leases. Almost overnight, the Mackenzie River changed from Indian fishing ground to industrial highway. The barges of the Northern Transportation Company Limited, staging out of Hay River on Great Slave Lake, with rail and highway connections to Edmonton, moved whole drilling rigs and enormous quantities of drill pipe, prefabricated trailer units, winter rations, sacked cement and tons of the special mud required to lubricate and cool the diamond drill bits.

The formation that contained the Prudhoe Bay field extends eastward to the estuary of the Mackenzie itself and northeast, under the polar ice, far into Canada's Arctic archipelago. When I first arrived in Inuvik, the oil companies had only just begun to contemplate the awesome engineering that would be required to move off-shore into the grinding pack ice of the Beaufort Sea itself. The federal government's Polar Continental Shelf Project, charting the undersea dimensions of Canada's Arctic territory, had barely begun the map. Drill ships, artificial islands, undersea pipelines — technology that would later propel Canadian enterprise to the leading edge of polar oil exploration — were still only a body of theories in the minds of bright young scientists and engineers. In 1971, most of the discussion revolved around plans for pipelines. The biggest scheme called for an immense system to carry chilled natural gas from Prudhoe Bay down the Mackenzie River valley to Alberta and thence to the urban markets of Chicago and the American midwest. Smaller but no less formidable was a proposal for a pipeline to carry hot oil from the delta through the permafrost to refineries in the south. The industrial ferment that was transforming the farthest reaches of Canada's North was also working powerful changes among its native people.

Down the whole Mackenzie Valley, shepherded by a street-smart grade-eight drop out, a new political consciousness was in the process of birth. Stuart Hodgson, born in poverty on the wrong side of the Vancouver tracks, had been a most improbable appointment to head up the colonial old boys' club that formed the government of the Northwest Territories. He sprang from the radical crucible of organized labour in British Columbia's forest industry. Hodgson shot through B.C.'s troubled labour skies like a comet. Labour friends like to tell how he was shop steward on a Monday, member of the plant committee on Friday, chairman of Local 217 on Sunday and, finally, a financial secretary for the International Woodworkers of America.

If the relatively young Hodgson was a key figure in one of western Canada's most powerful and militant unions, the rising star had all the right credentials for his job with the union executive. A two-fisted organizer, he had driven six-inch spikes into the tires of logging trucks running hot cargo during IWA strikes. He had been chosen to lead an organizing drive in Joey Smallwood's Newfoundland — and had been run out by union-busting goons. He was later to recall that he had been so frightened by his narrow escape that when he looked in the mirror the next morning his hair had gone white, but only because he'd gotten drunk enough on the flight south to mistake his toothpaste for his Brylcreem. Whatever his close calls, Hodgson was not known for timidity. He'd been a tough, fearless point man in the union's decision to purge itself of the communist extremists who had percolated into the executive while people like Hodgson were keeping the supply lines to Stalin open on the Murmansk run.

When this new commissioner of the Northwest Territories contemplated the government he had just taken over in 1967, he found a beast entirely alien to his principles and sensibilities. Political life in the IWA may have been brutal, bloody and turbulent, but there was no disputing the say of its membership in a fundamental, sweat-stained democracy. The government of the Northwest Territories, on the other hand, was like a moribund clone of the Family Compact. The territorial council was largely appointed, often for reasons of political patronage; the commissioner held despotic powers and ruled from the absentee splendour of Ottawa, governing a third of Canada from thousands of kilometres away like a consul of Imperial Rome. One of the commissioner's major jobs was to maintain the momentum of economic development of the North's mineral resources, another was to continue a paternalistic relationship with native people that was fast vanishing from the rest of the Commonwealth.

The first thing Hodgson did as dictator of the North was behave like one. He moved his government, lock, stock and barrel, from the comforts of Ottawa to the political centre he intended to build at the sleepy mining town of Yellowknife. In fact, Hodgson moved before his civil service did, setting up his office in the battered kitchen of St. Patrick's School. While the bureaucrats went through their mid-career crises in the south, Hodgson sat on the floor of a shack in his new capital, drinking coffee he'd brewed in an empty corn can. He flipped through job applications for his territorial administration, fully aware that many of them came from the candidates he least wanted — overly ambitious career bureaucrats who saw a quick route to the top and a plush Ottawa office as a reward, or failures desperate to get as far from the scene of their crimes as possible and hang on in obscurity until their pensions came due. He would have to surround himself with a core of competent advisers, find a loyal lieutenant who could keep the mandarins off his case and fight the fires left by his own mistakes as they arose.

Hodgson found his loyal lieutenant rooted in the rock of Yellowknife itself. His name was John Havelock Parker, and he was a geologist and mining engineer. Parker had run the Rayrock Mine for the legendary Norm Byrne, one of Yellowknife's founding spirits, and had later led his own company, Precambrian Mining Services. Steady as the Canadian Shield granite he stood on, Parker was a competent administrator and much respected among the powerful mining establishment. Gold was the only reason for Yellowknife's existence, and the people connected with it formed the elite of the new capital's society. Parker's claim on the golden upper crust of Yellowknife society dated back to 1954 when the young mining engineer's sharp eye had uncovered the fifty thousand dollar swindle in which painted lead bricks had been substituted for bullion in a shipment south. Yellowknifers had first elected Parker mayor and then returned him by acclamation. Hodgson appointed him deputy commissioner. It was the shrewdest of choices.

Yellowknife's elite was about to discover it would have to

share its power with the native people it frequently — and often contemptuously — dismissed as drunks and layabouts. Parker did not share these views, but he was the establishment's man. He would run the administration while Hodgson worried about his grand strategy — how to change the Northwest Territories from an atrophied colonial organ to a self-governing democracy. This was no matter of simply holding elections overnight. Great interests in Ottawa had to be disengaged from the seductive pleasures of appointed government in the continent's last colony.

The Ottawa bureaucracy had no intention of surrendering its authority without a struggle, and the new commissioner's tenure was marked by a sudden proliferation of federal regulatory agencies, all of which served to project a network of parallel powers into his jurisdiction. On one occasion following an oil spill, no less than seven government agencies responded, quarrelling fitfully about who was responsible for what. At the same time that federal authorities had to be weaned, the consciousness of the native community had to be nudged toward full understanding of democratic process and the power that went with it. The white establishment in Yellowknife and other centres of northern government had to be eased into acceptance of the ultimate consequences of democracy in a territory where the majority was non-white.

Hodgson's first task was to systematically dismantle the appointed territorial council and replace it with a fully responsible elected legislature. His second task was to start pulling the triggers which would generate local government and to encourage the emergence of a native political leadership, although it was clear from the beginning that this would be a thankless and hurtful task. Whatever the commissioner's role behind the scenes might be, whatever his own aspirations for democratic government, he would be the inevitable lightning rod for the anger, bitterness, frustration and criticism that would surely accompany the arrival of a generation of Dene, Inuit and Métis leaders with real power — power dispensed not from government but from the grass roots of their own communities. Hodgson, whatever his origins in labour socialism, was now the figure-head of decrepit colonialism and distant imperial mandate.

Inevitably, the policies of his government for all Northerners would come into conflict with the interests of political organizations representing specific aboriginal constituencies. A good example lay in the complicated new politics of native land claims. The original treaties had been signed with Ottawa, not the government of the Northwest Territories, and many native leaders would refuse to recognize the legitimacy of the very government Hodgson was determined to create. Nevertheless, with the same decisiveness that had earned him a reputation for courage in the union halls, he put the process in motion.

By the time Hodgson had left the North, the politicization had thrown on to the national stage leaders like Inuvik's Wally Firth, the first native elected to the House of Commons from north of the sixtieth parallel. Firth was not a brilliant MP, but he was the first, and in short order he was followed into parliament by Willie Adams, an Inuit senator from Rankin Inlet in the Keewatin district on the west shore of Hudson Bay. A young Dogrib named James Wah-shee headed up the fledgling Indian Brotherhood of the Northwest Territories. It would become the Dene Nation under his militant successor Georges Erasmus, who would himself go on to lead the national Assembly of First Nations. Nick Sibbeston, a young Métis from Fort Simpson, was just thinking about law school at the University of Alberta. He would return as the fiery leader of the Northwest Territories government itself. Tagak Curley was organizing the Inuit Tapirisat; he, too, would lead the government. Nellie Cournoyea, a CBC employee in Inuvik, was to lead the Committee for Original Peoples' Entitlements. As minister of health, she would wrest control of the northern medical service from Ottawa and bring it home after a thirty-four-year struggle. Peter Ernerk, born in a snow house, had been red-circled by the commissioner himself, pulled into the civil service for seasoning and sent on to serve as senior minister in critical portfolios and as a major advocate for Nunavut, an independent Inuit territory which called for separation from the western lands of the Dene Nation. Jim Bourque, a president of the Northwest Territories Métis Association, became the only person of native ancestry to head a wildlife department, one that is rated among the finest in Canada.

Stephen Kakfwi, a tough and uncompromising leader of the Dene Nation, had been a homesick kid at a residential school when Hodgson unleashed a radical young educator named Paul Robinson and gave him a mandate to remake the northern curriculum. Robinson believed that learning materials in northern schools should reflect the reality of life in the Arctic, not the values of a distant and alien southern culture. Robinson's texts were simple, cheap and often mimeographed to cut costs, but they were written in the language of Northern youngsters, filled with references to trappers and hunters, chain saws and canoe kickers. The approach brought a revolution in thought which transformed the teaching landscape. Almost overnight, this home-grown curriculum became an international model for other countries with struggling aboriginal minorities. Twenty years later, Kakfwi completed the circle begun by Hodgson, taking over as minister of education for the Northwest Territories, the first person of aboriginal descent in Canadian history to hold such a vital post.

All of these individuals expressed varying degrees of hostility to Hodgson's perceived colonial paternalism, yet to an outsider, unencumbered by the vested interests of cultural politics, it was clear that the source of their new power lay in the commissioner's unswerving efforts to create a responsible government that they would ultimately control. From his first day in office, Hodgson drove hard to eliminate appointed power wherever he could, and I watched fascinated from the press gallery, often the only journalist there from southern Canada, as he gradually withdrew himself from debate on the floor, deliberately making himself less and less of a quasi-premier and more and more of a state figure-head.

In the midst of this, determined that Yellowknife would not become the remote and isolated capital that Ottawa had been, the commissioner maintained an exhausting schedule of personal appearances designed to take government directly to the people who would be electing the legislatures of the future. From Ellesmere Island beside Greenland to Cantung Mines on the Yukon border, Hodgson strove to appear personally before the newly elected hamlet and village councils, responding directly to their questions and demands. It was at these meetings, sweeping aside the red tape of his own bureaucracy's procedures, that Hodgson earned his reputation with the civil servants as an irresponsible Santa Claus. The important thing, he said, was not the pride of bureaucrats but the symbolic acknowledgment that to be an elected official, however small the office, was to have the right to command public servants. Hostility to Hodgson's approach inside his administration, on the other hand, was rooted in a colonial past where the bureaucrat's power had been supreme. The commissioner intended to demolish that tradition and seized every opportunity to do so.

At one tiny settlement, high on the northern shoulder of Baffin Island, Hodgson arrived for a meeting with the town council. Spring, with its clear, cold skies and brilliant sunlight, had just arrived in the High Arctic, and after the meeting one of the Inuit councillors generously invited some of Hodgson's officials to go out with him the next morning to look at the scenery. He told them that it was a special time of year, that the early light on the sea ice and glaciers was particularly beautiful. The officials arranged for the councillor to pick them up with his motor toboggan just before first light the next morning. But when he showed up, he found that the officials had all slept in. The volunteer guide waited until sunrise, then he went about his business. When the commissioner discovered that nobody had turned out for the arranged tour, he summoned his officials and formally gave them a public tongue-lashing that is still talked about in the eastern Arctic.

"He reamed us out, then he reamed us out again," one of them later recalled. "He was so mad they could hear him at the other end of the settlement. I still cringe when I think about it sixteen years later."

The commissioner told his officials that for a hundred years stupid bureaucrats had joked about the impossibility of getting things done in the North because the native people were all operating on "Indian time."

"You tell them they have to adapt to your schedules," he said. "Adapt to our ideas about time. Then you fail to show up for a councillor who has come to show you how beautiful his country is. You make us into liars. You make me into a liar. That man is a hunter. It's a damn sight more honourable profession than yours. These people have better things to do with their time than idle their Ski-doo outside the door waiting for a bunch of lazy bureaucrats operating on white man's time."

If there was a calculating element to Hodgson's demonstrations of the responsiveness of the public service to the elected arm of government, there was also a personal generosity of spirit that went beyond political strategy. On one occasion, dropping into the summer fish camp of four bachelor brothers on the Mackenzie River, the commissioner found a log cabin with its interior plastered with hockey pictures clipped from magazines. When he asked if there was anything he could do for the elderly men, they shyly asked if they could see a hockey game. They were great fans of Bobby Hull, then playing for the Winnipeg Jets of the new World Hockey League, but their experience of the sport was restricted to radio broadcasts. They had never seen hockey played in the flesh.

Promising to get the Winnipeg Jets to play in the Northwest Territories was beyond even Hodgson's powers, but he didn't hesitate to ask the *Edmonton Journal* to lay on tickets the next time the Jets and the Oilers squared off. He sent his plane back to

Fort Wrigley that winter with instructions to bring the brothers out for their hockey game. It was the coldest day of the year, the temperature hanging at seventy below zero, and the word came down from the old men's winter trapping camp: "Too cold for dogs to travel." Hockey might be fun and the commissioner might have sent his plane five hundred kilometres from Yellow-knife, but the rights of their animals came before the pleasure of their masters.

If Hodgson believed that it was his responsibility to create the concept of powerful, home-grown government in the minds of the people who would ultimately seize his authority for them-selves, he also believed that one of his most important missions was to place the North on the bigger map of Canadian cons-ciousness, to make the rest of the country take heed of this vast and important region. His political enemies accused him of a profligate administration, addicted to bread and circuses and big gestures, but the flamboyance of this commissioner was less ego than calculation. Abstemious and unassuming in his private life, the kind of guy, one trapper told me, who would piss in the same snow bank as his dog handler, Hodgson had a sophisti-cated understanding of political statements in the new age of television. If the Imperial Roman style was what competed suc-cessfully with Pierre Trudeau, Peter Lougheed and W.A.C. Ben-nett in the eyes of CBC producers, then bread and circuses they would get.

Hodgson organized royal tours; lured princes and prime min-isters on to the ice pack — and under it; bestowed official gifts of Inuit art and Indian crafts on every visitor; invited influential writers and journalists to accompany him on tours to places that were impossible to reach. The man, who privately brewed his coffee in a billy can and wore a cheap Mickey Mouse watch, publicly threw spectacular parties at every excuse, the most lav-ish of them a formal ball in honour of the RCMP's one hun-dredth birthday. But mostly, whirling about his million-and-a-half-square-kilometre sultanate like a dervish, he spoke tirelessly to southerners — and to Northerners — about his vision of a democratic Northwest Territories that could be a full partner in Confederation. When he left office at the end of 1978, having put in one year more than the ten he had promised, the North was part of our national consciousness as never before.

The man who had started as the only true dictator in North America left behind him the only legislature in the New World with a freely elected majority of aboriginal people. It is the only democratic government in the western hemisphere that can claim that three of the last four government leaders have been an Indian, an Inuit and a Métis. While Hodgson was commissioner, the Canadian Armed Forces established Northern Command, with headquarters in Yellowknife, and the Northwest Territories acquired its own independent and autonomous court system.

It remained for the loyal lieutenant to nurture the seeds planted by his frequently misunderstood captain. In that choice, too, Hodgson proved resoundingly astute. John Parker, the gentle, reserved geologist, took up Hodgson's mantle as commissioner, the first true Northerner to hold the job. He presided with grace and good humour over the turbulent politicization of the North and its peoples that had been launched by his predecessor. Parker willingly served as steward, keeping a low profile while native people developed their own organizations and learned the ropes of political power. Without any active intervention, he watched the great debates over aboriginal rights, resource development, environment, even the proposed division of his beloved Northwest Territories. All the time, he believed that these decisions should not be in the hands of Ottawa mandarins or appointed officials like himself but of elected, responsible, northern politicians. In 1986, he took the next to last step, removing himself as the last appointed agent of the federal government in the elected forum and stepping down from his powerful seat on the executive council of the Northwest Territories legislature. It was a measure of the stature and integrity of both men that they worked so diligently not to cling to power but to shed it.

The power they surrendered was real power. Native peoples organized to stop the plans of multinational consortiums to build pipelines down the mighty valley of the Mackenzie River that had sustained their cultures for so long. The settlement of aboriginal claims on northern lands displaced development as the top political priority north of the sixtieth parallel. The nature of government itself and the rights of northern people to determine their own forms of democracy suddenly emerged as legitimate issues on the national agenda.

Hodgson wrote to me after hearing of Parker's decision to remove himself as the last appointed official from the legislative process: "Yes, sir — Stu the First and John the Last, I wouldn't have wanted it any other way." If the major legacies of these two political leaders are written largely in the intangibles of process and attitude, sometimes it is the small achievement that endures both in memory and in physical form. As my plane banked over Fort McPherson, squaring on its navigation beacon for the

descent to Inuvik, I was able to look down on the supple sweep
of the Peel River where it enters the muddy Mackenzie. Almost
a generation before, as I prepared to leave the Delta for what I
knew might be the last time, I had taken a final trip up the Peel
and into the wilderness that had swallowed up the last stampede to riches. I wanted to feel again the untouched splendour
of the place, to burn it into the hidden memories of my senses
like Wordsworth's daffodils, something to spring into the
mind's eye of the imagination with a power and vividness that
external records can never evoke.

The sky was brassy under the deflected light of the midnight
sun and the shallow-bottomed plywood skiff I'd hired seemed
to stand motionless on the polished surface of that immense,
jade-green current. Above me, in the gloomy spruce woods that
crowd the banks, there slowly passed a procession of pitiful,
decaying shelters. These were cabins and lean-tos abandoned by
Overlanders on their way to perish in the grisly scurvy camp at
Rat River they named Destruction City. How many survived the
trek from Edmonton to the Klondike gold fields in 1898 is unknown to this day, but it was a starving handful of those who
left their bones on the unforgiving tributaries of the Peel and the
desolate passes of the Ogilvie Range, "rock-ribbed and ancient as
the sun."

Like so many others, like myself, the Overlanders had come
and gone, but the man I was going to visit had lived on the Peel
all his life. And his father and grandfather and great-grandfather
before him. Counting the rough measure of long generations in
an oral tradition, it was four hundred years of memory. One of
those ancestors had greeted Alexander Mackenzie in 1789, and
the memory of that wondrous event had been passed down in
the family like the most precious of heirlooms.

I tracked into the sandy beach below Peter Vittrekwa's camp
by following the rich scent of the fresh doughnuts his wife
Rebecca had just fried and found Peter himself wreathed in the
pungent shadows of the log house where he cured fish. The sun
that had rolled just under the horizon was beginning to climb
again when I stepped into Peter's smoke house. He was throwing handfuls of aromatic chips on the glowing bank of coals. My
entry stirred the air, sent a blue eddy swirling up and released
an eerie, flickering light that was accompanied by a strange
sound. Startled, I looked up. Above us, hung on the drying racks
in the peak of the roof, a silvery school of freshwater herring rus-
tled and danced like some magician's wind chimes. Beneath
them hung the chunky shapes of split white fish and coney fish.

Peter laughed at my surprise and took me up past the cabin of his eighty-year-old father, William, for a breakfast of Rebecca's doughnuts.

Over coffee, he marvelled on a recent event. One morning not long before my visit he had been awakened by the sound of strangers in his camp. He had gone out to see who they were while Rebecca had bustled about preparing for unexpected visitors. Outside, he found two men in yellow hard hats pounding survey stakes into the grassy clearing on either side of the cabin he'd lived in for half a century. When he asked what they were doing, they cheerfully told him: The clearing was smack in the middle of the right of way for the federal government's promised highway from Whitehorse to Inuvik. The highway was coming through and this was Crown land, so he'd just have to move. When he objected to the federal government, it was pointed out by Ottawa's public works department lawyers that, technically speaking, the Vittrekwas were squatters. He should apply for legal aid and hire a lawyer of his own, they told him. The justice department's bureaucrats rendered that advice academic. Civil land disputes did not merit legal aid. When Peter pointed out that his family had been squatting on the site before Canada was even an idea; long enough, indeed, to have the adjacent tributary into the Peel carry his surname, the public works bureaucracy magnanimously agreed to move the highway one hundred metres — less, I suspect, from some miserly form of compassion than from a desire to avoid compensation for the log cabins.

"My goodness, I don't know what to do," Peter told me while Rebecca brewed more coffee. "I don't want to give this place up. It is in my mind that this is my home. What am I going to do?"

I didn't know either. But when Stu Hodgson heard the story, he knew what to do. And that is why, when you look down on the first channels of the delta, descending to Inuvik from thirty thousand feet, you see this public works irregularity, this sudden, odd dog-leg in the arrow-straight Dempster Highway, just where it approaches the ferry crossing to Fort McPherson, about twenty-five kilometres downstream from where the Vittrekwa River gushes into the Peel.

SINGING UNDER ENDLESS STARS

Bill Smith was watering a marvellous crop of marigolds when I encountered him for the first time. The flowers boiled up out of the dark earth, a brilliant yellow drift in one of those barren boulevards that traffic engineers throw in as a sop to the urban landscape whenever they transform a quiet residential street into a truck route. The tiny garden was a small act of insurgency, an aesthetic ambush in the constant guerrilla war between the secret Canadian love of dishevelled nature and our public propensity to bureaucratic discipline.

In this jab at officialdom, one of Bill's young neighbours had ignored the environmental impact studies, development permits, rezoning applications and bank stability studies demanded by protocol. He simply dug up the boulevard, planted his marigolds, turned the operation over to Bill as chief horticulturist and left on a foreign aid project. Not surprising from a resident of the old Edmonton pocket community that residents insist upon calling Skunk Hollow in defiance of city ordinances naming places after dead politicians and departed school trustees. To make things worse, before he vanished into Africa, the casual revolutionary had taken his chain saw, cut a big chunk out of the fence behind the sidewalk and installed a seat where the weary might rest and gaze upon the flowers.

This created a crisis among the drones of urban planning. But, at ninety, Bill Smith was more than a match for the clucking mandarins at city hall. He outflanked them in public relations, outmanoeuvred them in the press and out-hustled them in winning neighbourhood support. When I wrote about the contretemps as a small victory against the tyranny of orthodoxy, I made the mistake of referring to Bill as a frail, elderly gentleman.

The next time we met, he seized me with a grip that was all sinewy muscle and offered to wrist wrestle any damn time I'd care to choose. But that wasn't why I wound up in his cheery apartment on a late summer evening, drinking whisky straight from a shot glass and watching the strawberry light flood through the birches and saskatoons in the valley of the North Saskatchewan. I was there because of a revelation, an epiphany rooted in the immigrant nature of Canada herself. I had discovered that Bill and I were bound up in the ancient bondage of blood and sacrifice that we remember each November 11.

How could this be? What conceivable connections could I have with a man who was more than half a century old the day that I was born on the other side of the planet? How small the world has become. How deep its currents run. Bill Smith and my grandfather landed on the same blood-stained beach in the same bloody battle of the war that marks the beginning of the modern world and its industrial slaughters. Bill Smith was a peach-fuzz kid, barely shaving, when he was recruited to the Royal Welch Fusiliers with an appeal to adolescent patriotism and a promise of adventure. My grandfather Thomas Dodd Hume was a hard-bitten career soldier who had served with the Imperial Army, late of the Lancashire Fusiliers. He had served in Egypt in the nineteenth century and had campaigned on the Indian Frontier, where he was busted from sergeant back to private following a drunken escapade that involved instructing raw recruits in the tactics of evading patrolling MPs after a bar-smashing night on the town.

And both of them hit the beach at Suvla Bay in Gallipoli. And both of them got shot to hell. And every November 11, I rise to remember: not the bombast of patriotism, not the glory of our national honour, just these two men who never met and yet remain strangely connected through me, mingled in memory.

My grandfather died in my far away childhood, his life spent in the Empire's service on distant frontiers he neither knew nor wanted, a kind of legend to his scattered kinfolk. He was seventy-seven, missing an eye and most of one shoulder, and even now, dim and uncertain as a puddled reflection in my street kid's recollection, he beckons me behind the rain barrel in his little Black Country garden and presses upon me his medals, lustrous and wondrous. Always, my life will be transfixed upon the mystery stamped into that metal, that naked man on a silver horse, riding through a field of skulls. And always, my father weeps and makes me give them back, and we leave for the grey Atlantic and a passage to Canada.

Bill Smith became part of my history before my own father did. That occurred on August 4, 1914, when he left his job at the steelworks in Shotton, North Wales, and went to volunteer to serve his country in the Great War. At 8 p.m., he took the King's shilling.

Why did he go? "Well, I had some pals in the Territorials. You know, when I was a kid, The Continent was the other end of the world!" Bill Smith was the first volunteer from the village of Hawarden, where he had been born, and because he signed on four-and-a-half hours before the declaration of World War One he was entitled to mobilization pay: "They called it blood money. I was entitled to it and I got it. Oh yes, I got my blood money."

He was eighteen years old and had never heard of Canada. They paraded him before the Colonel of the regiment. Sitting in his apartment, squinting at the long arrows of sunlight slanting into the rank profusion of the river valley, he remembered back across two of my lifetimes: there was a table and piled upon it, in gleaming stacks, gold sovereigns. He got five pounds and returned to his billet. It was a barn behind a stable and, when they mustered for mess, the ale came not in mugs but in foaming buckets. They dipped for it. On his first leave, he walked the six miles home to give his mother three pounds of his "blood money."

A year later, he sailed for the Dardanelles. This was Winston Churchill's scheme. What he called the soft underbelly of Europe. Bill Smith and my grandfather were supposed to slice through the slack abdomen of the Ottoman Empire and into the entrails of the Kaiser's power. It was a wonderful plan. It had only one flaw. It assumed that the Turks couldn't fight. But the Turks could fight. They annihilated the flower of Britain, Australia and New Zealand's youth in one bitter year.

Bill Smith told me of sailing for the Dardanelles on July 13, 1915. He was aboard the S.S. *Caledonia* and, although quarters were cramped for the two thousand men, he was not so badly off. Assigned to run tea to the bridge for the captain and his watch, his topside cabin compensated for a farm boy's queasy first experience of Atlantic swells. "I was sick as a dog," he told me. His hammock was slung above the tables of the mess hall, but at least he wasn't in the bowels of the ship. He and his chums were up on A deck in the first-class tourist quarters, where he could be close to his duties on the bridge.

"All the Welsh boys would sit on the decks at night and sing," he said. "And Captain Thomas, he was a Welshman. I'd take him his mug of tea and he'd be up on the bridge listening and crying. 'You think you're going on a bloody Sunday school outing,' he'd say." The stupidity that Captain Thomas feared and that came to represent the whole command of the Gallipoli campaign revealed itself early. "The officers took away our army boots because the hobnails were scuffing the wood of A deck — that was the posh deck. When we finally got to Alexandria our feet were so swollen we couldn't get the boots back on. Some of the lads had sunburned feet."

Yet, that arrival in Alexandria remained vivid and powerful in the memory of a young man who had grown up in a world of grey mountains, mists and the soft green landscape of the Vale of Clwyd. First, there was the white flash of the houses, blinding in the vigour of the sun. Then, there was the clear water — so clear the troops could see to the pale and sandy bottom of the bay. It was not all beauty. The ships would dump the contents of their latrines into the water and it would seethe with feeding mackerel: "I've always been off fish ever since that day."

The *Caledonia* anchored among the long grey shapes of Royal Navy destroyers off Egypt's second capital. "You know, those Egyptians would dive to the bottom to collect coal spilled from the ships. We would wrap ha'pennies in silver foil and pitch them into the sea. The Egyptians would dive for what they thought were shillings. They'd be so angry when they found what they had — but we were so young. We just laughed."

One night in dock, the *Caledonia* suddenly developed a sharp list. It wasn't sabotage but the weight of two thousand young soldiers rushing to the rail: "Two Egyptians had a woman on the docks. The troops would throw coins and they'd raise her skirts. I spent my last tuppence on that!" The show lasted only long enough for the military police to arrive with clubs. They arrested the two men and sent the woman on her way.

Deep into the whisky bottle, he recalled a route march through the blast furnace of Alexandria by day: "We were in full gear. The long Lee Enfield rifle weighed nine-and-a-half pounds. We had one hundred rounds of ammunition. Rations. A great coat. Kit. Bayonet and all that." As the eight companies of the battalion marched through Alexandria, thirsty soldiers would toss shillings to Egyptian kids and dispatch them for bottles of cold beer. "The problem was that to the Egyptian kids, one British soldier looked like another and they'd run up and down the column with people trying to get the beer. And the other soldiers on the streets, they'd salute the officers as they went past, and show US their bottles of beer! Major Head was at the rear of the column on his horse and he saw this Egyptian kid selling beer. The streets were cobbled and the horses were shod — how the sparks flew as he galloped up and laid his quirt into that kid.

"Major Head. He was one of the first ones that got himself killed on the Dardanelles with us. We heard that he got hit and that he jumped up again to cheer on the troops and got shot between the eyes." There were many more who fell following the heroic Major Head. There was Bill's chum, Tommy Walker.

"Tommy Walker. Illiterate. He had a girlfriend but he couldn't read her letters. I'd read them to him. He'd tell me what to write. He was killed on the Dardanelles, Tommy was." And there was Captain Bill Beswick and his brother, Lieutenant Ed Beswick, both from the Roman-walled city of Chester and both killed. And Harry Williams. And the Chuck brothers who joined the band — but, of course, there was no place for musicians as the casualties began to mount, so they went into the front lines as stretcher bearers and were slain. And there were the Cheshires. And the Borderers. And the Wiltshires. And the Inniskillings. And the Aussies. And the Kiwis. And my grandad's Lancashire Fusiliers.

Today, reading the cool, dispassionate histories, it is hard for the mind to grapple with the slaughter of those battles. Even Bill found the numberless dead a presence that resided in the marrow of his bones, something that eluded intellect and reason. "The Royal Welch Fusiliers landed on that beach one thousand strong on August 10th," he told me. "When they took us off in November there were 145."

Bill was not one of them. Like my grandfather, who fell on his first day, never even reaching the wire where the bodies piled thirty deep, who lay maimed and mutilated at the water's edge, the empty socket of his eye filled with buzzing bluebottles, Bill lasted scarcely longer. On his fourth day, a ragged piece of shrapnel, moving slowly enough that he could watch it pinwheel toward him, ripped his right breast away. He never again joined a combat unit, although he went back to Flanders and served the rest of the war in a labour battalion and as a clerk.

Yet, even in his wounds, there is this connection between us. Bill went home in the hospital ship S.S. *Aquitania*, a Cunard trans-Atlantic liner requisitioned for naval service. She was the vessel that carried me to Canada in 1948, a baby in the arms of parents sickened by the carnage of a second world war and leaving Europe to its fate. It was the final voyage of the *Aquitania*, the ship that had carried Bill Smith toward his rebirth into a changed world, carrying the small bundle of my own life toward the same destination, the same dusty street in the same prairie city.

The quest that brought Bill Smith to Alberta in 1919 was as plain and forthright as the man himself. He came to Canada seeking peace for his soul, a soul troubled to its depths by the chaos and cynicism of the Great War's killing fields — a war he said had forever swept away the world he knew and loved. His friends, his culture, values and traditions he held dear, all seemed to have been broken and ploughed under in the Dardanelles and in the mud and carnage of the Western Front.

My grandfather bowed to the weight of things as they were, accepted the depression and the grim factories of his industrial midlands, lost two of his four children to the disease and poverty of the slums. But Bill Smith, as my father would do a generation later, turned his back on the smoking ruin of Europe and looked to the New World, a world filled with possibilities and futures.

"It was only about four or five of us came back to my little town after the war," he said. "It's why I came to this country. You'd see Mrs. Williams coming down the street and she'd want to know if I was there when Harry got killed.

"I got some literature about Canada, the Last Best West, and there was a mention of Peace River. I got the impression it was a new country, named after peace. And I went up to the city of Chester and I got my ticket to the land of Peace."

What he found, of course, was not an ideal, but a muscle-and-blood frontier of toil and sweat. In the midst of it, through the Dirty Thirties and the Second World War spawned out of his own war to end war, he raised four children, who in turn gave him the eight grandchildren and twelve great-grandchildren that he prized. When he died a few months short of his ninety-second birthday, he was surrounded by the family he said was the greatest gift he could give to his new country.

His long journey had begun in a village still tied to another time. His own first memory was of a traditional ritual descended from a past so ancient nobody can remember the origins. As a male child, he was "britched," formally initiated into the community of men. And almost a century later, nearly blind, sitting on his bed in the hospital, already losing his last, sudden battle with illness, age and time, he could still ring off the names of his slain companions from that village of his youth: "I can see their faces as clear as if I were with them . . . but their faces are not like mine. They have the faces of young boys and there is a brightness upon them." Holding my hand, he wept for all the Welsh boys he remembered singing their hymns under the glittering canopy of Aegean stars, singing in perfect harmony as they sailed to their graves.

"And I alone survived," goes a line from the ancient Welsh poetry in which Bill Smith took immense pride, the poetry he loved to cite as the foundation of all our modern poetic traditions. "And when I came again to my own country, not one friend remained," goes another.

So he turned his face to the farthest west and came to a new country with new dreams. What did Bill Smith find at the end of his long 1919 voyage across Canada in the cold, smoky rattle of a colonists' car? He found what my father found in his time, and what I found in mine — freedom from the expectations of privilege and class, freedom to make a way unhindered by the burdens of convention and the brutal limitations of Britain's unacknowledged caste system.

He found a job as a cowhand for one dollar a day. He found the tranquillity of the old log church in Peace River where he was confirmed, of the high, white course of the Milky Way, pouring across a sky so clear he saw stars he had never known. He found the wonders of science and out of that wonder founded, in 1923, the first commercial radio station in the Peace River block. And one cold night, he found a greasy spoon in a settlement called McLennan. It had not much going for it except big helpings of plain food and an exceptionally pretty waitress who did not take exception to his interest. She was Alice Luella English, whom he courted and married in 1925.

Bill Smith found a career with the Northern Alberta Railway, retiring as head of his department in 1959, but not retiring from life. As a member of the Retired Railway Veterans Association, he spent the next twenty-seven years visiting members confined to hospital, until, finally,the hospital claimed him.

And he invented a new role for himself as a vital contributor to civic affairs in the city of Edmonton. He was a gad-fly activist who almost single-handedly pestered the politicians into moving the cenotaph from an obscure site to a place of honour before the city hall chambers. In his final year, he was still at the fore-front of the battle to prevent the bureaucrats from meddling with the marigold patch his young neighbours in Skunk Hollow had planted in the dusty boulevard. He watched with an eagle eye from his balcony and each day made the expedition down six floors to water those flowers.

The summer he died, the flowers dried up and blew away. It

was as though the vivid blooms had faded with Bill, who loved them so much. But the next year, they came back, a kind of defiant illumination in the shadow of death. I picked a few and laid a bouquet at the cenotaph. A ritual not so much for the dead as for the living. For it is only in the hearts of the living, in the hearts of you and I, who have this obligation to remember, it is only there that we find Tommy Walker and Harry Williams and the Beswick boys and the Chuck brothers and my grandfather and Bill Smith, uncorrupted and untarnished, singing under endless stars.

SURRENDER TO THE DAY

Don't look for Zipper Creek on a map because you won't find it. The name is a lie and the location a deliberate mystery. I will confess to a clear, bubbling stream that tumbles over pebbles and limestone ledges in its upper reaches, frothing like champagne in the little punch-bowls hollowed among boulders. Farther down, it swirls into long placid stretches, meandering through scrub willows and grassy meadows. On a typical summer day in the Far West, addressed by a sky of limitless prospects, the intensity of its blue punctuated by countless white clouds and the whole array scudding before a breeze that sets the silver-bellied aspen leaves quaking, it is difficult to imagine a place that is closer to heaven.

Under the cool tickle of back eddies, perfectly camouflaged by shadows that curl along the green banks, you may sometimes spot the dappled shoulders of a fanning trout. In the heat of the day, they lie still as iron in the slow current, but the spring-fed waters remain icy even in the glare of solar noon. Everywhere, the careful watcher will see the stealthy surface dimples over rising fish.

These dark-backed beauties are my excuse for coming here, but in reality it is the stream itself which draws me. It is a living thing, always present yet infinitely changeable, a universe to the small creatures that dwell upon and within it, yet itself a tiny, fragile part of a changing and vulnerable landscape.

I have always had this affinity for moving water. I draw sustenance from the sound and sight of it, from the thundering rivers like the Nahanni, plunging in boiling columns down Virginia Falls, to the black glass of the Skeena at first light, slipping seaward under veils of mist. The steel-blue sweep of the Thompson under arid table land; the chrome-flecked slash of the Coppermine rushing to Bloody Falls. The olive drab of the lazy North Saskatchewan. The glistening, patterned boulders in the green ribbon of the Similkameen, twining like a diamond-back past sage-brush and cactus, through deserts of smashed rock and alkali pans. The muscular immensity of the St. Lawrence and its brawny match, the mile-wide Mackenzie — not one of them fails to rivet my attention.

There is something about water moving on the face of rock, carving its endless patterns into tundra and prairie, oxbow and coulee, chute and canyon, something that defines the spiritual shape of the country in which we live. These sculpted images recur again and again in the paintings of A.Y. Jackson, Arthur Lismer and Lawren Harris and in the writings of Roderick Haig-Brown, Bruce Hutchison, Howard O'Hagan and Hubert Evans. And yet, for all the awe inspired by rivers, it is small streams that course the landscape of my affections. I call them all by the same name — Zipper Creek. They flow out of the dreams of my past to wind through the turmoil of the present, subterranean currents of solitude and peace. Like any parent with many children, I have my favourites, and yet I could not imagine the world without one of them.

There is the island stream where I caught my first trout, a hand's length of cutthroat hammering out of a foaming chute to near straighten the hook on my little silver spinner. I'd scoured the frost-covered logjams down that whole stretch of water, stocking my tackle box with the snagged tee-spoons and spinning gear of other more grown up fishermen who came after steelhead and the yellow-bellied sea-run browns.

At the mountain stream where I laid out my first fly, I stood on a huge metamorphic boulder above the hidden creek that rushes through volcanic canyons, pool cascading into mossy pool, with only a luminous strip of sky above. At night, I'd roll my blankets under the overhanging cliffs, still warm with the late sun, and fall into the blackness of a deep, dreamless sleep that was somehow filled with the sound of rushing water.

There is the enduring mystery of the vanishing stream with its vanishing fish. It dries to a trickle in summer and there are no fish at all in the brackish puddles, yet it returns with the October rains, foams under the fallen trees and fills with the slab-sided coho salmon that whiz through the shallows of the estuary like silver comets. And there's the Zipper Creek of my high Alberta summers, tumbling down from the highlands to wander through meadows beneath the big bonnet of the Rocky Mountain sky.

Roderick Haig-Brown, our national philosopher of moving water, observed that a river never sleeps and that for all the splendour of water in its other states — the pristine cornices of snow-capped peaks or the slow majesty of glacial ice — it is the motion of water that seems most beautiful and profound. Perhaps this is because the great river systems and their tributaries defined our national consciousness. Analogy fashions the rivers as a nervous system, the portages as synapses, the traffic of canoes and York boats as the impulses that organized into thought and consciousness. And from that network of early commerce, we shape our sense of national self. We are a people of continental fringes stitched together by those great uncharted rivers running into an unknown interior. They are the channels to that powerful, restless Canadian unconscious which has always absorbed its energy from the archetypes of our elemental landscape.

Someone, I think it was Izaak Walton, said of the gentler chalk streams of his native England, that every hour spent fishing can be added to the end of one's life. So, as with Roderick Haig-Brown, I claim the trout as my excuse. Here at Zipper Creek, in the baby toe of Alberta's foothills, one finds some of the best trout fishing in the world. Brown trout, brookies, cutthroat, rainbow and Dolly Varden, not to mention Rocky Mountain white fish and sail-finned grayling — you can pick your stream, your species and your fishing style. You may fish still waters in the shade of cottonwoods, or you may test your skills on a rising freshet; you may try the riffles at the tail of a clear pool or challenge murky eddies over muddy bottoms. But each fisherman must bring intelligence and patience along with tackle, tricks and technical skill.

I'm a fly fisherman myself, although I'm not above dragging a worm off the end of a dock if that's what it takes to provide supper. When I cannot challenge the wild strength of a sea-run cutthroat, working the rising tide in a misty estuary, then I prefer the silent stealth of a brown trout in ambush.

Alberta browns are cautious and wary. They are spooked as easily by a heavy step on the bank or a sudden shadow against the sun as they are by wallowing in the stream like a hippopotamus or the splashing bird's nest of an ill-cast line. For me, the first sortie always involves a long, slow stroll by the stream, pausing frequently to watch for trout rising to take the insects that hatch in the warmth and pop through the surface film. Next comes the keen observation of insect life. What are the fish eating? Is there a hatch of caddis-fly or stone-fly? Check the fly box. Do I have a pattern that resembles the hatching flies? If not, can I tie one?

Finally, the stalk. On come the chest waders — I prefer supple waterproofed nylon to the drier, warmer but inevitably awkward rubber — and out into the icy current. I approach the fish from downstream, trying to lay a long, gentle line into the current. The big browns like to lie below the bends of the stream, conserving energy by idling in the back eddy and sliding out to feed on what the current brings to them. They are wary, and the fly must drift unencumbered over the trout's station.

Watching a fish rise slowly through crystal water to take the tiny fly you have tied yourself is a moment of beauty and exhilaration. For myself, I hardly care whether I catch a fish any more. Those that I do are most often released. The long days and purple evenings on Zipper Creek are the real treasure.

On this day, not even the minnows are stirring. Overhead, there's a red-legged hawk wheeling under skies gone ragged with fast-moving cloud. The lowing of distant cattle wafts in from ranch land beyond the tree line. This stretch of current runs clear over brown pebbles and streaming weed, rippling in the green landscape. Here and there, leaves have begun to turn the tawny colours of autumn. It is the kind of scene that drew Izaak Walton again and again from the clamour of his seventeenth century ironmonger's shop to the contemplative pleasures of fishing. It was to the pastoral life of streams that he finally retreated and wrote for us his lovely little meditation, *The Compleat Angler*.

I've tried six pools now and nothing is stirring. I change flies. First, a backswimmer, iridescent filaments of peacock herl; then, my own spiky variant of a deerfly, made with clipped caribou hair; a glittery minnow imitation; a gaudy California coachman, yellow wool under polar bear fur; finally, in desperation, a garish black, silver and scarlet British pattern called The Butcher, sent by a far-removed relative on a forgotten birthday. The Butcher is a pig. It tracks in the current with all the grace of a sow's toe. I cast it several times more, wondering at the stupidity of the fish it is supposed to deceive. I surrender to the day.

Pushing through a thicket perfumed by wild roses, I head back upstream to a natural meadow. The underbrush is thick with canes of late-ripening raspberries, and I fill my fly box with the wild, red fruit and retire to sit by the stream, watching reflections of clouds sail by as I eat the sweet berries one by one.

My meditations are interrupted by the prickling sensation that comes of being secretly watched. I search the underbrush. The stream bank. The feeling persists, almost electric in its creeping at the nape of my neck.

I try a trick taught by a bush-wise Dogrib trapper. Don't look for anything in particular, empty the mind and leave the blank screen sensitive to any tiny, ill-defined movement at the periphery of vision. One only experiences the feeling of being watched when the unconscious mind has noticed something almost imperceptible to the normal senses, something screened out by the conscious mind. The truly ambushed never suspect their fate.

Sure enough, there is a flutter at the edge of my field of vision, and then I see it. Only a rod's length away, a tree stump begins to move. It is a great horned owl, near perfect in his grey camouflage. It is most unusual to meet such a nocturnal bird of prey abroad in bright daylight, but his presence explains the absence of bird song and squirrel chatter. The huge, golden eyes watch me for a long moment, then blink slowly, and the bird rises and wings away in a silent sweep of wings, another shadow blending with the longer shadows of a growing dusk.

And where, you are asking, is Zipper Creek. My lip is zipped. This much I promised the old fisherman who led me to it, as another led him to it many years ago. Like love, you'll have to find it for yourself. When you do, you will know that you are there.

BIBLIOGRAPHY

Akrigg, G.P.V. and Helen B. Akrigg. *British Columbia Chronicle 1778-1846*. Vancouver: Discovery Press, 1975.

Akrigg, G.P.V. and Helen B. Akrigg. *British Columbia Chronicle 1847-1871*. Vancouver: Discovery Press, 1977.

Anderson, Frank W. *Hillcrest Mine Disaster*. Chapbook No. 18. Calgary: Frontier Publishing Ltd., 1969.

Asch, Michael. *Home and Native Land: Aboriginal Rights and the Canadian Constitution*. Toronto: Methuen, 1984.

Back, Sir George. *Narrative of the Arctic Land Expedition*. Edmonton: Hurtig, 1970.

Balickci, Asen. *The Netsilik Eskimo*. New York: The Natural History Press, 1970.

Barbeau, Marius. *The Downfall of Temlaham*. Toronto: Macmillan, 1928.

Barlee, N.L. *Similkameen: The Pictograph Country*. Summerland: self-published chapbook, 1978.

Barlee, N. L. *West Kootenay: Ghost Town Country*. Surrey: Canada West Publications, 1984.

Beattie, Owen and John Geiger. *Frozen In Time: Unlocking the Secrets of the Franklin Expedition*. Saskatoon: Western Producer Prairie Books, 1988.

Bennett, Ben. *Death, Too, For The-Heavy-Runner*. Missoula: Mountain Press Publishing, 1982.

Bennett, John W. *Northern Plainsmen: Adaptive Strategy and Agrarian Life*. Chicago: Aldine Publishing Co., 1969.

Berton, L. B. *I Married the Klondike*. Toronto: McClelland & Stewart, 1967.

Brody, Hugh. *The People's Land*. Markham: Penguin, 1975.

Brody, Hugh. *Maps and Dreams*. London: Jill and Norman Hobhouse, 1982.

Caragata, Warren. *Alberta Labour: A Heritage Untold.* Toronto: James Lorimer and Company, 1979.

Cardinal, Harold. *The Rebirth of Canada's Indians.* Edmonton: Hurtig, 1977.

Clark, Ella Elizabeth. *Indian Legends of Canada.* Toronto: McClelland & Stewart, 1960.

Cole, Douglas. *Captured Heritage: The Scramble for Northwest Coast Artifacts.* Vancouver: Douglas & McIntyre, 1985.

Colombo, John Robert, editor. *Poems of the Inuit.* Ottawa: Oberon Press, 1981.

Cousins, William James. *A History of the Crow's Nest Pass.* Lethbridge: Historic Tails Society of Alberta, 1981.

Crisafio, Robert, editor. *Backtracking with Fernie & District Historical Society.* Fernie: The Fernie and District Historical Society, 1977.

David, Richard. *Hakluyt's Voyages, A Selection.* London: Chatto & Windus, 1981.

Dancocks, Daniel G. *Legacy of Valour: The Canadians at Passchendaele.* Edmonton: Hurtig, 1986.

Dempsey, Hugh A. *Red Crow, Warrior Chief.* Saskatoon: Western Producer Prairie Books, 1980.

Dempsey, Hugh A. *Crowfoot, Chief of the Blackfeet.* Edmonton: Hurtig, 1976.

Denig, Edwin T. *Five Indian Tribes of the Upper Missouri.* Oklahoma City: University of Oklahoma Press, 1961.

Diaz, Bernal, translated by J. M. Cohen. *The Conquest of New Spain.* Markham: Penguin, 1974.

Donkin, John George. *Trooper in the Far North-West.* Saskatoon: Western Producer Prairie Books, 1987.

Drushka, Ken. *Against Wind and Weather: The History of Towboating in British Columbia.* Vancouver: Douglas & McIntyre, 1981.

Eccles, W.J. *The Canadian Frontier 1534-1760.* Albuquerque: University of New Mexico Press, 1983.

Edmonds, Alan. *Voyage to the Edge of the World.* Toronto: McClelland & Stewart, 1973.

Erasmus, Georges and Jim Bourque. *Public Government for the People of the North.* A discussion paper on aboriginal rights. Yellowknife: Dene Nation and the Métis Association of the N.W.T., 1981.

Fardy, Bernard. *Demasduit, Native Newfoundlander.* St. John's: Creative Publishers, 1988.

Flanagan, Thomas, editor. *The Diaries of Louis Riel.* Edmonton: Hurtig, 1976.

Ferguson, Ted. *A White Man's Country: An Exercise in Canadian Prejudice.* Toronto: Doubleday, 1975.

Forester, Anne D. and Joseph E. Forester. *Fishing: British Columbia's Commercial Fishing History.* Saanichton: Hancock House, 1975.

Fowke, Edith. *Folklore of Canada.* Toronto: McClelland & Stewart, 1976.

Freire, Paulo. *Pedagogy of the Oppressed*. New York: Seabury Press, 1970.

Friesen, J. and H.K. Ralston, editors. *Historical Essays on British Columbia*. Toronto: McClelland & Stewart, 1976.

Fuller, John G. *Tornado Watch #211*. New York: Morrow, 1987.

Gillespie, Beryl. *Handbook of North American Indians, Vol. 6, Subarctic*. Territorial Groups Before 1821: Athapaskans of the Shield and the Mackenzie Drainage. Washington: Smithsonian Institution, 1981.

Gillespie, Beryl. "Yellowknife." In *Handbook of North American Indians, Vol. 6, Subarctic*. Washington: Smithsonian Institution, 1981.

Gillespie, Beryl. "Mountain Indians." In *Handbook of North American Indians, Vol. 6, Subarctic*. Washington: Smithsonian Institution, 1981.

Gilman, Sander L. *Difference and Pathology: Stereotypes of Sexuality, Race, and Madness*. Ithaca: Cornell University Press, 1985.

Goldring, Philip. *Whisky, Horses and Death: The Cypress Hills Massacre and its Sequel*, Canadian Historic Sites: Occasional Papers in Archaeology and History Number 21. Ottawa: Parks Canada, 1979.

Gray, Earle. *The Great Canadian Oil Patch*. Toronto: Maclean-Hunter Ltd., 1970.

Gregson, Harry. *A History of Victoria*. Victoria: Victoria Observer Publishing Ltd., 1970.

Haig-Brown, Roderick. *A River Never Sleeps*. Toronto: Collins, 1974.

Haig-Brown, Roderick. *Measure of the Year*. Toronto: Collins, 1968.

Harrington, Richard. *The Inuit, Life As It Was*. Edmonton: Hurtig, 1981.

Hearne, Samuel. *A Journey from Prince of Wale's Fort in Hudson's Bay to the Northern Ocean*. Edmonton: Hurtig, 1971.

Henry, Walter, contributing editor. *Uncharted Skies*. Edmonton: Reidmore Books, 1982.

Hewson, John. *The Pulling and Liverpool Manuscripts*. Newfoundland Quarterly, Vol. 84, No. 1. St. John's: Newfoundland Quarterly Foundation, 1988.

Hoagland, Edward. *Notes From The Century Before*. New York: Random House, 1969.

Horrall, S. W. *Sir John A. Macdonald and the Mounted Police Force for the Northwest Territories*. Canadian Historical Review, Vol. 53, No. 2. Toronto: University of Toronto Press, 1972.

Hume, Andrew, and Pat Morrow. *The Yukon*. Vancouver: Whitecap Books, 1979.

Hunt, George T. *The Wars of the Iroquois: A Study in Inter-tribal Trade Relations*. Madison: University of Wisconsin Press, 1940.

Inglis, Alex. *Northern Vagabond, The Life and Career of J.B. Tyrrell*. Toronto: McClelland & Stewart, 1978.

Janes, Robert R. *Archaeological Ethnography Among Mackenzie Basin Dene, Canada*. Technical Paper 28. Calgary: The Arctic Institute of North America, 1983.

Jenness, Diamond. *The Indians of Canada*. Originally published in 1932 as Bulletin 65, Anthropological series No. 15, of the National Museum of

Canada. Toronto: University of Toronto Press, 1984.

Jenness, Diamond. *Report of the Canadian Arctic Expedition 1913-1918*. Vol. 13, Eskimo Folk-lore, Part A: Eskimo Myths and Traditions from Alaska, the Mackenzie Delta and the Coronation Gulf. Ottawa: King's Printer, 1924.

Johnston, Alex. *Plants and the Blackfoot*. Occasional Paper No. 15, Lethbridge Historical Society. Lethbridge: Lethbridge Historical Society, 1987.

Johnson, Les. *Sea-Run*. Portland: Frank Amato Publications, 1979.

Joseph, Chief of the Nez Percé, as told to Rt. Rev. W. H. Hare. *Chief Joseph's Own Story*. The North American Review, April, 1879. Facsimile reprint, Seattle: The Shorey Book Store, 1967.

Jupp, Ursula. *Home Port: Victoria*. Victoria: self-published, 1967.

Jupp, Ursula. *From Cordwood to Campus in Gordon Head*. Victoria: self-published, 1975.

Larsen, Henry, Frank Sheer and Edvard Omholt-Jensen. *The Big Ship, An Autobiography*. Toronto: McClelland & Stewart, 1967.

Lowes, Warren. *Indian Giver: A Legacy of North American Indian Peoples*. Penticton: Canadian Alliance in Solidarity with Native People, 1986.

MacEwan, Grant. *Sitting Bull, The Years in Canada*. Edmonton: Hurtig, 1973.

MacEwan, Grant. *Tatanga Mani, Walking Buffalo of the Stonies*. Edmonton: Hurtig, 1969.

MacEwan, Grant. *Eye Opener Bob*. Saskatoon: Western Producer Prairie Books, 1974.

MacLaren, I. S.. *The Aesthetic Map of the North, 1845-1859*. Arctic, Vol. 38, No. 5. Calgary: The Arctic Institute of North America, 1985.

Maclean, Norman. *A River Runs Through It*. Chicago: University of Chicago Press, 1976.

MacRae, Archibald O. *History of the Province of Alberta*. The Western Canada History Company, 1912.

M'Clure, Robert. *Discovery of the North-West Passage*. Edmonton: Hurtig, 1969.

McDonald, Ven. Archdeacon. *A Grammar of the Tukudh Language*. London: The Society For Promoting Christian Knowledge, 1911.

McMillan, Alan D. *Native Peoples and Cultures of Canada: An Anthropological Overview*. Vancouver: Douglas & McIntyre, 1988.

Mayse, Susan. *Canu Heledd*. Edmonton: unpublished paper, 1979.

Mayse, Susan. *A Coal Town History*. Edmonton: unpublished oral histories, 1984-1986.

Middleton, John, editor. *Myth and Cosmos, Readings in Mythology and Symbolism*. New York: The Natural History Press, 1967.

Mitcham, Allison. *The Northern Imagination: A Study of Northern Canadian Literature*. Moonbeam: The Penumbra Press, 1983.

Moore, Joanne R. *Nahanni Trailhead*. Toronto: Deneau & Greenberg, 1980.

Morice, Rev. A.G. *History of the Northern Interior of British Columbia.* Toronto: William Briggs, 1904.

Moyles, R.G. *British Law and Arctic Men.* Saskatoon: Western Producer Prairie Books, 1979.

Murray, Peter. *The Devil and Mr. Duncan: A History of the Two Metlakatlas.* Victoria: Sono Nis Press, 1985.

Nanton, Paul. *Arctic Breakthrough, Franklin's Expeditions 1819-1847.* Toronto: Clarke, Irwin & Company Ltd., 1981.

National and Regional Interests in the North. Transactions of the Third National Workshop on People, Resources and the Environment North of 60 Degrees. Ottawa: Canadian Arctic Resources Committee, 1984.

Nicholson, George. *Vancouver Island's West Coast.* Victoria: George Nicholson's Books, 1962.

Oliver, E.H., editor. *The Canadian North-West: Its Early Development and Legislative Records, Minutes of the Councils of the Red River Colony and the Northern Department of Rupert's Land.* Ottawa: The Government Printing Bureau, 1915.

Owen, Roger C., James J.F. Deetz and Anthony D. Fisher, editors. *The North American Indians· A Source Book.* Toronto: Macmillan, 1967.

Parkman, Francis. *The Oregon Trail: Sketches of Prairie and Rocky-Mountain Life.* New York: Macmillan, 1910.

Pitseolak, Peter and Dorothy Eber. *People from our side: An Inuit record of Seekooseelak — the land of the people of Cape Dorset, Baffin Island.* Edmonton: Hurtig, 1975.

Raczka, Paul, editor. *Winter Count: A History of the Blackfoot People.* Brocket: Oldman River Culture Centre, 1979.

Rasky, Frank. *The Polar Voyagers.* Toronto: McGraw-Hill Ryerson Ltd., 1976.

Rasky, Frank. *The North Pole or Bust.* Toronto: McGraw-Hill Ryerson Ltd., 1977.

Rasmussen, Knud, translator. *Beyond The High Hills.* Poems collected during the Fifth Thule Expedition, 1921-1924. New York: The World Publishing Company, 1961.

Ray, Arthur. *Indians in the Fur Trade: Their Role as Hunters, Trappers and Middlemen in the Lands Southwest of Hudson Bay 1660-1870.* Toronto: University of Toronto Press, 1974.

Richardson, John. *Arctic Ordeal.* Journals edited with a commentary by C. Stuart Houston. Kingston and Montreal: McGill/Queen's University Press, 1984.

Robertson, Heather. *Reservations Are For Indians.* Toronto: James Lewis & Samuel, 1970.

Robertson, Helen and Diamond Jenness. *Report of the Canadian Arctic Expedition 1913-1918.* Vol. 14: Eskimo Songs, Part A: Songs of the Copper Eskimo. Ottawa: King's Printer, 1925.

Rowe, Frederick. *Extinction: The Beothuks of Newfoundland.* Toronto: McGraw-Hill Ryerson, 1977.

Sampson, Anthony. *The Seven Sisters.* New York: Viking Press, 1975.

Schultz, James W. *Blackfeet and Buffalo, Memories of Life among the Indians.* Oklahoma City: University of Oklahoma Press, 1962.

Smith, Ian. *The Unknown Island.* Vancouver: J.J. Douglas Ltd., 1973.

Stefansson, Vilhjalmur. *Unsolved Mysteries of the Arctic.* New York: Macmillan and Company, 1939.

Stewart, Hilary, editor. *The Adventures and Sufferings of John R. Jewitt, Captive of Maquinna.* Vancouver: Douglas & McIntyre, 1987.

Stewart, Hilary. *Indian Fishing: Early Methods on the Northwest Coast.* Vancouver: J.J. Douglas, 1977.

Sturluson, Snorri. *King Harald's Saga.* Translated by Magnus Magnusson and Hermann Palsson. New York: Dorset Press, 1966.

Thomas, Lewis G., editor. *The Prairie West to 1905: A Canadian Sourcebook.* Toronto: Oxford University Press, 1975.

Trindell, Ted. *Métis Witness to the North.* Edited by Jean Morisset and Rose-Marie Pelletier. Vancouver: Tillacum Library, 1986.

Underhill, Ruth. *Red Man's Religion: Beliefs and Practices of the Indians North of Mexico.* Chicago: University of Chicago Press, 1965.

Vigfusson, Gudbrand and F. York Powell, translators. *Landnamabok.* Libellus Islandorum, Cristne Saga. Oxford: Clarendon Press, 1905.

Wah-Shee, James. *Our Land, Our Future.* Departmental discussion paper of the Northwest Territories Minister for Aboriginal Rights and Constitutional Development. Yellowknife: 1981.

Walbran, Capt. John T. *British Columbia Coast Names, Their Origin and History.* The Government Printing Bureau, Ottawa, 1909. Vancouver: Reprint by J.J. Douglas Ltd., 1973.

Watt, Frederick B. *Great Bear, A Journey Remembered.* Yellowknife: Outcrop Ltd., 1980.

Weeden, Robert B. *Northern People, Northern Resources, and the Dynamics of Carrying Capacity.* Arctic, Vol. 38, No. 2. Calgary: The Arctic Institute of North America, 1985.

Wejr, Patricia and Howie Smith. *Fighting For Labour: Four Decades of Work in British Columbia 1910-1950.* Sound Heritage Series, Vol. 7, No. 4. Victoria: Provincial Archives of British Columbia, 1978.

Wellman, Paul I. *Death on the Prairie: Thirty Years' Struggle for the Western Plains.* New York: Macmillan, 1934. Lincoln: Reprint by University of Nebraska Press, 1987.

Whittington, Michael S. and Glen Williams, editors. *Canadian Politics in the 1980s.* Toronto: Methuen, 1984.

Wild, Roland. *Amor De Cosmos.* Toronto: The Ryerson Press, 1958.

Wilkinson, Doug. *Arctic Fever, The Search for the Northwest Passage.* Toronto: Clarke, Irwin & Company, 1971.

Wright, Allen A. *Prelude To Bonanza.* Sidney: Gray's Publishing, 1976.

Zlotkin, Norman K. *Unfinished Business: Aboriginal Peoples and the 1983 Constitutional Conference.* Discussion Paper 15, the Institute of Intergovernmental Relations. Kingston: Queen's University, 1983.

Photo by Susan Mayse

Born in Britain, Stephen Hume emigrated to Canada with his parents as an infant in 1948. He lived in widely dispersed communities across western Canada where his father worked as a logger, deck hand, deliveryman and later as a newspaper editor, reporter, and political columnist.

Hume graduated from the University of Victoria in 1971 with a BA, taking second class honors in classical studies and anthropology. He then pursued special and advanced studies at the University of Alberta, the Banff School of Advanced Management, the American Press Institute and the Centre for Creative Leadership.

Stephen Hume is currently the general manager of the *Edmonton Journal*. In 1968 he joined the *Victoria Daily Times*, where he worked as both a reporter and copy editor while completing his university studies. In 1971 he joined the *Journal* and was assigned to the paper's northern bureau in Yellowknife, NWT, with responsibility for covering Alaska, the Yukon, and Greenland. In 1973 he returned to Edmonton to cover the oil patch. He joined the editorial board in 1974, was appointed city editor in 1975, news editor in 1978, editor in 1981, and general manager in 1987.

During his tenure as a senior editor, *Journal* editorial staff won both a Michener Award and a special Michener citation for excellence in public service journalism, a national newspaper award for editorial writing, and two B'Nai Brith awards for journalism in defence of human rights.

He is the author of two books of poetry, a collection of essays, and is a contributor to a number of anthologies.